Amos 4.0 User's Guide

James L. Arbuckle
Werner Wothke

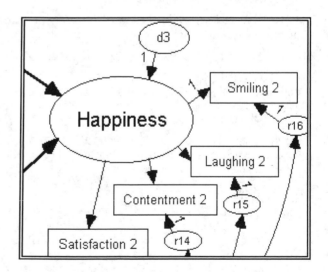

For more information, please contact:

Marketing Department
SPSS Inc.
233 S. Wacker Dr., 11th Floor
Chicago, IL 60606-6307, U.S.A.
Tel: (312) 651-3000
Fax: (312) 651-3668
URL: http://www.spss.com

SmallWaters Corporation
1507 E. 53rd Street, #452
Chicago, IL 60615, U.S.A.
Tel: (773) 667-8635
Fax: (773) 955-6252
URL: http://www.smallwaters.com

Amos 4.0 User's Guide
Copyright © 1995-99 by SmallWaters Corporation
All rights reserved.
Printed in the United States of America.

890 05

ISBN 1-56827-264-2

Contents

Introduction

Welcome to Amos! Let us start by dispensing with one of the most frequently asked questions: Amos (at least *this* Amos) is not a minor prophet. Amos is short for **A**nalysis of **MO**ment **S**tructures. But prophets have a reputation for standing outside the mainstream and shaking things up a bit. *This* Amos does share in that prophetic tradition by standing apart from many other statistical packages. Amos implements the general approach to data analysis known as *structural equation modeling* (SEM) — also known as *analysis of covariance structures*, or *causal modeling*. This approach includes as special cases many well-known conventional techniques, including the general linear model and common factor analysis.

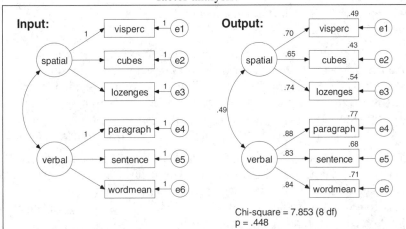

Amos (Analysis of Moment Structures) is an easy-to-use program for visual SEM. With Amos, you can quickly specify, view, and modify your model graphically using simple drawing tools. Then assess your model's fit, make any modifications, and print out a publication-quality graphic of your final model. Simply specify the model graphically (left). Amos quickly does the computations and displays the results (right).

Structural equation modeling (SEM) is sometimes thought of as an esoteric method that is difficult to learn and use. This is a complete mistake. In fact, the reason why SEM is such an important breakthrough is because of its ease of use. SEM opens the door for nonstatisticians to solve estimation and hypothesis-testing problems that once would have required the services of a specialist.

Amos was originally designed as a tool for teaching this powerful and fundamentally simple method. For this reason, I have made every effort to see that it is easy to use. Amos integrates an easy-to-use graphical interface with an advanced computing engine for SEM. Amos's publication-quality path diagrams provide a clear understanding of the model to students and fellow researchers. It also incorporates the results of extensively testing a variety of numerical algorithms. The methods implemented in Amos are among the most effective and reliable ones now available.

This User's Guide will help you explore many facets of SEM and show you how you can apply Amos to give more complete results when multivariate models are fit to all the data.

Features

Amos provides the following methods for estimating structural equation models:
- maximum likelihood
- unweighted least squares
- generalized least squares
- Browne's asymptotically distribution-free criterion
- scale-free least-squares

Amos goes well beyond the usual capabilities found in other structural equation modeling programs. When confronted with missing data, Amos performs state-of-the-art estimation by full information maximum-likelihood instead of relying on ad-hoc methods like listwise or pairwise deletion, or mean imputation. The program can analyze data from several populations at once. It can also estimate means for exogenous variables, and intercepts in regression equations.

The software makes bootstrapped standard errors and confidence intervals available for all parameter estimates, effect estimates, sample means, variances, covariances and correlations. It also incorporates percentile intervals and bias-corrected percentile intervals (Stine, 1989), as well as Bollen and Stine's (1992) bootstrap approach to model testing.

Multiple models can be fitted in a single analysis. Amos examines every pair of models where one model can be obtained by placing restrictions on the parameters of the other. The program reports several statistics appropriate for comparing such models. It provides a test of univariate normality for each observed variable, as well as a test of multivariate normality. It even attempts to detect outliers.

Amos accepts a path diagram as a model specification and displays parameter estimates graphically on a path diagram. Path diagrams used for model specification and those that display parameter estimates are of presentation quality. They can be printed directly or imported into other applications, such as word processors, desktop publishing programs, and general-purpose graphics programs.

New Features Added in Amos 4.0

This new release 4 of Amos has an improved graphical interface with a number of new capabilities. In addition, **Amos 4.0** comes with its own Basic interpreter, **Amos Basic** that can control all actions by the **Amos Graphics** program. **Amos Basic** is going to be the macro workhorse for simplifying many specialized modeling tasks—for example, the growth curve analysis of longitudinal data. Other object-oriented programming languages, such as **Visual Basic** or **C++** can also be used to control **Amos Graphics**.

The "$" commands of previous releases are no longer supported. Instead, **Amos Graphics** has a "point-and-click" interface for selecting its many analysis options. Users who preferred the nongraphical model specifications of the previous "Amos Text" program can continue working in keyboard mode by writing **Amos Basic** or **Visual Basic** programs.

Improvements to the interface

The redesign of the **Amos Graphics** interface has added new capabilities. Common operations can now be performed with fewer mouse and keyboard operations.

- The use of "$" commands has been supplanted by a point-and-click interface.
- A new **View Path Diagrams** window displays a thumbnail picture of one path diagram from each model in a directory. By selecting an individual model, you can view its description, modify and refit the model, or view the results of a previous analysis.
- A new **View Data** window allows you to inspect your data.
- A new **View Tables** window displays results in a spreadsheet format, making it easy to reformat the results for presentation. (The **View Text** window displays results in the traditional format.)
- **Amos 4.0** supports local languages. **Amos 4.0** can display variable names in all European languages as well as in the Japanese Kana and Kanji character sets. Program commands and messages can be displayed in English, German or Japanese, depending on the regional setting of the operating system. Additional languages may be supported in future versions of Amos.

The new and more powerful **Matrix View** window replaces the Amos 3.6 **View Spreadsheet** command. The **Matrix View** window can contain multiple matrices. Each matrix can be either a covariance matrix or a regression weight matrix. The **Matrix View** window can be used to view and to modify parameter constraints and to view parameter estimates.

Amos now takes advantage of the drag and drop feature in Windows® to make operations faster and more intuitive. You can, for example:

- drag text from another document and drop it into an analysis title, a figure caption, a variable name, or a parameter name.
- drag variable names from a data file to a path diagram.
- drag variable names from the path diagram to a matrix view.
- drag any property of one path diagram object to another path diagram object. For example, you can drag the name of a regression weight from one single-headed arrow to another single-headed arrow. Or you can drag a rectangle's color to another rectangle.
- drag a file that contains a path diagram from Windows Explorer® to the **Amos Graphics** window.
- drag a data file from Windows Explorer® to a **View Data** window.
- drag an Amos output file to the **View Text Output** window.
- drag a path diagram from the **Browse Path Diagrams** window to the **Amos Graphics** window.

You will discover improved integration with Windows Explorer. Double-clicking on an Amos output file opens a window for viewing the file. Right-clicking on a data file in one of the formats that Amos supports opens a window for viewing the data. (As in previous versions, execute **Amos Graphics** by double-clicking on a file that contains an Amos path diagram.)

Amos 4.0 can read data in these database formats:

- comma-delimited ASCII (`*.csv`), or in regions where decimal commas are used, semicolon-delimited text
- SPSS® versions 7.5, 8 and 9
- dBase® 3, 4 and 5
- Microsoft® Excel® 3 through 8
- Microsoft® FoxPro® 2.0, 2.5 or 2.6
- Lotus® 1-2-3 files (with `*.wk1`, `*.wk3` and `*.wk4` extensions)
- Microsoft Access® through Access 97

You can now delete a group from a multiple group analysis.

Further, names for variables, parameters, groups and models can be up to 1000 characters, instead of the previous limit of 29. **Amos 4.0** even allows embedded spaces.

Additional analyses

Amos 4.0 provides estimates of the following quantities:
- Total effects
- Standardized total effects
- Indirect effects
- Standardized indirect effects
- Direct effects
- Standardized direct effects

You have the option of estimating standard errors from the matrix of exact second-order derivatives, rather than from the expected second-order derivatives.

Programmability

Use Amos as a component in other computer programs. Your program can preprocess the data, specify the model, and display the results — or save the results in whatever format you choose.

Other Sources of Information

Although the *Amos 4.0 User's Guide* contains a good bit of expository material, it is not by any means intended to be a complete guide to the correct and effective use of structural modeling. Bollen's (1989) comprehensive text is an important reference that can also serve well as an introduction to structural modeling. The SmallWaters online bookstore makes this and several other textbooks on structural equation modeling available via the World Wide Web at:

        http://www.smallwaters.com/books/

Structural Equation Modeling: A Multidisciplinary Journal contains methodological articles as well as applications of structural modeling. It is published by

    Lawrence Erlbaum Associates, Inc.
    Journal Subscription Department
    10 Industrial Avenue
    Mahwah, NJ 07430 USA
    phone: 201-236-9500
    fax: 201-236-0072

Carl Ferguson and Edward Rigdon established an electronic mailing list called Semnet to provide a forum for discussions related to structural modeling. You can find comprehensive information about joining and searching Semnet, plus how-to instructions for unsubscribing from the list, on the World Wide Web at:

        http://www.gsu.edu/~mkteer/semnet.html

In short, to subscribe to Semnet, send the message:

```
subscribe semnet firstname lastname
```

to `listserv@bama.ua.edu`. For example, James Arbuckle would subscribe by sending the message:

```
sub semnet James Arbuckle
```

After subscribing, you will receive messages that are distributed to all subscribers to the list. You will also be able to send messages that will be seen by other subscribers.

Edward Rigdon also maintains a list of frequently asked questions (FAQs) about structural equation modeling. That list is located on the World Wide Web at:

```
http://www.gsu.edu/~mkteer/semfaq.html
```

Last but not least, SmallWaters maintains an Amos-specific list of frequently asked questions at:

```
http://www.smallwaters.com/amos/faq
```

and a more general SEM FAQ list at:

```
http://www.smallwaters.com/faq-sem
```

You can also find white papers on particular SEM applications at:

```
http://www.smallwaters.com/whitepapers
```

Acknowledgments

Many people contributed to the development of Amos. Morton Kleban and Rachel Pruchno were two early Amos users who helped to influence the development of the program. Jonathan Brill is a frequent source of good advice. Michael Friendly used several versions of the program and provided useful feedback. Amos has had the benefit of extensive testing by David Burns, an active structural modeler who generously takes the time to report his experiences as well as to contribute new ideas. The "Name Parameters" macro was just one of David's many contributions. Kenneth Bollen made a number of valuable suggestions, including the idea of a one-step procedure for drawing latent variables along with their indicators and residual variables. Many subsequent enhancements to the graphics interface flowed from this single idea. Students in Jim Arbuckle's structural modeling class and Amos users in the field have been a perennial source of feedback and new ideas.

At SmallWaters, Tom Stribling and Werner Wothke copyedited and typeset the Amos documentation, while Erin Pruitt and Michael Reinhard prepared the Japanese localization of the program. Werner also worked on the German localization. Many portions of the User's Guide were substantially rewritten at SmallWaters, including the first nineteen examples.

At SPSS, Hans Cheng and Tom Chiu delighted in pointing out bugs in the many Amos beta versions, so that they could be fixed in the production release. Yvonne Smith and JoAnn Ziebarth provided excellent editorial advice for typesetting this User's Guide. At SPSS's Tokyo office, Etsuko Murata, Rui Arai and Akemi Tabei, with the generous assistance of Professors Yukata Kano and Akihiro Inoue, finalized and tested the Japanese localization of Amos 4.0.

Amos 4.0 was field-tested extensively before its release. Some forty structural equation modelers participated in the Amos 4.0 beta testing program. We are especially grateful for the detailed feedback provided by Tony Babinec, Lynd Bacon, Christopher Burant, Barbara Byrne, Gordon Cheung, Wynne Chin, David Fresco, Rachel Fouladi, Gregory Hancock, Aribert Heyder, Joop Hox, Charles Martinez, Tor Neilands, Jonathan Nevitt, Alan Olinsky, Bo Palaszewski, Dale Pietrzak, Ed Rigdon, David Rindskopf, Steven Safren, Mike Saltis, Peter Schmidt, Randall Schumacker and Diane Spangler.

A word of warning is still in order: While SmallWaters, SPSS and the program's author have engaged in extensive program testing to ensure that Amos operates correctly, all complicated software, Amos included, is bound to contain some undetected bugs. We are committed to correcting any program errors. If you encounter any odd-looking or seemingly erroneous results, please report them to the SmallWaters or SPSS technical support staff.

James L. Arbuckle
Ambler, Pennsylvania

Werner Wothke
Chicago, Illinois

March, 1999

A Note from the Author of Amos

Although Amos introduces some new techniques, the program is primarily the implementation of other people's ideas. I would like to mention that Amos's computations rely heavily on the chapter by Browne (1982). This document helped to shape my view of the field of structural modeling, as well as serving as a blueprint for the numerical portions of Amos.

Additionally, I wish to take note of the singular role of Karl Jöreskog in demonstrating that structural modeling, as we now know it, is possible, and in persuading people that the method is useful. Developing a program like Amos is made immeasurably easier by the knowledge that one is dealing with a problem that is both soluble and worthwhile.

No computer program is ever finished as long as people keep using it. I am already working on the next version of Amos. Your suggestions would be appreciated.

James L. Arbuckle

Overview of Amos 4.0

About the Amos Documentation

Amos 4.0 has extensive written documentation and online help. The written documentation comes in two volumes: the *Amos 4.0 Installation Instructions* and the *Amos 4.0 User's Guide* (which you are reading now).

Two other volumes are available as downloadable Portable Document Format (PDF) files from the **Amos 4.0** CD-ROM. These are the *Amos 4.0 Graphics Reference Guide* and the *Amos 4.0 Programming Reference Guide*. We have included a complimentary copy of the Adobe® Acrobat® Reader 3 software on the **Amos 4.0** CD-ROM so you can easily view and print these PDF files. You can also download the most recent version of the Adobe Acrobat Reader directly from their website at: www.adobe.com/acrobat.

The *Amos 4.0 Installation Instructions* walk you through the installation process.

The *Amos 4.0 User's Guide* contains this overview of the most common Amos functions, three initial tutorials and a leisurely walk through 21 worked examples. The tutorials get you started with **Amos Graphics** and **Amos Basic**. The subsequent examples serve as an introduction to structural modeling and the use of Amos.

Examples 1 through 4 show how you can use Amos to do some conventional analyses—analyses that could be done using a standard statistics "package." These examples show a new approach to some familiar problems while also demonstrating all of the basic features of Amos. There are sometimes good reasons for using Amos to do something simple like estimating a mean or correlation, or testing the hypothesis that two means are equal. For one thing, you might want to take advantage of Amos's ability to handle missing data. Another reason would be to use Amos's bootstrapping capability, particularly to obtain confidence intervals.

Examples 5 through 8 illustrate the basic techniques that are commonly used nowadays in structural modeling.

Example 9 and those that follow demonstrate advanced techniques that have so far not been used as much as they deserve. These techniques include a) simultaneous analysis of data from several different populations, b) estimation of means and additive constants in regression equations, c) maximum likelihood estimation in the presence of missing data, and d) bootstrapping to obtain estimated standard errors. Amos makes these techniques especially easy to use, and we hope that they will become more commonplace.

The *Amos 4.0 Graphics Reference Guide* gives definitions of all **Amos Graphics** commands and the program outputs. It also has a Technical Appendix describing the computational formulas used.

Extensive, advanced reference material for the Amos API (Amos Programming Interface) is included in the *Amos 4.0 Programming Reference Guide*.

Both the *Amos 4.0 Graphics Reference Guide* and the *Amos 4.0 Programming Reference Guide* are also available as Help files. Simply look in the Help menu in either **Amos Graphics** or **Amos Basic**.

Starting Amos 4.0

One common way to start up **Amos 4.0** is to click the **Start** icon on the Windows® desktop and then **Programs**. Select **Amos 4**:

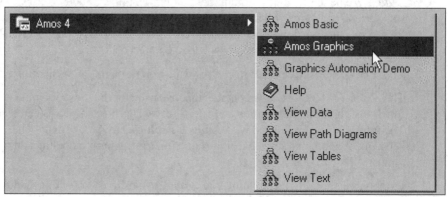

You will notice that **Amos 4.0** is actually a program group. Typically, you will want to select **Amos Graphics**, but you do have other options:

- **Amos Basic** is **Amos 4.0**'s function for developing macros without the graphical interface

- **Amos Graphics** is the graphical interface for drawing path diagrams

- **Graphics Automation Demo** gives sample macros for speeding up common drawing tasks

- **Help** activates **Amos 4.0**'s extensive online help system

- **View Data** displays data files in all supported formats

- **View Path Diagrams** lets you browse all Amos graphics diagrams

- **View Tables** displays Amos table output in a directory of earlier analyses

- **View Text** displays Amos text output in a directory of earlier analyses

Other ways to start Amos programs include:

1. You can double-click on either the **Amos Graphics** or **Amos Basic** icon (depending on what you want to do) if these shortcuts have been installed on your Windows desktop.

2. You can double-click on any path diagram (***.amw**) file created with **Amos Graphics** to go directly into Amos Graphics.

3. You can double-click on a path diagram displayed by Amos's **View Path Diagrams** utility.

4. If you have the SPSS® version of Amos, you can also start **Amos Graphics** from SPSS by the **Statistics** → **Amos** command.

Tutorial: Get Running with Amos Graphics

Purpose

Remember your first statistics class when you sweated through memorizing formulas and laboriously calculating answers with pencil and paper? The professor had you do this so you would understand some basic statistical concepts. Later you discovered that a calculator or software program could do all these calculations in a split second.

This tutorial is a little like that early statistics class. There are many short cuts to drawing and labeling path diagrams in **Amos Graphics** that you will discover as you work through the Examples in this User's Guide, or as you review the *Amos 4.0 Graphics Reference Guide*. The intent of this tutorial is to simply get you started using **Amos Graphics** in Microsoft Windows. It will cover some of the basic functions and features of Amos and guide you through your first Amos analysis. Once you have worked through this tutorial, you can learn more advanced functions in the companion *Amos 4.0 Graphics Reference Guide* (either the PDF document or Help file). Or you can continue to incrementally learn about Amos and its statistical applications by working through the Examples in this User's Guide.

Please note that there are two versions of this tutorial. The exercise `Getstart.amw` uses data from a Microsoft Excel file, while `Startsps.amw` points to input data in SPSS format. Both exercises are located in the `Tutorial` subdirectory, underneath **Amos 4**, typically in `C:\Program Files\Amos 4\Tutorial`.

Prerequisites

This tutorial assumes that Amos has been installed on your computer. If you have not yet installed Amos, you might want to install it now, before continuing with this tutorial. Also, this tutorial assumes that you already have some basic experience using Windows programs. We assume you already know how to select an item from a menu, how to move the mouse pointer, clicking and double-clicking the mouse, and so on.

The data

Hamilton (1990) provided several measurements on each of 21 states. Three of the measurements will be used for the present example: 1) average SAT score, 2) per capita income expressed in $1,000 units, and 3) median education for residents 25 years of age or older. The data are provided in the **Tutorial** directory, inside the Excel 8.0 workbook **Hamilton.xls,** in the single worksheet named **Hamilton**. Here is a listing:

SAT	Income	Education
899	14.345	12.7
896	16.37	12.6
897	13.537	12.5
889	12.552	12.5
823	11.441	12.2
857	12.757	12.7
860	11.799	12.4
890	10.683	12.5
889	14.112	12.5
888	14.573	12.6
925	13.144	12.6
869	15.281	12.5
896	14.121	12.5
827	10.758	12.2
908	11.583	12.7
885	12.343	12.4
887	12.729	12.3
790	10.075	12.1
868	12.636	12.4
904	10.689	12.6
888	13.065	12.4

The path diagram in **Figure 1** shows a model for these data:

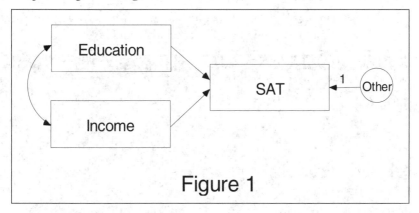

Figure 1

It is a simple regression model where one observed variable, SAT, is predicted as a linear combination of the other two observed variables, Education and Income. As with nearly all empirical data, the prediction will not be perfect. The latent variable Other therefore serves to absorb random variation in the SAT scores and systematic components for which no suitable predictors were provided.

Each single-headed arrow represents a regression weight. The number "1" in the figure specifies that Other must have a weight of one in the prediction of SAT. Some such constraint must be imposed in order to make the model *identified*, and it is one of the features of the model that must be communicated to Amos. You need to provide Amos with information about both the Hamilton data and the model in **Figure 1**.

Starting Amos Graphics

The are several ways to start up **Amos Graphics**:

1. You can double-click on the **Amos Graphics** icon on the Windows desktop.

2. From the Windows taskbar, you can launch **Amos Graphics** with the command path

    Start → Programs → Amos 4 → Amos Graphics

3. You can double-click on any path diagram (***.amw**) file created with **Amos Graphics**.

4. You can double-click on a path diagram displayed by Amos's **View Path Diagrams** utility.

5. If you have the SPSS version of Amos, you can also start **Amos Graphics** from SPSS by the **Statistics → Amos** command.

After **Amos Graphics** has started up, click on **File** → **New** to start a new model. You will see a window containing a large rectangle and several menu titles:

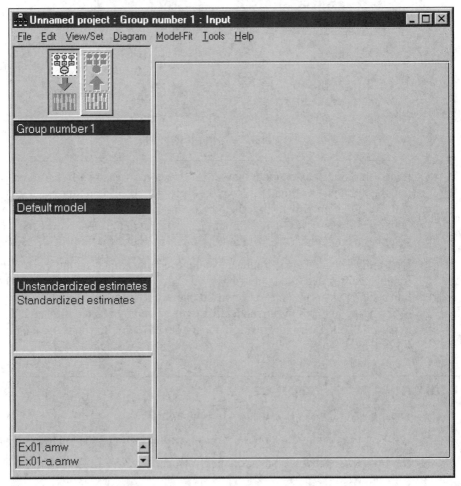

The large rectangle (in the center of the window) represents a sheet of paper. Its shape depends on how your printer is set up. In this example, the printer is set up in *portrait* mode, so the rectangle is taller than it is wide. If your printer is set for *landscape* printing, the rectangle will be wider than it is tall.

In addition to the **Amos Graphics** main window, Amos displays a toolbar window with "button" or icon commands that are shortcuts for drawing and modeling operations (as shown on the left).

You have a choice of running **Amos Graphics** commands either by clicking on their toolbar icons or by selecting their corresponding menu commands.

Actually, Amos features even more icon shortcuts than the ones shown here on the default toolbar. The *Amos 4.0 Graphics Reference Guide* (either the PDF document or Help file) covers how to customize your toolbar so you have immediate access to your most-used shortcuts.

Attaching the data

The next step is attaching the Hamilton data to the model. While inputting ASCII (or text) based data input is possible, **Amos Graphics** supports input of several common database formats, including SPSS ***.sav** files. For the tutorial, we will attach a Microsoft Excel 8.0 file of the Hamilton data. Do this by selecting:

File → **Data Files...** → **File Name**

We placed the data for this tutorial in the **Tutorial** subdirectory. The directory path is:

Program Files → **Amos 4** →**Tutorial**

In the Files **of type** listbox, select **Excel 8.0 (*.xls)** as the desired file type and double click on the **Hamilton.xls** file:

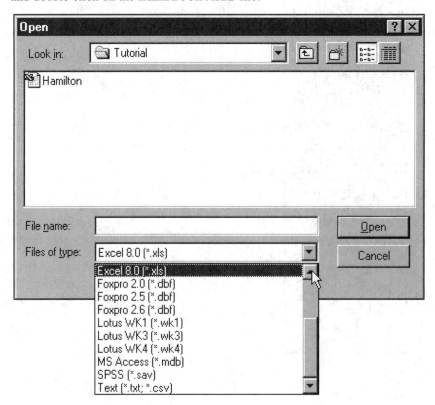

This will bring you back to the **Data Files** dialog box. Click on **OK**:

Reading data from an SPSS system file

The SPSS version of **Amos 4.0** reads the current SPSS working file when Amos is started directly from the SPSS Statistics menu. Even when run in standalone mode, all versions of **Amos 4.0** can read SPSS (***.sav**) files saved to disk. To read an SPSS file, such as the file **Hamilton.sav** in the **Tutorial** subdirectory, simply follow the same steps outlined in the previous section. However, when you get to **Files of type**, click on **SPSS (*.sav)** as the desired file type and double click on the **Hamilton.sav** file.

There is one difference to naming variables when working with SPSS data files. SPSS system files support variable names of up to eight characters. Thus, if the Hamilton data file was in the SPSS format, the variable name Education would have to be shortened to Educatn.

Specifying the model and drawing variables

First, draw three rectangles to represent the three observed variables in the model. Begin by clicking on the **Draw observed variables** icon on the toolbar, or by clicking on the **Diagram** menu and selecting **Draw Observed**:

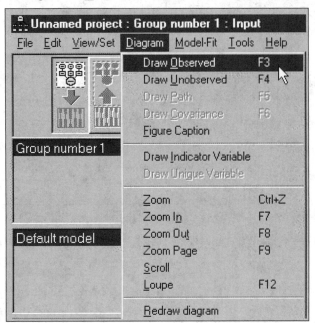

When you click on an icon, you will know it is activated because its appearance will change. The color surrounding the icon image will be brighter, as if illuminated. Move the mouse pointer to the place where you want the Education rectangle to appear in the drawing area. Do not worry too much about the exact size or placement of the rectangle — you can change it later on. Once you have picked a spot for the Education rectangle, press the left mouse button and hold it down while making some trial movements of the mouse. Movements of the mouse will affect the size and shape of the rectangle. When you are reasonably satisfied with its appearance, release the mouse button. Now, use the same method to draw two more rectangles for Income and SAT. As long as the **Draw observed variables** icon is illuminated, a new rectangle will appear every time you press the left mouse button and move the mouse.

Next, draw an ellipse to represent Other. Ellipses are drawn the same way as rectangles, except that you begin by clicking on the **Draw unobserved variables** icon, or selecting **Draw Unobserved** from the **Diagram** menu. After drawing the ellipse, your screen should look more or less like **Figure 2** (except on a gray background).

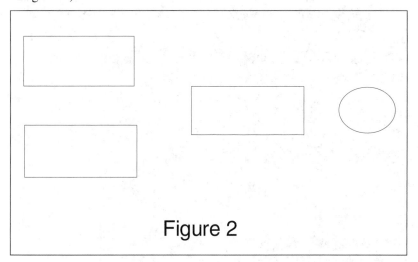

Figure 2

Naming the variables

To assign names to the four variables, double click on one the objects in the path diagram. It does not matter which one you start with. For this example, we will start by double clicking on the rectangle that is supposed to represent Education. The **Object Properties** dialog box appears. Click on the **Text** tab and enter the word Education in the **Variable name** field:

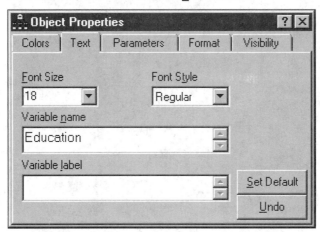

Notice that while you are typing in the field, the word Education is appearing in your first rectangle. Click once on the next rectangle and enter Income in the **Variable name** field.

> *Remember that SPSS files cannot be longer than eight characters.*
> *To compensate, you would need to enter Educatn in the **Variable***
> ***name** field and the proper Education in the **Variable label** field.*
> *This modification is not needed for this tutorial because we are*
> *using an Excel file.*

Follow this procedure until you have labeled all four objects. To close the **Object Properties** box, click on the **X** in the upper right hand corner of the dialog box. Your path diagram should look like **Figure 3**:

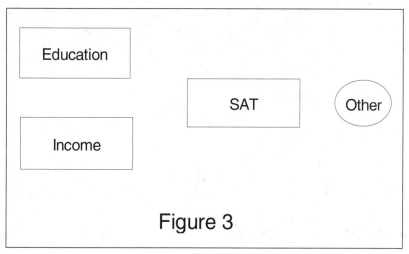

Figure 3

Drawing arrows

 To draw a single-headed arrow, click on the **Draw paths** icon from the toolbar. When you move your mouse into the drawing arrow, you will notice that mouse pointer has the word PATH underneath it to remind you that you are drawing a path. You will also notice that when your pointer touches an object, the object changes color. Click and hold down your left mouse button from the right edge of the Education rectangle to the left edge of the SAT rectangle. Release the mouse button and the arrow will be fixed into place. Repeat this procedure for each of the remaining single-headed arrows. Use **Figure 1** on page as your model.

 Drawing double-headed arrows is similar to drawing single-headed arrows. Simply click on the **Draw covariances** icon on the toolbar. Then, click and hold down your left mouse button from the left edge of the Income rectangle to the left edge of the Education rectangle. The reason why we suggested starting at the bottom variable is because the initial curvature of the two-headed arrow follows an arc in a clockwise direction. That means going from bottom to top will curve the arrow to the left. If you accidentally arc your arrow in the wrong direction, you can always change it. We will discuss how to make changes to your path diagram a little later.

Your path diagram should now look like **Figure 4**:

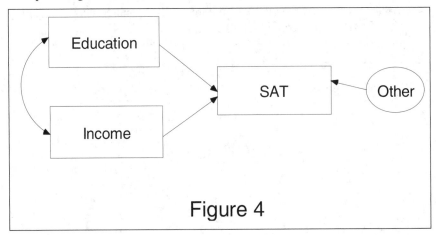

Figure 4

Constraining a parameter

To identify the regression model, you must define the scale of the latent variable Other. You can do this by fixing either the variance of Other or the path coefficient from Other to SAT at some positive value. Suppose you want to fix the path coefficient at unity. Double click on the arrow between Other and SAT. Once again the **Object Properties** dialog appears. Click on the **Parameters** tab and enter the value "1" in the **Regression weight** field:

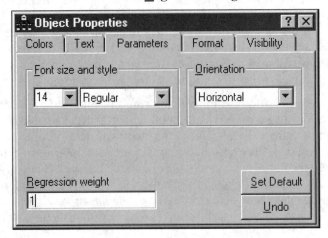

This adds a "1" above the arrow between Other and SAT. To close the **Object Properties** box, once again click on the **X** in the upper right hand corner of the dialog box. This completes the path diagram except for any changes you might want to make to improve its appearance. It should look something like **Figure 5**:

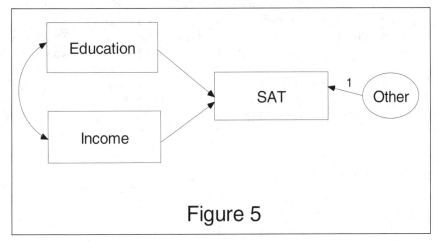

Figure 5

Improving the appearance of the path diagram

You can change the appearance of your path diagram by moving objects around, and by changing their sizes and shapes. These changes do not affect the meaning of a path diagram. That is, they do not change the model's specification. To move an object, click on the **Move** icon on the toolbar. You will notice that the picture of a little moving truck appears below your mouse pointer when you move into the drawing area. This lets you know the **Move** function is active. Then click and hold down your left mouse button on the object you wish to move. With the mouse button still depressed, move the object to where you want it, and let go of your mouse button. **Amos Graphics** will automatically redraw all connecting arrows.

To change the size and shape of an object, first press the **Change the shape of objects** icon on the toolbar. You will notice that the word shape appears under the mouse pointer to let you know the **Shape** function is active. Click and hold down your left mouse button on the object you wish to re-shape. Change the shape of the object to your liking and release the mouse button.

Change the shape of objects also works on two-headed arrows. Follow the same procedure to change the direction or arc of any double-headed arrow.

Of course, if you make a mistake, there are always three icons on the toolbar to quickly bail you out: the **Erase** and **Undo** functions. To erase an object, simple click on the **Erase** icon and then click on the object you wish to erase.

To undo your last drawing activity, click on the **Undo** icon and your last activity disappears. Each time you click **Undo**, your previous activity will be removed.

 If you change your mind, click on **Redo** to restore a change.

No matter how carefully you try to adjust the size, shape and location of individual objects in your path diagram, the path diagram as a whole will probably end up looking slightly out of kilter. You might, for example, want the Education and Income rectangles to look exactly alike, but it is very hard to do this simply by eyeballing it. Amos has many other tools for achieving the "picture perfect" path diagram, but we will not take the time to explain them all in this "Getting Started" tutorial. For more details about drawing functions, refer to the *Amos 4.0 Graphics Reference Guide* (either the PDF document or Help file).

Performing the analysis

The next step is to decide what properties you wish to analyze. Amos gives you an array of options by following the path: **View/Set** → **Analysis Properties** and clicking on the **Output** tab. There is also an **Analysis Properties** icon you can click on the toolbar. Either way, the **Output** tab gives you these options:

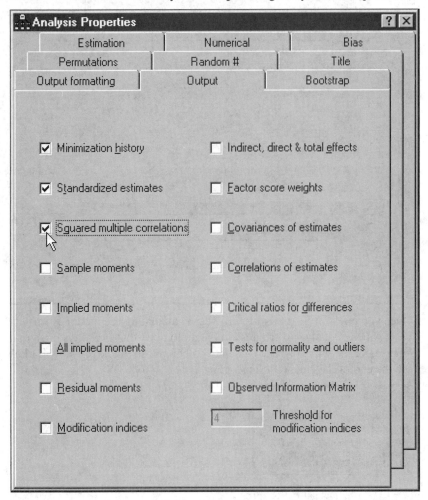

For this example, check the **Minimization history**, **Standardized estimates**, and **Squared multiple correlations** boxes. We are doing this because these are so commonly used in analysis. In the Examples section, we explore the meaning and impact of a variety of analytical property options.

Click the **X** in the corner of the **Analysis Properties** dialog box, so you can better see your drawing area. The only thing left to do then is to have Amos perform the actual calculations. To do this, click on the **Calculate estimates** icon on the toolbar. Amos will want to save this problem to a file, so if you have given it no filename, the **Save As** dialog box will appear. Give the problem a filename; let us say, `tutorial1`:

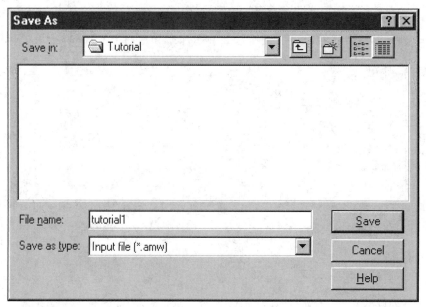

Once you click on **Save**, Amos will begin calculating the model estimates. You can view Amos' calculating progress in the dialog box that is always open in the lower left area of the window. The calculations happen so quickly, you will likely only see the end of the calculation progress:

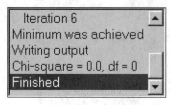

Viewing the text output

When Amos has completed the calculations, you have three options for viewing the output: text output, table (spreadsheet) output, or graphics output. For text output, click the **View Text** icon on the toolbar. Here is a portion of the text output for this problem:

```
Minimum was achieved


Chi-square =      0.000
Degrees of freedom =    0
Probability level cannot be computed

Maximum Likelihood Estimates
---------------------------


Regression Weights:               Estimate    S.E.     C.R.
-------------------               --------   -------  -------

     SAT <---------- Education     136.022   30.555    4.452
     SAT <------------ Income        2.156    3.125    0.690


Standardized Regression Weights:  Estimate
-------------------------------   --------

     SAT <---------- Education       0.717
     SAT <------------ Income        0.111


Covariances:                      Estimate    S.E.     C.R.
-----------                       --------   -------  -------

     Education <------> Income       0.127    0.065    1.952


Correlations:                     Estimate
------------                      --------

     Education <------> Income       0.485


Variances:                        Estimate    S.E.     C.R.
---------                         --------   -------  -------

                     Education       0.027    0.008    3.162
                        Income       2.562    0.810    3.162
                         Other     382.736  121.032    3.162


Squared Multiple Correlations:       Estimate
-----------------------------        --------

                            SAT       0.603
```

Viewing the table (spreadsheet) output

 For table output, click on the **View Table Output** icon on the toolbar. The open dialog box on the left side of the spreadsheet gives you a variety of output options:

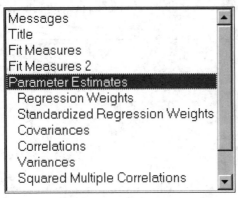

Click on **Parameter Estimates** to view the following portion of the table output for this problem:

	A	B	C	D	E	F	G
1							
2	**Regression Weights**						
3				Estimate	S.E.	c.r.	P
4	SAT	<--	Income	2.16	3.13	0.69	0.49
5	SAT	<--	Education	136.02	30.56	4.45	0.00
6							
7	**Standardized Regression Weights**						
8				Estimate			
9	SAT	<--	Income	0.11			
10	SAT	<--	Education	0.72			
11							
12	**Covariances**						
13				Estimate	S.E.	c.r.	P
14	Income	<-->	Education	0.13	0.07	1.95	0.05
15							
16	**Correlations**						
17				Estimate			
18	Income	<-->	Education	0.49			
19							
20	**Variances**						
21				Estimate	S.E.	c.r.	P
22			Income	2.56	0.81	3.16	0.00
23			Education	0.03	0.01	3.16	0.00
24			Other	382.74	121.03	3.16	0.00
25							
26	**Squared Multiple Correlations**						
27				Estimate			
28			SAT	0.60			

Notice that output goes to the second decimal place. If you wish to change the decimal setting, click on either the **Increase decimal** or **Decrease decimal** icon on the **Table Output** toolbar. **Amos 4.0** will display up to four decimal places.

Viewing the graphics output

To view the graphics output, click the **View output** icon next to the drawing area. Your model will display all the properties you specified. However, you must chose to view either unstandardized or (if you selected this option) standardized estimates by click one or the other in the **Parameter Formats** panel next to your drawing area:

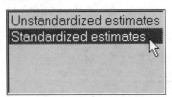

If you selected **Standardized estimates** and assuming that you selected both standardized estimates and squared multiple correlation in the **Output** tab of the **Analysis Properties** menu, your path diagram should look like **Figure 6**:

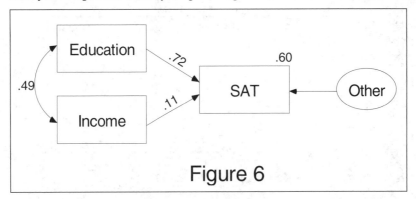

Figure 6

The value .49 is the correlation between Education and Income. The entries .72 and .11 are standaridized regression weights. The number .60 is the squared multiple correlation of SAT with Education and Income.

Now to see the unstandardized estimates, simply click on **Unstandardized estimates** in the open dialog box next to your drawing area. Your path diagram should now look like **Figure 7**:

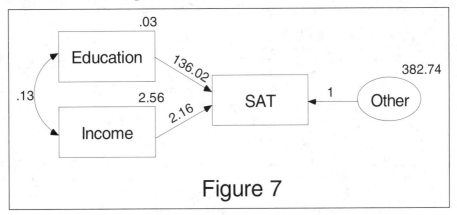

Figure 7

In the graphics output, you can click between standardized and unstandardized estimates, if you have specified the analysis of both. But note that you have to re-run the model (**Calculate estimates**) after every change to the model, data, or properties to be analyzed. This is to keep the parameter estimates up to date.

Printing the path diagram

 To print the path diagram click on the **Print** icon in the toolbox. The **Print** dialog box will appear:

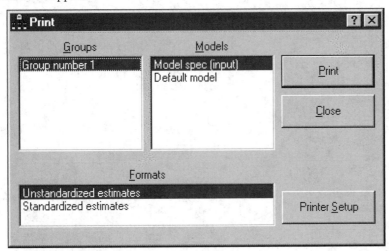

For the purposes of this tutorial, you can accept all the printing defaults and simply click on **Print**.

Copying the path diagram

Amos Graphics lets you easily export your path diagram to many word processing programs, such as Microsoft Word or WordPerfect®. Simply follow the path:

<u>E</u>dit → Cop<u>y</u> (to Clipboard)

Then, in your word processing program, use the **Paste** function to import in the diagram as a picture or text box. **Amos Graphics** will only export the diagram itself, and not the (typically gray) background. You will likely need to resize and crop the diagram, as **Amos Graphics** will copy the entire drawing area to the clipboard, typically leaving lots of extra space around your diagram.

You can also copy table or text output by clicking once and then dragging your mouse over the desired area (so the text is highlighted). After highlighting the data, hold down the **Control** key and the "c" key simultaneously (<Ctrl> - c). This will copy the highlighted text to the clipboard. Then, switch your word processing or spreadsheet program and use its **Paste** function (or press **Control** and the "v" key simultaneously; <Ctrl> - v) to import the text.

Tutorial: Learning to Write in Amos Basic

Purpose

Amos 4.0 has a programming interface called **Amos Basic**. With **Amos Basic**, you can specify models as sets of equations, rather than via the "boxes and arrows" notation introduced earlier. **Amos Basic** can be unbeatable as a workhorse for larger models and batch-oriented model estimation. It also allows you to manipulate and save the estimation results. Whenever you are more interested in the parameter values than in the paths themselves, equation mode can be the more efficient interface.

This tutorial will get you started learning to write in **Amos Basic** under Microsoft Windows. Once you have worked through this section, you can continue to incrementally learn about **Amos Basic** and its statistical applications by working through the Examples section of this User's Guide. Extensive, advanced reference material for **Amos Basic** is included in the *Amos 4.0 Programming Reference Guide*. This volume is available as a downloadable Portable Document Format (PDF) file from the **Amos 4.0** CD-ROM or as a Help file under either the **Amos Graphics** or **Amos Basic** Help menu.

Prerequisites

This tutorial assumes that **Amos 4.0** has been installed on your computer. If you have not yet installed Amos, it might be a good idea to install it now. Also, this tutorial assumes that you already have some basic experience with both text and graphics operations under the Microsoft Windows operating system. You should know how to select an item from a menu, use the mouse, and edit plain text files with a system editor such as Microsoft Notepad[®].

Data and model

Hamilton's (1990) data, featured in the **Amos Graphics** tutorial are used once again in this example. We will consider the path model in the **Amos Graphics** example and reproduced here in **Figure 1**:

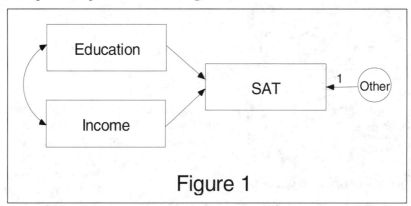

Figure 1

The path model can be expressed as a traditional regression equation of the SAT deviation scores:

SAT = b_1 • Education + b_2 • Income + Other

You will need to provide **Amos Basic** with information about both the data and this predication model.

Specifying the model

Begin by clicking on **Amos Basic** in the **Amos 4.0** program group. After the **Program Editor** has opened, click on **File** → **New Engine Program**:

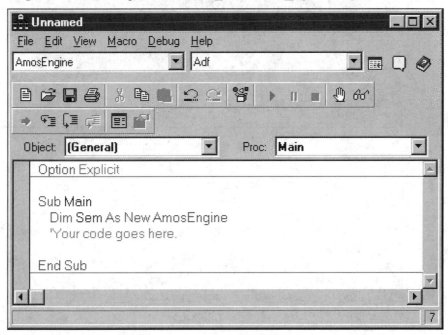

Then, begin to enter code after the cursor. Note that the line 'Your code goes here. starts with a single quote ('). When **Amos Basic** encounters a single quote, it treats the quote itself and all text to its right as a comment. Comments appear in green on a color display. In place of the comment, immediately following the line Dim Sem As New AmosEngine, type in the code for this problem.

Of course, if you do not wish to write out the code, **Amos Basic** contains the code pre-written in the file **Getstart.AmosBasic**. To get to it, click on **File** → **Open**. The default path of this file is
C:\Program Files\Amos 4\Tutorial\Getstart.AmosBasic.

Either way, when you are done, the **Amos Basic** Program Editor should look like this:

This **Amos Basic** program may not look like much of a model yet, but each line informs the program which data to read, what parameters to estimate and in what order.

The following table is a line by line explanation of what functions these **Amos Basic** commands perform.

Amos Basic Command	Explanation
Sub main()	Starts the **Amos Basic** program.
Dim Sem As New AmosEngine	Declares **Sem** as an object of type **AmosEngine**.
Sem.TextOutput	Writes the results of the analysis to a text file to be displayed by Amos's **View Text** program.
Sem.Standardized	Calculates standardized regression weights and correlations among predictor variables.
Sem.Smc	Calculates the squared multiple correlation of the dependent variable **SAT**.
Sem.BeginGroup "Hamilton.xls", "Hamilton"	Begins the model specification for a single group (or population). Additionally, **BeginGroup** specifies that the input data will be from the worksheet (data table) **Hamilton** contained in the Excel workbook **Hamilton.xls**. Amos determines from the name extension **.xls** that the data are in the Excel format. Other formats have different extensions. This worksheet/workbook nesting of data files is a new development in spreadsheet and database organization. For many other formats (such as SPSS), you will only need to specify the actual filename.
Sem.Structure "SAT = Education + Income + (1) Other"	Used to specify a model.
Sem.FitModel	Calculates parameter estimates and model fit.
End Sub	Terminates the **Amos Basic** program.

Note that the Sem.Structure line comes after the Sem.BeginGroup statement. The structure declaration must come *after* BeginGroup. Otherwise, Amos may not recognize the variable names as observed variables.

Reading data from an SPSS system file

There is one difference to naming variables when working with SPSS data files. SPSS system files support variable names of up to eight characters. Thus, if the data file Hamilton was in the SPSS format, the variable name Education would have to be shortened to Educatn.

Here is what the **Amos Basic** Program Editor should look like using the SPSS `Hamilton.sav` file:

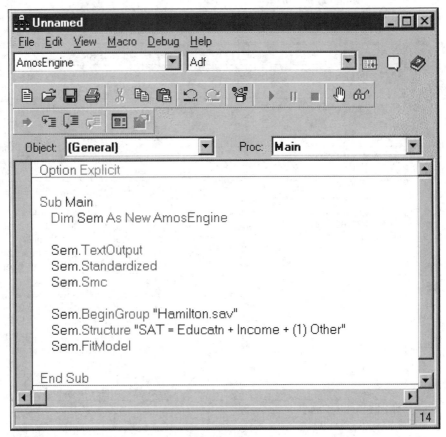

Once again, if you do not wish to write out the code, **Amos Basic** contains the code pre-written in the file `Startsps.AmosBasic`. To get to it, click on **File** → **Open**. By default, the file reference is
`C:\Program Files\Amos 4\Tutorial\Startsps.AmosBasic`.

Now, click on the **Start/Resume** arrow in order to have Amos interpret the command file and data. A small window will appear and keep you informed about the progress of the computations:

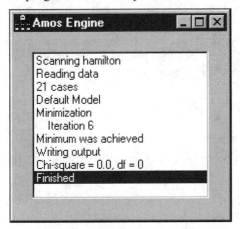

When **Amos Basic** has finished the computations, the output will immediately appear. In this example, we specified text output, so (a portion of) the output will look like this:

```
   Maximum Likelihood Estimates
   ----------------------------


Regression Weights:              Estimate    S.E.      C.R.
-------------------              --------   -------   -------

     SAT <---------- Education    136.022    30.555    4.452
     SAT <------------ Income       2.156     3.125    0.690


Covariances:                     Estimate    S.E.      C.R.
------------                     --------   -------   -------

     Education <------> Income      0.127     0.065    1.952


Variances:                       Estimate    S.E.      C.R.
----------                       --------   -------   -------

                     Education      0.027     0.008    3.162
                        Income      2.562     0.810    3.162
                         Other    382.736   121.032    3.162
```

If you have made any mistakes in entering the model or the data, an error message will be located at the end of this file. These maximum likelihood estimates are identical to the standard least-square solution for regression coefficients. Amos standard errors (S.E.) are asymptotically correct. The Critical Ratio (C.R.) is defined as:

C.R. = Estimate/S.E.

Optional output

So far, we have only been discussing the Amos default output that would be obtained without any special requests. You can request additional calculations in **Amos Basic** by adding more **Amos Engine** methods. For instance, the Sem.Structure command in the sample code calculates standardized regression weights, and the Sem.Smc command calculates the squared multiple correlation of the dependent variable SAT. You will find a complete list of Engine methods in the optional *Amos 4.0 Programming Reference Guide*.

Print functions

To print the command structure (input), simply click on the **Print** icon on the toolbar, or select **File** → **Print** from the menu.

To print text output (from the command line Sem.TextOutput), select **File** → **Print...** from the menu. The **Print Setup** box will appear:

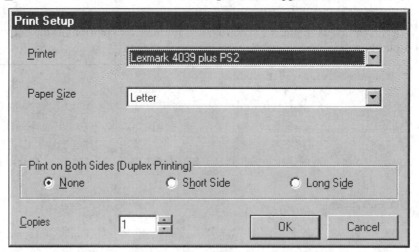

Make any changes to the settings you wish and click on **OK**.

To print table output (from the command line Sem.TableOutput), click on the **Print** icon on the toolbar. The **Print** dialog box will appear:

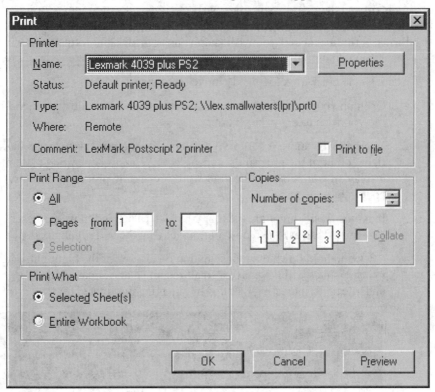

Make any changes to the settings you wish and click on **OK**.

Copy functions

Amos Basic lets you easily import your command structure (input), text output, or table output into many word processing programs, such as Microsoft Word or WordPerfect. To copy any text, click once and then drag your mouse over the desired area (so the text is highlighted). After highlighting the data, hold down the **Control** key and the "c" key simultaneously. This will copy the highlighted text to the clipboard. Then use the **Paste** function (or press **Control** and the "v" key simultaneously) to import the text into your word processing or spreadsheet program.

If you are copying the command structure, you also have the option of highlighting the text structure (as described earlier) and then selecting **File** → **Copy** from the menu. Then, as described earlier, use the **Paste** function (or press **Control** and the "v" key simultaneously) to import the text into your word processing or spreadsheet program.

Similarly, to copy table output, highlight the portion of the table you wish to copy and select **File** → **Copy** from the menu. Then, use the **Paste** function (or press **Control** and the "v" key simultaneously) to import the text into your word processing or spreadsheet program. The copy function will not copy the table format (grid lines), so if you wish keep your original table format, you will need to paste the table output into an empty table.

There is one other trick to quickly move text output:

1. Open up your word processing program to the desired file and place within the file you wish to copy the text to.

2. Minimize the entire program (typically using the **underscore** icon in the upper right corner of the program's screen. Your Windows operating system will display an icon representing your word processing program (typically) at the bottom of your screen.

3. In **Amos Basic**, highlight the text you wish to cut and move (as described earlier) and release the mouse button, leaving the text highlighted.

4. Click and hold down the mouse button on an area of the highlighted text. Your mouse pointer will now have a small rectangle and square with a "+" underneath it, indicating that it is moving the highlighted text:

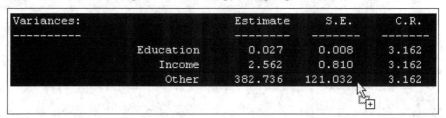

Variances:	Estimate	S.E.	C.R.
Education	0.027	0.008	3.162
Income	2.562	0.810	3.162
Other	382.736	121.032	3.162

5. Still holding down the mouse button, move the mouse pointer to the icon representing your minimized word processing program (at this point you will only see the rectangle underneath the mouse pointer):

Your word processing program and document will automatically maximize on your desktop screen.

6. Still holding down the mouse button, move the mouse pointer to the place in your word processing document where you wish to paste in the text.

7. Release the mouse button and the selected text will be moved directly into your document.

Tutorial: Learning to Program Amos with Visual Basic

Purpose

You can use **Amos 4.0** as a component in the computer programs you write. It is a relatively easy process because Amos lets you work in a general-purpose programming language instead of having to learn some special language. To use **Amos 4.0** with your program, you need to program in a language or environment that can control automation servers, *e.g.*, Microsoft **Visual Basic**, Microsoft **C++**, the **SPSS** scripting facility, **SAS**, DEC **Visual FORTRAN** or Borland **Delphi**[1].

The program that you write can carry out a single Amos analysis, or multiple Amos analyses. It can also include statements that:

- specify a model
- give the location of data files
- select options, such as: which discrepancy function to use, whether to obtain bootstrap confidence intervals, and so on.

This section demonstrates in detail how you can call **Amos 4.0** from the Microsoft **Visual Basic Professional Edition**[2], Version 5.0. It assumes that Microsoft **Visual**

---

[1] At the time of this writing, there have not been any attempts to use **Amos 4.0** with SAS, Visual Fortran, or Borland Delphi.

Basic Professional Edition is installed on your system. The **Visual Basic** files for this tutorial are `StartVB.vbp` (VB project) and `StartVB.bas` (VB code). You will find both located in the `Tutorial` subdirectory underneath the **Amos 4.0** program directory.

1. Create a new Visual Basic project

First, launch **Visual Basic**. In the **New Project** window, click on the **New** tab and double-click on **Standard EXE**.

---

[2] Microsoft offers several other **Visual Basic** packages with varying capabilities. Most of these can be used with **Amos 4.0**, but different steps may be required to reference the Amos Engine.

2. Remove Form1

If this is the first time you have used **Visual Basic** since its installation, the **Visual Basic** window will probably look something like this:

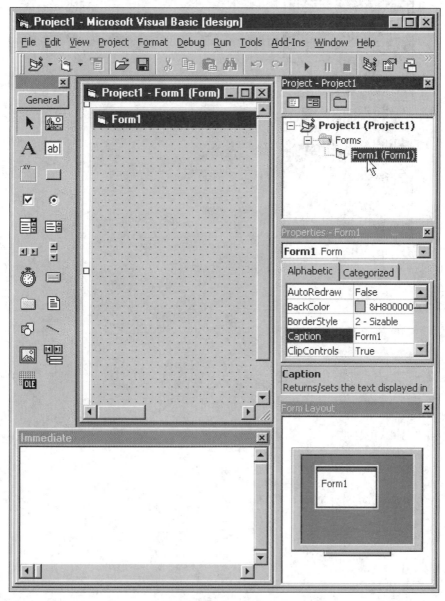

Many of the elements in the **Visual Basic** window are useful only when you are writing a program that has a graphical interface. These elements are not needed for this tutorial, so we will get rid of them.

In the **Project1** window, use the *right* mouse button to click on **Form1 (Form1)** as indicated by the mouse pointer in the preceding figure. When the following pop-up menu appears, select **Remove Form1**:

3. Hide unnecessary windows

 Hide the VB toolbar by clicking the **X** button indicated by the mouse pointer in the following figure:

Also, hide the three sub-windows titled **Project - Project1**, **Properties - Project1**, and **Form Layout - Project1**. (Do not hide the sub-window titled **Immediate**.)

The resulting **Visual Basic** window should look like this:

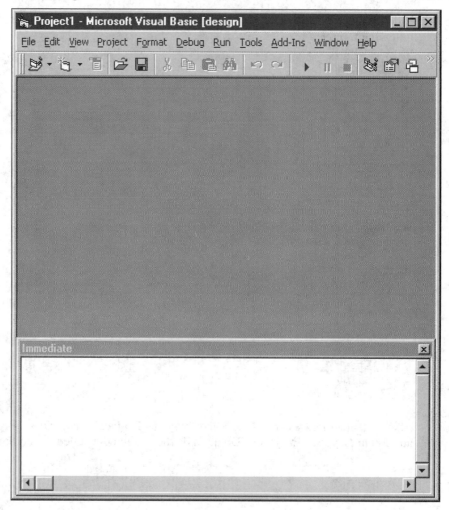

4. Create a code window for your program

On the menu, select **Project** and then **Add Module**:

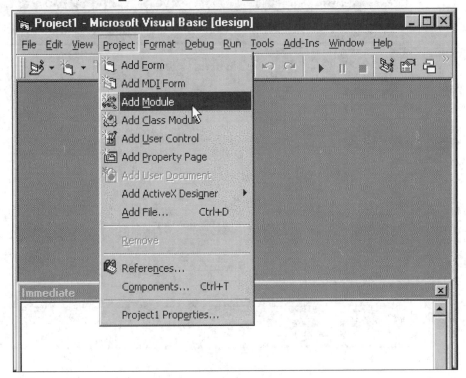

In the **Add Module** window, select the **New** tab and double-click on **Module**:

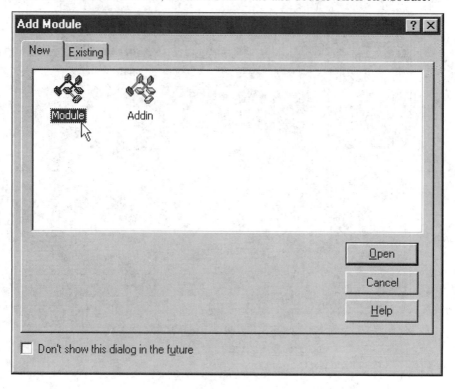

The **Visual Basic** window will then look something like this:

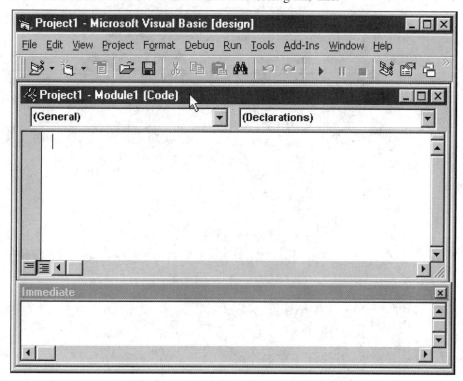

5. Tell Visual Basic how to find the Amos Engine

In order to let **Visual Basic** know that you want to use the Amos Engine, select **Project** from the main menu, and then **References**:

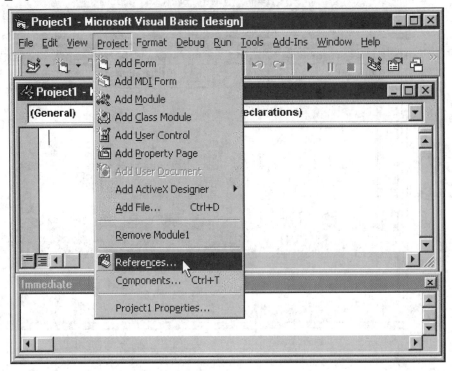

When the **References - Project1** dialog appears, make sure that the **Amos Engine** box is has a check mark in it. If necessary, click on the **Amos Engine** box to add a check mark. Then press the **OK** button to close the dialog:

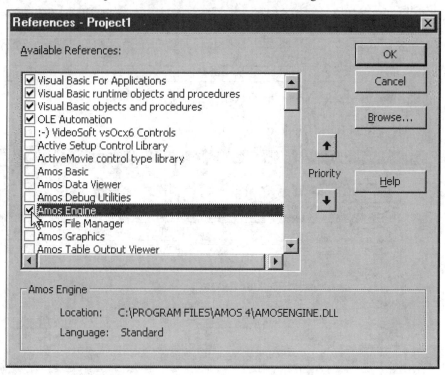

6. Enter your program

Type the following program in the large panel in the **Visual Basic** window.

```
Option Explicit

Sub main()
    Dim Sem As New AmosEngine

    Sem.TextOutput

    Sem.BeginGroup Sem.Dir & "Tutorial\Hamilton.dbf"
    Sem.Structure "SAT = (w1) Education + (w2) Income + (1) Other"
    Sem.FitModel

    Debug.Print "Regression weight 1 is "; Sem.ParameterValue
("w1")
    Debug.Print "Regression weight 2 is "; Sem.ParameterValue ("w2")
    Debug.Print "Chi square = "; Sem.Cmin
    Debug.Print "Degrees of freedom = "; Sem.df

End Sub
```

Instead of typing these commands, you can also insert the **StartVB.bas** file from **Amos 4.0**'s **Tutorial** subdirectory. With the code window active, run **Edit → Insert File...** and select **StartVB.bas** located by default in the **C:\Program Files\Amos 4\Tutorial** directory. Sem.Dir is an Amos Engine property that returns the path to where the Amos program is found. The VB string expression:

```
Sem.Dir & "Tutorial\Hamilton.dbf"
```

pinpoints exactly where the data file resides.

The **Visual Basic** window should look like this:

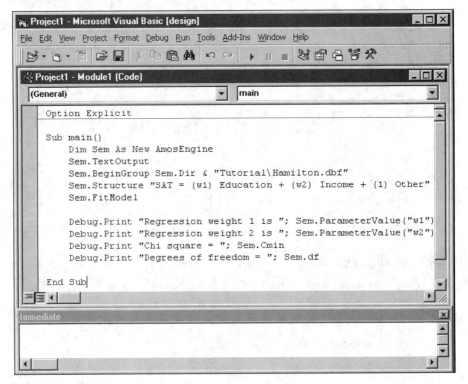

7. Run the program

To run the program, select **Run** from the main menu, and then **Start with Full Compile**:

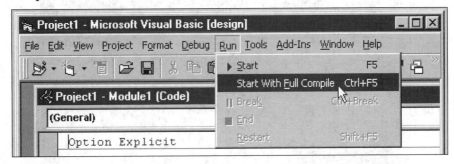

When the program has finished running, the output from the Debug.Print statements appears in the **Immediate** panel:

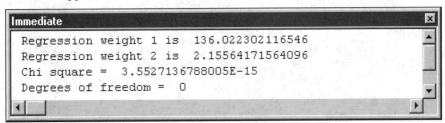

8. Try out the help system

Before closing the **Visual Basic** window, try the help system. Click somewhere within one of the words that describes an Amos method in your program:

> TextOutput
> BeginGroup
> Structure
> FitModel
> ParameterValue
> Cmin
> Df

Then press the **F1** key. A dialog box will appear giving documentation for that method. To get a list of all available methods, press the **F2** key to display **Visual Basic's Object Browser**. In the **Classes** listbox, click on **AmosEngine**.

All the available methods will appear in the listbox labeled **Members of 'AmosEngine'**:

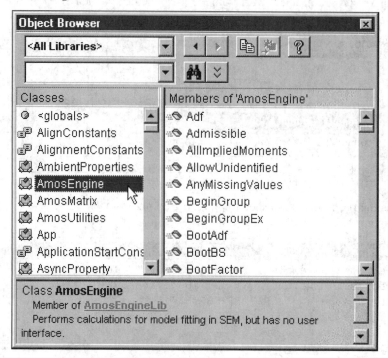

Click once on a method to see a short summary of its function in the bottom panel. Press **F1** to see the full documentation of the method.

Beyond the basics

Still seeking more information about how to use **Amos 4.0** as a component in the computer programs you write? Extensive, advanced reference material for the Amos API is also included in the *Amos 4.0 Programming Reference Guide*. This guide is available as a downloadable Portable Document Format (PDF) file from the Amos 4.0 CD-ROM or as a Help file from either the **Amos Graphics or Amos Basic** Help menu.

Worked Examples

21 Worked Examples

Most people's learning style is "learning by doing." Knowing this, we have developed 21 examples to quickly demonstrate practical ways to use Amos — without bogging down in a lot of detail. The initial examples introduce Amos's program functions with simple statistical problems. You will learn which icons to select, how to access the several supported data formats, and how to maneuver through the output. Later examples tackle Amos's handling of more advanced statistical capabilities and are less concerned with program interface issues.

> *If you have questions about a particular Amos feature, you can always refer to Amos's extensive online Help or the* Amos 4.0 Graphics Reference Guide *(PDF or Help file).*

Example 1: Estimating Variances and Covariance

Purpose

- Show how Amos can be used to estimate population variances and covariances.

- Illustrate the general format of Amos input and output.

The data

Attig (1983) showed forty subjects a booklet containing several pages of advertisements. Then each subject was given three memory performance tests:

test	explanation
recall	The subject was asked to recall as many of the advertisements as possible. The subject's score on this test was the number of advertisements recalled correctly.
cued	The subject was given some cues and asked again to recall as many of the advertisements as possible. The subject's score was the number of advertisements recalled correctly.
place	The subject was given a list of the advertisements that appeared in the booklet, and asked to recall the page location of each one. The subject's score on this test was the number of advertisements whose location was recalled correctly.

Attig repeated the study with the same forty subjects after a training exercise intended to improve memory performance. There were thus three performance measures before training and three performance measures after training. In addition, he recorded scores on a vocabulary test, as well as age, sex and level of education.

You will find Attig's data files in Amos's **Examples** directory. We have saved the data in various formats to demonstrate how Amos automatically recognizes most spreadsheet software files. In this demonstration, we will read the data from a Microsoft Excel workbook.

Begin by following these menu commands to initially open **Amos Graphics**:

Start → **Programs** → **Amos 4** → **Amos Graphics**

Then in **Amos Graphics**, follow this path to open a new model:

File → **New**

You will see a box with an empty drawing space.

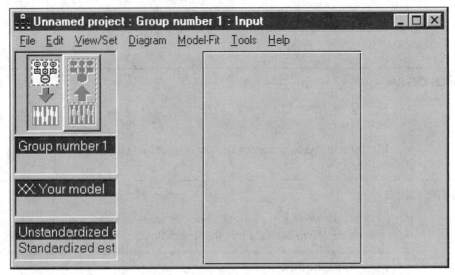

The next step is attaching data to the model. Do this by selecting:

File → **Data Files...** → **File Name**

Pull down the **Files of type** field to display the various file formats Amos can support. For this example, we will select data from an Excel workbook:

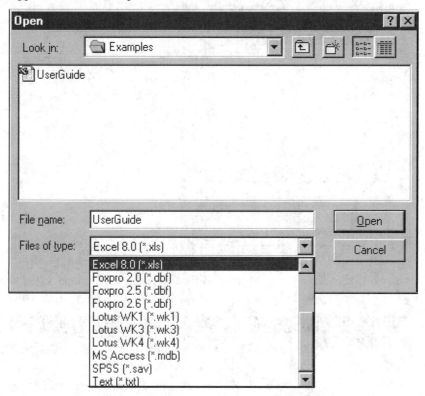

The Excel workbook **UserGuide** contains all data files for the examples. Click **UserGuide** and **Open**.

> *If you do not see the* **UserGuide** *workbook icon at this point, then* **Amos 4.0** *is probably pointing to a different directory. You can usually find the data by following the directory path*
>
> **C:** → **Program Files** → **Amos 4** → **Examples**

Amos next displays a list of worksheets in the **UserGuide** workbook:

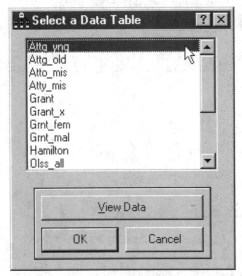

The worksheet **Attg_yng** has the data for this problem. Click on **Attg_yng** and **View Data**. You will see the Excel worksheet for the **Attg_yng** data file:

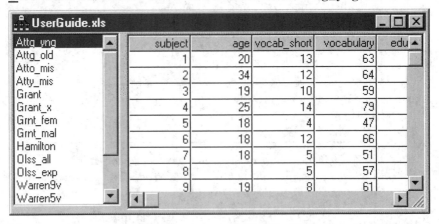

If you scroll across the worksheet, you will see all of Attig's test variables:

- subject - subject ID
- age - age of subject
- vocab_short - raw score on WAIS subtest
- vocabulary - raw score on WAIS
- education - years of schools
- sex - 0 = female, 1 = male
- recall1 - recall pretest
- recall2 - recall posttest

- cued1 - cued recall pretest
- cued2 - cued recall posttest
- place1 - place recall pretest
- place2 - place recall posttest

We will initially focus on the **recall** and **place** variables.

 Once you have reviewed the data, exit the data view by clicking on the **X**. Then close the file opening displays by clicking on each of the **OK** buttons.

Analyzing the data

Now that you have called up the Attig data, you can move on to the analysis. In this example, the analysis is to estimate the variances and covariances of the **recall** and **place** variables before and after training. Amos offers two ways of performing these estimates. The first method uses the path diagrams in **Amos Graphics**. The second method is equation oriented modeling, which is used in **Amos Basic**. Since either method has advantages, we present both ways.

> *In every example, we will present both* **Amos Graphics** *and* **Amos Basic** *methods. Although you will probably find using* **Amos Graphics** *a lot easier, please read both sections. Statistical information you need may be included in one section, but not in the other.*

Modeling in Amos Graphics

In **Amos Graphics**, click **File** and **New** to specify a new model.

Follow these steps to place four rectangles on the screen. The rectangles indicate that the model has four observed variables:

1. Click on the **Draw observed variables** (rectangle) icon.

2. Move your mouse to the area of the drawing space where you want create the first rectangle.

3. Hold down the left mouse button and drag the pointer to create a rectangle.

4. Click on the **Duplicate objects** (copy machine) icon.

5. Move the mouse back to your rectangle. Hold down the left mouse button and drag out a duplicate rectangle, moving it next to the original one.

6. Continue to drag out duplicate rectangles until you have four rectangles side by side:

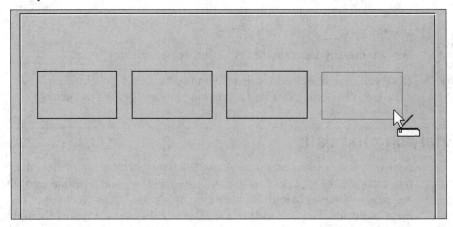

 If you want to reposition your rectangles, click the **Move objects** (truck) icon and then point the mouse at the object you want to move. Hold down the left mouse button until you have positioned the object, then release it. From now on, "click" will mean "click with the left mouse button."

> *Amos 4.0 gives you more than one way to accomplish the same task. For every button, there is a menu option that performs exactly the same task. For many tasks, Amos also provides keyboard shortcuts.*

You could have also created an observed variable rectangle by using menu options. For instance, you could have clicked on the **Diagram** menu (or pressing **D** while holding down the **Alt** key, called "Alt-D"), and then clicked on the **Draw Observed** command (or pressing **O**). To duplicate an object by using the menu, click on the **Edit** menu, and then on the **Duplicate** command.

You can also activate some buttons by pressing one or two keyboard shortcuts. For example, the keyboard shortcut for **Draw Observed** is **F3**. You know that Amos has activated the command if the cursor has a miniature rectangle (for **Draw Observed**) beneath it. Use whatever way works best for you. At this point, it does not matter how you obtained the command, continue as if you had just pressed the button.

> *These examples will not list the menu commands and keyboard shortcuts for each task. You will find a complete listing of each in the* Amos 4.0 Graphics Reference Guide *(PDF or Help file). Familiarize yourself with whatever option you find easiest to use.*

The next step is to give the rectangles variable names. Do this by clicking on the **List Variables in data set**. A dialog box will open displaying the names of all the variable names from the data file.

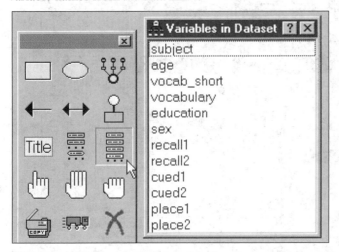

Click on a variable name and drag it (keeping your left mouse button depressed) to a rectangle:

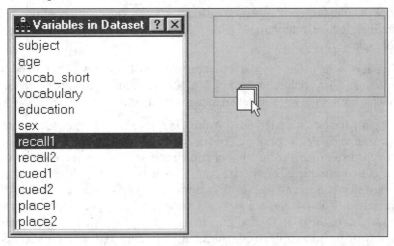

When you release the mouse, the variable name will appear in the box. Repeat the drag and drop procedure until you have labeled all four variables.

At this point you may want to change the font, size, or some other property of your variable. To make changes, simply double click on the variable you wish to alter. Dotted lines will surround the selected rectangle and the **Object Properties** dialog box will appear.

For instance, to increase the font size, select the **Text** tab and enter a new font size:

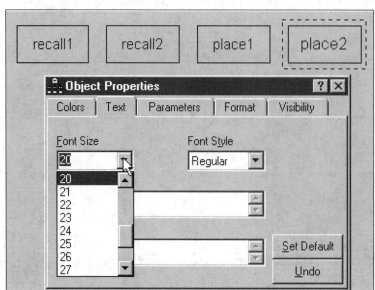

Notice that the **Object Properties** dialog box gives you a variety of options if you wish to customize your variable names. In this example, we changed the font size to 20 point.

This diagram identifies the four variables. Note that Amos does not mention the remaining eight variables in the data file. Amos automatically disregards any variable that has not been included in the path diagram.

If the path diagram were left as is, **Amos Graphics** would estimate the variances of the four variables, but not the covariances between them. In **Amos Graphics**, the rule is to assume a correlation or covariance of zero whenever arrows do not connect two variables. To estimate the covariances between the observed variables, we must first connect all pairs with two-way arrows. Do this by selecting the **Draw covariances** (double-headed arrows) icon, and dragging connecting arrows from one variable to the next. By dragging from the right variable to a left variable, the arrows will automatically go underneath the variables. **Amos 4.0** is smart enough to know what are acceptable covariances and will not allow you to draw inappropriate linkages.

If you make a mistake, simply click on the **Erase** icon and then click on the double-headed arrow you wish to erase. In the end, you should have drawn six two-way arrows.

As you draw the last covariance, the input path diagram will look somewhat like the portion of this screen:

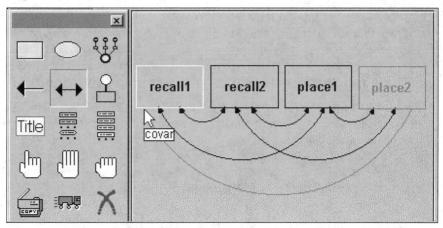

Amos Graphics output

To estimate the model parameters with Amos, simply click on the **Calculate estimates** (abacus) icon. Amos will then prompt you for a filename for saving the path diagram to disk. We have already set up this example (and all of the others), and saved it under the name **Ex01.amw**.

Immediately after saving the diagram, Amos calculates the parameter estimates. To view the results, click on the **View Output** icon. Amos displays the output path diagram with parameter estimates inserted:

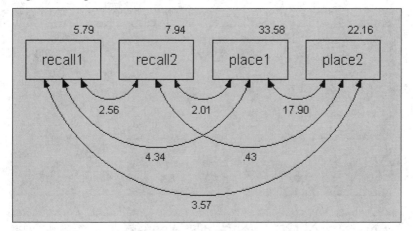

In the output path diagram, the numbers displayed next to each box are the variance estimates, and the numbers displayed next to the two-way arrows are the estimated covariances. For instance, the variance of **recall1** is estimated at 5.79, and that of **place1** at 33.58. The estimated covariance between these two variables is 4.34.

 To view the estimates in spreadsheet form, click on the **Table Output** icon or **Table Output** from the **View/Set** menu. We will provide a detailed explanation of the analysis after introducing how to specify models using **Amos Basic**.

Modeling with Amos Basic (programming interface)

Amos 4.0 has a programming interface called **Amos Basic**. With **Amos Basic**, you can specify models as sets of equations, rather than via the "boxes and arrows" notation introduced earlier. **Amos Basic** can be unbeatable as a workhorse for larger models and batch-oriented model estimation. It also allows you to manipulate and save the estimation results. Whenever you are more interested in the parameter values than in the paths themselves, equation mode can be the more efficient interface.

Begin by clicking on **Amos Basic** in the **Amos 4.0** program group. After the **Program Editor** has opened, click on **File → New Engine Program**:

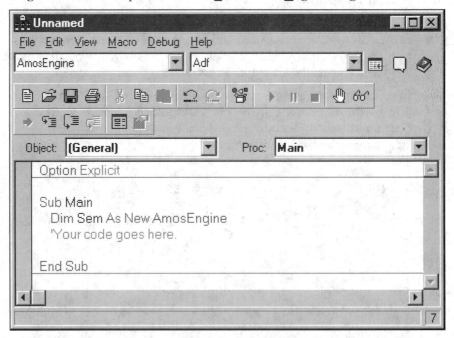

Then, begin to enter code after the cursor. Note that the line 'Your code goes here. starts with a single quote ('). When **Amos Basic** encounters a single quote, it treats the quote itself and all text to its right as a comment. Comments appear in green on a color display. In place of the comment, immediately following the line Dim Sem As New AmosEngine, type in the code for this problem.

When you are done, the **Amos Basic** Program Editor should look like this:

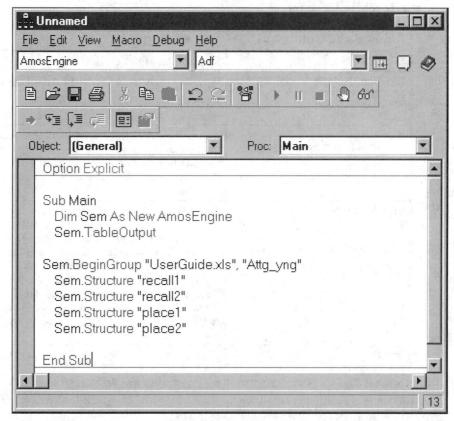

> **Amos Basic** *contains all these examples pre-written, so you do not have to write out all these commands. Simply click on* **Open** *and select an example — in this case* **Ex01**. **Amos Basic** *program files have the extension* ***.AmosBasic**.

This **Amos Basic** program may not look like much of a model yet, but each line informs the program which data to read, what parameters to estimate and in what order.

The following table is a line by line explanation of what functions these **Amos Basic** commands perform.

Amos Basic Command	Explanation
Sub main()	Starts the **Amos Basic** program.
Dim Sem As New AmosEngine	Declares **Sem** as an object of type **AmosEngine**.
Sem.TableOutput	Sends the analysis results to an Excel-type spreadsheet or table.
Sem.BeginGroup "UserGuide.xls", "Attg_yng"	Begins the model specification for a single group (or population). Additionally, **BeginGroup** specifies that the **Attg_yng** worksheet in the Excel workbook **UserGuide.xls** is to be used as input data.
Sem.Structure "recall1" Sem.Structure "recall2" Sem.Structure "place1" Sem.Structure "place2"	Used to specify a model. The four **Structure** commands declare the variances of **recall1**, **recall2**, **place1** and **place2** as free parameters. The other eight variables in the **Attg_yng** file are left out of this analysis. With **Amos Basic**, observed exogenous variables are assumed to be correlated by default. In other words, **Amos Basic** will automatically include the six covariance parameters with the variance term of the four exogenous variables.
End Sub	Terminates the **Amos Basic** program.

Note that the four Sem.Structure lines come after the Sem.BeginGroup statement. The structure declaration must come *after* BeginGroup. Otherwise, Amos may not recognize the variable names.

Now, click on the **Start/Resume** arrow in order to have Amos calculate the estimates of variances and covariances and display them in spreadsheet form. Then, click on **Parameter Estimates** to view the Covariances and Variances:

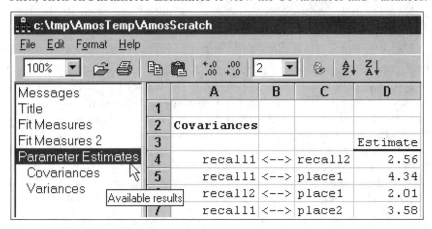

Expand the table to view the analysis.

	A	B	C	D	E	F	G
1							
2	Covariances						
3				Estimate	S.E.	c.r.	P
4	recall1	<-->	recall2	2.56	1.16	2.20	0.03
5	recall1	<-->	place1	4.34	2.34	1.86	0.06
6	recall2	<-->	place1	2.01	2.64	0.76	0.44
7	recall1	<-->	place2	3.58	1.90	1.88	0.06
8	recall2	<-->	place2	0.43	2.13	0.20	0.84
9	place1	<-->	place2	17.91	5.22	3.43	0.00
10							
11	Variances						
12				Estimate	S.E.	c.r.	P
13			recall1	5.79	1.31	4.42	0.00
14			recall2	7.94	1.80	4.42	0.00
15			place1	33.58	7.60	4.42	0.00
16			place2	22.16	5.02	4.42	0.00

Explanation of the table output

The first estimate is of the covariance between **recall1** and **recall2**. The covariance is estimated to be 2.56. Right next to that estimate, in the S.E. column, is an estimate of the standard error of the covariance, 1.16. The estimate 2.56 is an observation on an approximately normally distributed random variable centered around the population covariance with a standard deviation of about 1.16 — that is if the assumptions in Appendix A (found in the Appendices section of this User's Guide) are met. You can use these figures to construct, say, a 95% confidence interval on the population covariance by computing $2.56 \pm 1.96 \times 1.160 = 2.56 \pm 2.274$. Later you will see that you can use Amos to estimate many kinds of population parameters besides covariances, and follow the same procedure to set a confidence interval on any one of them.

Right next to the standard error, in the C.R. column, is the critical ratio obtained by dividing the covariance estimate by its standard error ($2.20 = 2.56/1.16$). This ratio is relevant to the null hypothesis that, in the population from which Attig's forty subjects came, the covariance between **recall1** and **recall2** is zero. If this hypothesis is true, and still under the assumptions of page , the critical ratio is an observation on a random variable that has an approximate standard normal distribution. Thus, using a significance level of .05, any critical ratio that exceeds 1.96 in magnitude would be called significant. In this example, since 2.20 is greater than 1.96, you would say that the covariance between **recall1** and **recall2** is significantly different from zero at the .05 level.

The P column, to the right of C.R., gives the approximate two-tailed probability for critical ratios this large or larger. The calculation of P assumes the parameter estimates to be normally distributed, and is only correct in large samples. See Appendix A in the Appendices section of this User's Guide for a more detailed explanation.

The assertion that the parameter estimates are normally distributed is only an approximation. Moreover, the standard errors reported in the S.E. column are only approximations, and may not be the best available. Consequently, the confidence interval and the hypothesis test just discussed are also only approximate. This is because the theory on which these results are based is *asymptotic*. Asymptotic means that it can be made to apply with any desired degree of accuracy, but only by using a sufficiently large sample. We will not discuss whether the approximation is satisfactory with the present sample size because there would be no way to generalize the conclusions to the many other kinds of analyses that you can do with Amos. However, you may want to re-examine the null hypothesis that **recall1** and **recall2** are uncorrelated, just to see what is meant by an approximate test.

We previously concluded that the covariance is significantly different from zero because 2.20 exceeds 1.96. The p value associated with a standard normal deviate of 2.20 is .028 (two tailed), which of course is less than .05. By contrast, the conventional t statistic (*e.g.*, Runyon and Haber, 1980, p. 226) is 2.509 with 38 degrees of freedom   (p = .016). In this example, both p values are less than .05, so both tests agree in rejecting the null hypothesis at the .05 level. However, in other situations, the two p values might lie on *opposite* sides of .05. You might or might not regard this as especially serious — at any rate, the two tests can give different results. There should be no doubt about which test is better. The t test is exact under the assumptions of normality and independence of observations, no matter what the sample size. The test based on Amos' critical ratio depends on the same assumptions, but with a finite sample the test is only approximate.

> *For many interesting applications of Amos, there is no exact test or exact standard error or exact confidence interval available for statistical comparisons.*

On the bright side, when fitting a model for which conventional estimates exist, maximum likelihood point estimates (*i.e.*, the numbers in Amos' Estimate column) are generally identical to the conventional estimates.

Now click on **Fit Measures**. The first few lines play an important role in every Amos analysis:

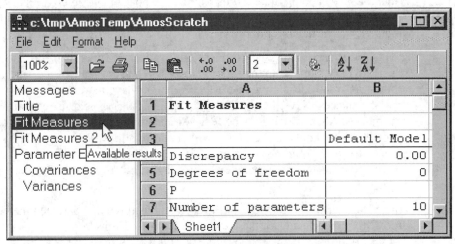

In the present analysis, there are four variables for Amos to work with: **recall1**, **recall2**, **place1** and **place2**. There are four sample variances and six sample covariances, for a total of ten elements. As for the parameters to be estimated, they are the corresponding population variances and covariances. There are, of course, four population variances and six population covariances, which makes ten parameters to be estimated (line 7, column B). The degrees of freedom is the amount by which the number of elements exceeds the number of parameters to be estimated. In this example, there is a one-to-one correspondence between the elements and the parameters to be estimated, so it is no accident that there are zero degrees of freedom (line 5, column B).

As we will see beginning with Example 2, any nontrivial null hypothesis about the parameters will effectively reduce the number of parameters that have to be estimated. The result will be positive degrees of freedom. For now, there is no null hypothesis being tested.

Discrepancy (line 4, column B) normally gives the discrepancy or fit chi-square value. A chi-square value of zero would ordinarily indicate no departure from the null hypothesis. But in the present example, the zero value for degrees of freedom and the zero chi-square value merely reflect the fact that there was no null hypothesis in the first place. If there had been an hypothesis under test in this example, the chi-square value would have been a measure of the extent to which the data were incompatible with the hypothesis.

Optional output

So far, we have only been discussing the Amos default output that would be obtained without any special requests. You can request additional calculations in **Amos Basic** by adding more **Amos Engine** methods. You can do the same in **Amos Graphics** by clicking on the **Analysis Properties** icon and then the **Output** tab, to view a variety of options.

You may be surprised to find estimates of covariances rather than correlations, which are more familiar in the social sciences. When the scale of measurement is arbitrary or of no substantive interest, correlations have more descriptive meaning than covariances. Nevertheless, Amos and similar programs insist on estimating covariances. Also, as will soon be seen, Amos provides a simple method for testing hypotheses about covariances, but not about correlations. This is mainly because it is easier to write programs that way. On the other hand, it is not hard to derive correlation estimates once the relevant variances and covariances have been estimated.

Amos Basic displays estimates of the correlations if the Standardized method is used. More specifically, in the Example 1 commands, insert the line Sem.Standardized between the Dim Sem As New AmosEngine and Sem.TableOutput lines.

To get standardized estimates in **Amos Graphics,** simply click on the **Analysis Properties** icon and the **Output** tab. Then, check **Standardized estimates**:

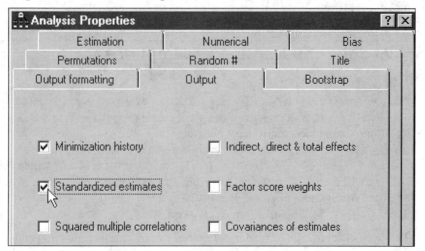

Then, run the model once again. To display the standardized correlation estimates in the path diagram, click the **View Output** icon and **Standardized estimates** in the **Parameter Formats** box:

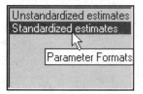

You can also display the correlations as text output or table output, simply by selecting either the **View Text** or **View Table Output** icon.

In either case the resulting output will be:

	A	B	C	D	E
1					
2	**Correlations**				
3				Estimate	
4	recall1	<–>	recall2	0.38	
5	recall2	<–>	place1	0.12	
6	place1	<–>	place2	0.66	
7	recall2	<–>	place2	0.03	
8	recall1	<–>	place1	0.31	
9	recall1	<–>	place2	0.32	

These correlation estimates are obtained in the usual way from the estimated covariances and variances shown previously. Being functions of maximum likelihood estimates, they are also maximum likelihood estimates.

Technical note: Distribution assumptions for Amos models

Amos's default method of computing parameter estimates is called *maximum likelihood*. It is beyond the scope of this document to say much about the maximum likelihood criterion, except that it produced estimates with very desirable properties. For more information about the maximum likelihood method, visit the FAQ pages on the SmallWaters website: www.smallwaters.com. However, be assured that the maximum likelihood method is a sound, modern approach to computing parameter estimates. Unless you requested otherwise, Amos estimates will be maximum likelihood.

The claim that Amos's estimates are indeed maximum likelihood depends, of course, on certain statistical distribution assumptions that have to be met by the input data. Hypothesis testing procedures, confidence intervals and claims for efficiency in maximum likelihood or generalized least squares estimation by Amos depend on certain statistical distribution assumptions. First, observations must be independent. For instance, the forty young people in the Attig study have to be picked independently from the population of young people. Second, the observed variables must meet certain distributional requirements. For instance, it will suffice if the observed variables have a multivariate normal distribution. Multivariate normality of all observed variables is a standard distribution assumption in many structural equation modeling and factor analysis applications.

There is another, more general situation to apply maximum likelihood estimation. If some exogenous variables are fixed (*i.e.*, they are either known beforehand or measured without error) their distribution may have any shape, provided that:

- For any value pattern of the fixed variables, the remaining (random) variables have a (conditional) normal distribution.

- The (conditional) variance-covariance matrix of the random variables is the same for every pattern of the fixed variables.

- The (conditional) expected values of the random variables depend linearly on the values of the fixed variables.

A typical example of a fixed variable would be an experimental treatment, classifying respondents into a study and a control group, respectively. This is alright as long as the other exogenous variables are normally distributed for study and control cases alike, and with the same conditional variance-covariance matrix.

Note that an experimental grouping variable is regarded as fixed, because the group assignment is completely determined by the experimenter.

Predictor variables in regression analysis (*cf.*, Example 4) are usually regarded as fixed, exogenous variables. Example 5 will demonstrate a test of this type of assumption.

Many people are accustomed to the requirements for normality and independent observations, since these are the usual requirements for many conventional procedures. However, with Amos, you have to remember that meeting these requirements lead only to asymptotic conclusions (*i.e.*, conclusions that are approximately true for large samples).

Example 2: Testing Hypotheses

Purpose

- Demonstrate how Amos can be used to test simple hypotheses about variances and covariances.

- Introduce the chi-square test for goodness of fit.

- Elaborate on the concept of degrees of freedom.

Data

We will again be using Attig's (1983) spatial memory data. The data were described in Example 1. To demonstrate Amos's flexibility with different data input formats, the example will use the SPSS version of this file, as opposed to the Excel version used in Example 1.

Placing constraints on parameters

Modeling using Amos Graphics

Here is the path diagram that was used in Example 1. We can think of the variable objects as having small boxes nearby (representing the variances) that are filled in once Amos has computed the parameter estimates.

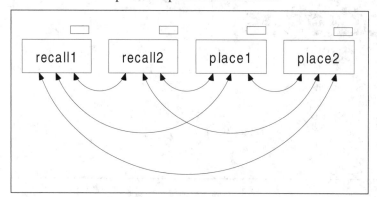

Actually, you can fill these boxes in yourself. If you wish to constrain the variance of any variable to a fixed value, follow the steps in this example. Suppose you wanted to set the variance of **recall1** to 6. Start by double clicking on **recall1**. The **Object Properties** dialog box will appear. Select the **Parameters** tab and enter the value 6 in the **Variance** field.

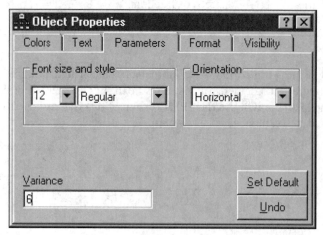

While the **Object Properties** dialog window is open, click on **recall2** and set its variance to 8. After leaving the **Object Properties** dialog box, **Amos Graphics** displays the newly fixed parameter values in the path diagram:

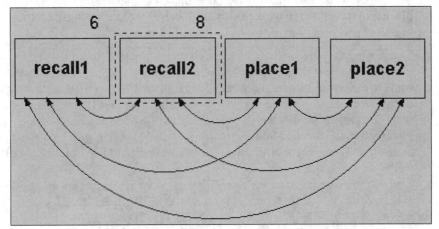

Of course, this was probably not a very realistic example because the numbers, 6 and 8, were just picked out of the air. Realistic value constraints must be based on good theory, previous analyses of similar data, or derived from study design or model identification rules. However, you can enter other things besides numbers into the **Variance** field.

Frequently, you will be interested in the plausibility of the variances being equal in the population, particularly in related variables such as **recall1** and **recall2**. You might believe this (or at least want to investigate the possibility) without having a particular value for the variances in mind. In such a scenario, again click on the **Object Properties** dialog box and then the **Parameters** tab function. But instead of equating the two variance parameters to different numeric values, simply equate them to a common symbolic name, such as the label **v_recall**.

> *Note that parameter labels may be up to 1000 characters long and must begin with a letter. If the variances of both variable objects are set to the same label, then any subsequent analysis will set these variances equal.*

We are going to tamper with the input file a little more before looking at any results, but first we will answer why you would want to specify that two parameters, like the variances of **recall1** and **recall2**, are equal. Here are two benefits:

- If you specify that two parameters are equal in the population, and if you are correct in this specification, then you will get more accurate estimates — not only of the parameters that are equal, but usually of the others as well. This is the only benefit if you happen to know that the parameters are equal.

- If the equality of two parameters is a mere hypothesis, requiring their estimates to be equal will result in a test of that hypothesis.

You may also want to consider the possibility that **place1** has the same variance as **place2**. In this example we are using the label v_place to constrain the variances of **place1** and **place2** to the same, estimated value.

Your model may also include restrictions on parameters other than variances. For example, you may hypothesize that the covariance between **recall1** and **place1** is equal to the covariance between **recall2** and **place2**. To do so, double click on the double-headed covariance path between **recall1** and **place1** (it will highlight in red). The **Object Properties** dialog box will again appear. Click on the **Parameters** tab function and set the value of this path to a symbolic constant, such as **cov_rp**. Then, set the covariance path between **recall2** and **place2** to **cov_rp** as well:

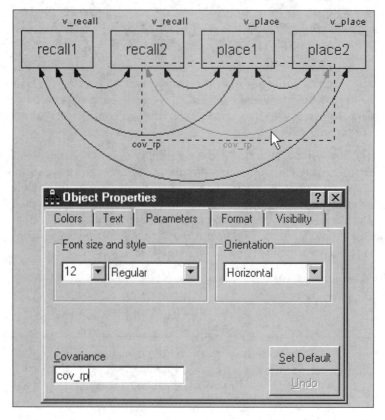

Moving variable objects

Up to now, and throughout the first example, we have displayed the four variable objects all in a line. While this is fine for small examples such as these, it is not practical for analyses that are more complex. Suppose we want to display the objects in a box-like fashion. Simply press the **Move objects** (moving truck) icon, click on the object you want moved, and with the mouse button still pressed, move the object (a shadow of the object will help you) to its desired location. This is the final path diagram found in **Ex02.amw**:

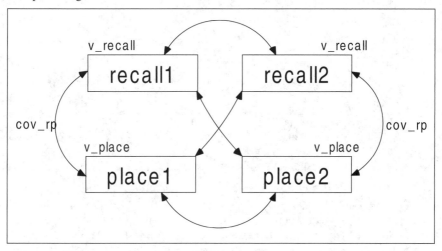

Some additional icons can be helpful in making your path diagram look just like the one above, in addition to the **Move objects** icon. The most important of these is the **Drag Properties** icon (also menu commands: **Edit** → **Drag Properties**). It is used to transfer (or copy) selected properties of a source object to one or more target objects. We will discuss other icons in later examples, but review the *Amos 4.0 Graphics Reference Guide* (PDF or Help file) for a complete description. Learning icon functions can greatly reduce the time it takes to produce a publication-quality path diagram.

Data input

As in Example 1, you need to attach data to the model by selecting:

File → **Data Files...** → **File Name**

In this example we will select SPSS (`*.sav`) as the file type:

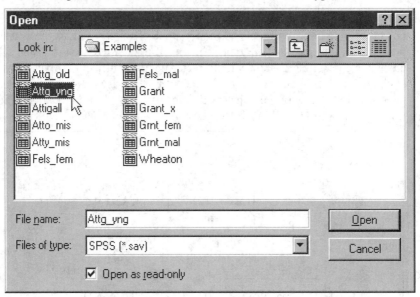

In Amos, viewing SPSS files works a little different from other file types. If SPSS (version 7.5 or later) is installed on your system, then Amos can launch SPSS to display the `*.sav` when requested. Run **File → Data Files...** and click on **View Data** to display the input data. If you have SPSS installed on your system, Amos will automatically start SPSS to display the `*.sav` files when you click **View Data**. Amos is always able to *read* SPSS files, but you must have SPSS installed on your system to *display* them. For many other file types (such as Excel and Lotus), Amos can both read and display the file without having the program installed on your system. Choose the `Attg_yng` worksheet in the SPSS format and click **Open.** Then in the **Data Files** dialog box, click on **View Data**.

If SPSS is installed on your system, you will see the following table:

	subject	age	v_short	vocab	educatio
1	1	20	13	63	14
2	2	34	12	64	14
3	3	19	10	59	13

As before, once you have reviewed the data, exit the data view by clicking on the **X**. Then close the file opening displays by clicking on each of the **OK** buttons.

Modeling in Amos Basic

Specifying the constrained model in **Amos Basic** requires a modification similar to that of adding the small boxes near each variable. Here, the boxes take the form of lines of code. Start by opening **Amos Basic**. **Amos Basic** will automatically open up an engine with an area to begin writing in your code. As in Example 1, simply begin to enter code in place of the comment, immediately following the line Dim Sem As New AmosEngine.

Once you have typed in the code for this example, the **Amos Basic** Program Editor should look like this:

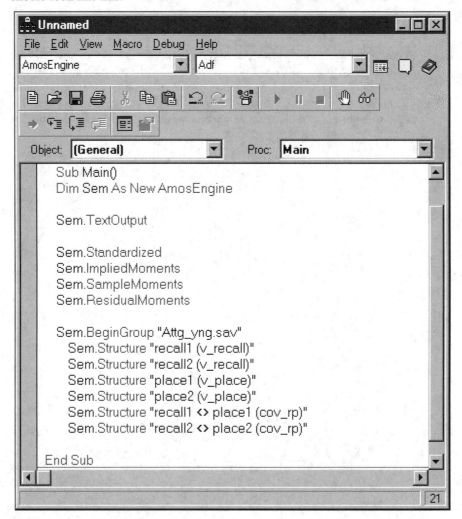

```
Sub Main()
Dim Sem As New AmosEngine

Sem.TextOutput

Sem.Standardized
Sem.ImpliedMoments
Sem.SampleMoments
Sem.ResidualMoments

Sem.BeginGroup "Attg_yng.sav"
    Sem.Structure "recall1 (v_recall)"
    Sem.Structure "recall2 (v_recall)"
    Sem.Structure "place1 (v_place)"
    Sem.Structure "place2 (v_place)"
    Sem.Structure "recall1 <> place1 (cov_rp)"
    Sem.Structure "recall2 <> place2 (cov_rp)"

End Sub
```

The following block of code is optional:

```
Sem.Standardized
Sem.ImpliedMoments
Sem.SampleMoments
Sem.ResidualMoments
```

We will explain its purpose later in this example.

This table is a line by line explanation of what functions the remaining **Amos Basic** commands perform.

Amos Basic Command	Explanation
Sub main()	Starts the **Amos Basic** program.
Dim Sem As New AmosEngine	Declares **Sem** as an object of type **Amos Engine**.
Sem.TextOutput	Writes the results of the analysis to a text file to be displayed by Amos's **View Text** program.
Sem.BeginGroup "Attg_yng.sav"	Begins the model specification for a single group (or population). Additionally, **BeginGroup** specifies that the SPSS file **Attg_yng.sav** is to be used as input data.
Sem.Structure "recall1 (v_recall)" Sem.Structure "recall2 (v_recall)" Sem.Structure "place1 (v_place)" Sem.Structure "place2 (v_place)" Sem.Structure "recall1 <> place1 (cov_rp)" Sem.Structure "recall2 <> place2 (cov_rp)"	Used to specify a model. The first four **Structure** statements constrain the variances of the observed variables via parameter labels in parentheses. **recall1** and **recall2** have the same free variance parameter, labeled **v_recall**. **place1** and **place2** have their variances constrained to a different value, **v_place**. The last two **Structure** statements use the two-character symbol "<>" for covariances. The two covariance terms have the identical label, **cov_rp**, so they will be estimated at the same value.
End Sub	Terminates the **Amos Basic** program.

Timing is everything

Note that the six Sem.Structure lines come after the Sem.BeginGroup statement. The structure statements must come *after* BeginGroup. Otherwise, Amos will not recognize the names of the observed variables in the Sem.Structure lines.

Amos statements, or *methods*, are divided into three general groups[1].

Group 1 — Declarative Methods

These are computational and output options that apply to the entire analysis. These methods tell the Amos Engine which statistics to compute and how to compute them. TableOutput and TextOutput are Group 1 methods we have used in these first two worked examples.

Group 2 — Data and Model Specification Methods

This group consists of data description and model specification commands for a sample of data with multigroup or multisample analyses. These commands may vary among samples. BeginGroup and Structure are Group 2 methods we have presented.

Group 3 — Methods for Retrieving Results

These are commands to...well, retrieve results. Examples using Group 3 methods are given in the *Amos 4.0 Programming Reference Guide*. The *Amos 4.0 Programming Reference Guide* is available as a downloadable PDF file on the **Amos 4.0** CD-ROM or as a Help file (look under the **Amos Graphics** or **Amos Basic** Help menu).

> When you write an Amos program, it is important to pay close attention to the order *you call the Amos engine methods. The rule is that groups must appear in order: Group 1, then Group 2, and finally Group 3.*

For more detailed information about timing rules and a complete listing of methods and their group number, see the *Amos 4.0 Programming Reference Guide*. The *Amos 4.0 Programming Reference Guide* is available as a downloadable PDF file on the **Amos 4.0** CD-ROM or as a Help file (look under the **Amos Graphics** or **Amos Basic** Help menu).

Text output from the analysis

Click on the **Start/Resume** arrow and Amos will calculate the estimates of variances and covariances and display them as text output. The following is a short digression to help you better understand the text output.

---

[1] There is also a fourth "special" group, called the **Initialize Method**. If the optional "Initialize Method" is used, it must come *before* even the Group 1 methods.

Moment estimates

> *The acronym **Amos** stands for Analysis of **Mo**ment **S**tructures —
> more specifically,* mean *and* covariance *structures. When fitting a
> model, Amos computes parameter estimates so that the resulting
> implied moments are closest (in terms of discrepancy function) to
> the sample moments.*

The following are the maximum likelihood estimates resulting from putting all
three constraints in place:

```
Covariances:               Estimate     S.E.      C.R.     Label
------------               --------    -------   -------   -------

 recall1 <----> place1       2.712      1.821     1.489    cov_rp
 recall2 <----> place2       2.712      1.821     1.489    cov_rp
 recall1 <---> recall2       2.872      1.208     2.377
 recall2 <----> place1       2.220      2.216     1.002
 recall1 <----> place2       4.608      2.166     2.127
 place1 <-----> place2      17.149      5.155     3.327


Variances:                 Estimate     S.E.      C.R.     Label
----------                 --------    -------   -------   -------

               recall1       7.055      1.217     5.798    v_recal
               recall2       7.055      1.217     5.798    v_recal
               place1       27.525      5.177     5.317    v_place
               place2       27.525      5.177     5.317    v_place
```

You can see that the parameters that were specified to be equal do have equal
estimates. The standard errors here are generally smaller than the standard errors
obtained in Example 1. For instance, the standard errors of the four variances, in
the order they are listed here, were 1.311, 1.799, 7.604, and 5.018 in Example 1.

Note that Amos shortened the name v_recall, for space reasons. You should be
aware that variable names can be shortened to as few as seven characters in the text
output, so that names that start with the same seven letters should be avoided.

Because of the constraints on the parameters, there are now positive degrees of
freedom:

```
Computation of Degrees of Freedom

              Number of distinct sample moments:    10
   Number of distinct parameters to be estimated:    7
                                                 ---------------
                              Degrees of freedom:    3
```

While there are still ten sample variances and covariances, the number of parameters to be estimated is only seven. Here is how the number seven is arrived at: The variances of **recall1** and **recall2**, labeled v_recall, are constrained to be equal, and thus count as a single parameter. The variances of **place1** and **place2** (labeled v_place) count as another single parameter. A third parameter corresponds to the equal covariances recall1 <> place1 and recall2 <> place2 (labeled cov_rp). These three parameters, plus the four unlabeled, unrestricted covariances, add up to *seven* parameters that have to be estimated.

The degrees of freedom ($10 - 7 = 3$) may also be viewed as the number of constraints placed on the original ten variances and covariances. One degree of freedom is gained from each of the three equality constraints, so there are three degrees of freedom in this example. With the three equality constraints in place, the fitted variances and covariances are not generally equal to the sample moments.

Optional output

So far, we have only been discussing the Amos default output that would be obtained without any special requests. As we discussed in Example 1, **Amos Graphics** allows you to see more output by following the command path: **View/Set** → **Analysis Properties** → **Output** or by clicking on the **Analysis Properties** icon and the **Output** tab.

The output tab looks like this:

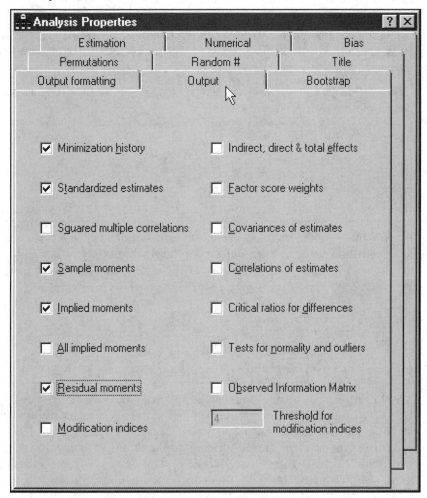

You should typically find **Minimization history** checked by default. In this example, the additional output options we have checked are:

> **Standardized estimates**
> **Sample moments**
> **Implied moments**
> **Residual moments**

You can request these same output options with corresponding Amos Engine methods as shown in the previous section "," starting on page .

Moment estimates

To see all the sample variances and covariances collected into one matrix, check the **Sample Moments** box. Click on the **Calculate Estimates** icon in the toolbox menu to recalculate the sample variances and covariances. Click on the **View Text** icon in the toolbox menu.

You will find the sample variances and covariances before the Computation of Degrees of Freedom section:

```
Sample Covariances

          place1    place2    recall1   recall2
         --------  --------  --------  --------
place1    33.578
place2    17.905    22.160
recall1    4.338     3.575     5.788
recall2    2.014     0.427     2.556     7.944
```

If you want to see the variances and covariances implied by the model, check the **Implied Moments** box on the **Output** tab. **Implied Moments** produces the matrix of estimated variances and covariances after the maximum likelihood estimates:

```
Implied Covariances

          place1    place2    recall1   recall2
         --------  --------  --------  --------
place1    27.525
place2    17.148    27.525
recall1    2.712     4.608     7.055
recall2    2.220     2.712     2.872     7.055
```

Note the differences between the sample and implied covariance matrices. Because the model imposed three constraints on the covariance structure, some or all of the implied variances and covariances come out differently than the sample values. For instance, the sample variance of **place1** is 33.578, but the implied variance is 27.525. To obtain a matrix moment differences (sample minus implied moment), click on the **Residual Moments** request on the **Output** tab.

The matrix of residual variances and covariances appears after the display of implied moments in the text output file:

```
Residual Covariances

          place1    place2    recall1   recall2
         --------  --------  --------  --------
place1     6.053
place2     0.757    -5.365
recall1    1.625    -1.033    -1.267
recall2   -0.206    -2.285    -0.316     0.890
```

As in Example 1, you can display the covariance and variance estimates in the output path diagram. Simply click on the **Unstandardized estimates** in the **Parameter Formats** list box and the **View Output** icon. Alternatively, you can request *correlation* estimates in the path diagram by clicking on **Standardized estimates** and the **View Output** icon.

Here is the path diagram for the correlations:

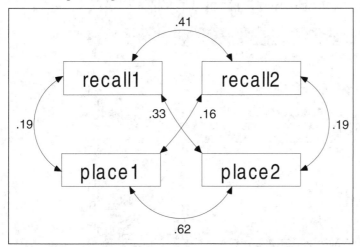

Particularly in larger models, it may be difficult to remember whether the displayed output are covariances or correlations. Amos provides for labeling the output so this is not a problem. Note that the file **Ex02.amw** contains a description at the bottom of the screen.

Double-clicking on this description displays the actual contents of the text caption:

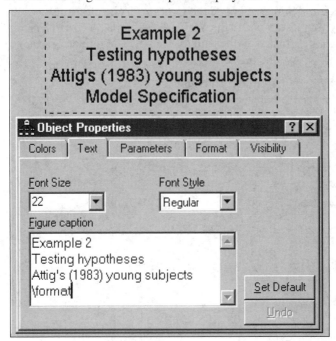

The line of interest is the word **\format** in the bottom line of the figure caption. You will need to press the down arrow key a few times to see it. **\format** and other words that begin with a backward slash are called *text macro s*. They are replaced with information about the currently displayed model. The text macro **\format** will be replaced by the heading "Model Specification," "Unstandardized estimates," or "Standardized estimates," or by a custom format defined by you, depending on which version of the path diagram is in view.

Hypothesis testing

The *implied* covariances are the best estimates of the population variances and covariances under the null hypothesis that the parameters required to have equal estimates are truly equal in the population, whereas the *sample* covariances are the best estimates obtained without making any equality assumptions. If the null hypothesis is correct, both the implied and sample covariances are maximum likelihood estimates of the corresponding population values, but the implied covariances are better estimates, as the standard errors are reduced. If however, the null hypothesis is incorrect, the sample covariances are preferred, and the implied covariances should not be used. Thus, it is of interest to test the veracity of the null hypothesis. The chi-square statistic is an overall measure of how much the implied and sample covariances differ, and is at least 0 (and that occurs only with a perfect fit). The more the implied and sample covariances differ, the bigger the chi-square statistic, and the stronger the evidence against the null hypothesis.

Here is the chi-square test against the null hypothesis that includes the two variance and one covariance constraint:

```
Chi-square =        6.276
Degrees of freedom =     3
Probability level =     0.099
```

If the null hypothesis is true, the chi-square statistic will follow an approximate chi-square distribution with three degrees of freedom, and will have a value in the neighborhood of the degrees of freedom. The probability that such a chi-square statistic equals or exceeds a value of 6.276 is about 0.099. In this situation, the evidence against the null hypothesis is not significant at the 5% level.

You can get the chi-square goodness of fit information to appear on the screen along with the path diagram, by typing **\cmin** and **\df** in a text field. These text macros are replaced by the chi-square statistic and the degrees of freedom, respectively, when Amos output is displayed. The text macro **\p** can be used to display the corresponding right tail probability under the chi-square distribution.

The following figure shows the completely labeled unstandardized output of
`Ex02.amw`:

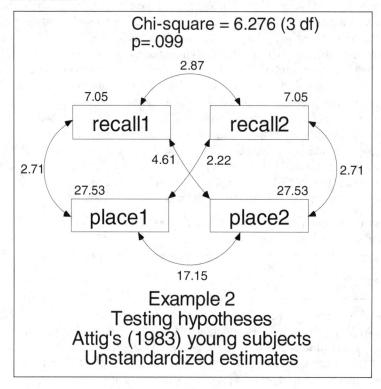

Chi-square = 6.276 (3 df)
p=.099

Example 2
Testing hypotheses
Attig's (1983) young subjects
Unstandardized estimates

Example 3: More Hypothesis Testing

Purpose

- Demonstrate how to test the null hypothesis that two variables are uncorrelated.

- Reinforce the concept of *degrees of freedom*.

- Show in a concrete way what is meant by an *asymptotically correct* test.

The data

The group of older subjects from Attig's (1983) spatial memory study will be used for this example. But now the two variables, **age** and **vocabulary**, will be used. Because we want to demonstrate how Amos handles various data formats, we will use data formatted as a comma-delimited text file:

```
subject,age,vocab_short,vocabulary, ... <more variable names>
1,65,12,72,16,1,5,11,5,11,30,32
2,68,14,77,18,0,12,16,14,16,35,32
3,64,14,74,17,1,11,11,10,11,33,30

    ... <34 similar records skipped> ...

38,70,14,80,14,0,8,13,8,13,32,31
39,64,14,78,13,0,12,13,12,14,26,31
40,63,13,66,12,0,9,10,11,11,29,31
```

You will find this text file by clicking on **Data Files...**, **Text (.txt)**, and then double clicking on **Attg_old.txt**.

Testing a hypothesis that two variables are uncorrelated

Among Attig's (1983) forty old subjects, the sample correlation between **age** and **vocabulary** is -0.09 — not very far from 0. Is this correlation still significant? To find out, we will test the null hypothesis that, in the population from which these forty subjects came, the correlation between age and vocabulary is zero. We will do this by estimating the variance-covariance matrix under the constraint that **age** and **vocabulary** are uncorrelated.

Modeling in Amos Graphics

Begin by drawing the two observed variables, **age** and **vocabulary**, in the path diagram. Use the same drawing tools that you used in Example 1 to create the following diagram:

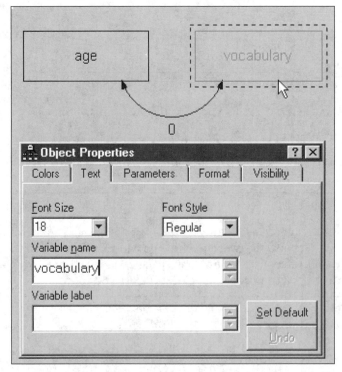

Amos Graphics then gives you two methods to constrain their covariance parameter to zero. The most obvious way to set the implied covariance of **age** and **vocabulary** to zero is by simply *not drawing* a covariance path between the two observed variables. In the **Amos Graphics** path diagram, the lack of a two-headed arrow corresponds to an implied covariance of zero, as long as the two variables are not connected indirectly via additional predictors. So, without drawing anything more, the model estimated from our simple diagram above constrains the covariance (and thus the correlation) between **age** and **vocabulary** to zero.

The second method of constraining a covariance parameter in **Amos Graphics** is the more general procedure introduced in Examples 1 and 2. In the toolbox menu, click on the **Draw covariances** icon and draw (click and drag) a double-headed arrow from **vocabulary** to **age**. Then, double-click on the arrow so that the **Object properties** dialog box appears. Click on the **Parameters** tab and enter a number (in this case 0) into the **Covariance** field. As demonstrated in Example 2, the **Covariance** field lets you constrain the covariance parameter to *any* desired value or variable.

This is the resulting path diagram (you can also find it in **Ex03.amw**):

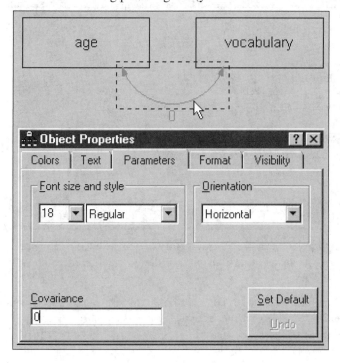

Modeling in Amos Basic

An **Amos Basic** input file that will accomplish the same covariance constraint is:

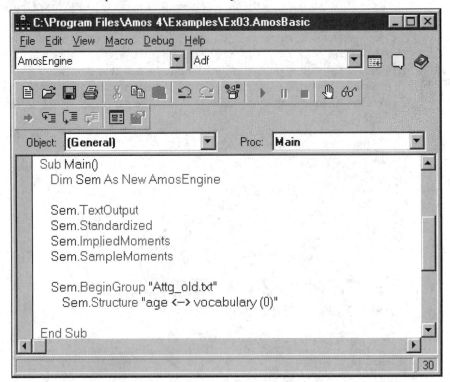

Note that the Structure method constrains only the covariance parameter. It says nothing about the variances of **age** and **vocabulary**, which are treated as free parameters by default.

The rule is that as long as a variable is mentioned in a Structure specification, **Amos Basic** will estimate its variance. Since **age** and **vocabulary** are both mentioned in the covariance specification, it is unnecessary to specifically request estimates of their variances.

Results of the analysis

The parameter estimates are not of primary interest in this analysis, but here they are:

```
Covariances:                        Estimate    S.E.      C.R.
-----------                         --------    ------    ------

        age <----------> vocabulary   0.000


Correlations:                       Estimate
------------                        --------

        age <----------> vocabulary   0.000


Variances:                          Estimate    S.E.      C.R.
----------                          --------    ------    ------

                    age   21.574     4.886     4.416
             vocabulary  131.294    29.732     4.416
```

In this analysis, there is one degree of freedom, corresponding to the single constraint that **age** and **vocabulary** be uncorrelated. The degrees of freedom can also be arrived at by the computation shown in the text output listing:

```
Computation of Degrees of Freedom

                Number of distinct sample moments:    3
       Number of distinct parameters to be estimated:    2
                                          ------------------------
                              Degrees of freedom:    1
```

Amos Graphics output

Amos Graphics provides a similar account of the parameters and degrees of freedom for the model when you click on the **Display degrees of freedom** (word "DF") icon.

This produces the following display:

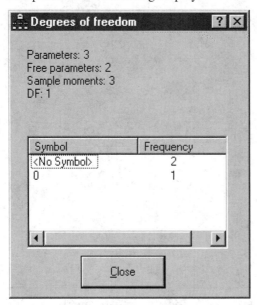

The three sample moments are the variances of **age** and **vocabulary**, and their covariance. The two free parameters to be estimated are the two population variances. The model covariance term is fixed at zero, not estimated from the sample information.

Here is the model specification for Example 3:

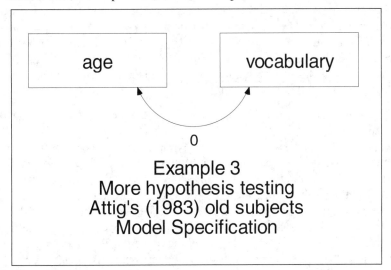

Now, here is the path diagram output of the unstandardized estimates, along with the test of the null hypothesis that **age** and **vocabulary** are uncorrelated:

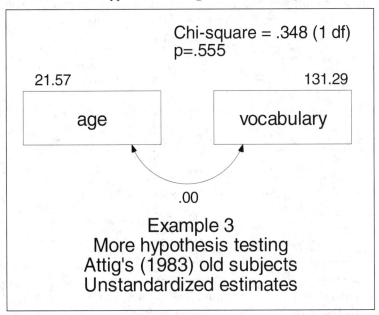

The probability of accidentally getting this, or even a larger departure from the null hypothesis, is 0.555. The null hypothesis would not be rejected at any conventional significance level.

The usual *t* statistic for testing this null hypothesis is 0.59 (*df* = 38, *p* = 0.72 one-sided). The probability level associated with the *t* statistic is exact, given the smaller sample size. The *chi-square* statistic is *off*, because it is only *asymptotically* distributed chi-square. In other words, the chi-squared statistic will be exact in larger samples, but not in small ones. But as you can see, even with a small sample size of 40, the results are not that far apart. In either case, the null hypothesis would not be rejected in this example.

Here is an interesting question: Suppose you use the probability level displayed by Amos to test the null hypothesis at either the .05 or .01 level. Then what is the *actual* probability of rejecting a true null hypothesis? In the case of the present null hypothesis, this question has an answer, although the answer depends on the sample size. The second column of Table 3.1 (below) shows, for several sample sizes, the real probability of a Type I error when using Amos to test the null hypothesis of *zero correlation* at the .05 level. The third column shows the real probability of a Type I error if you use a significance level of .01. The table shows that, the bigger the sample size, the closer the true significance level is to what it is supposed to be. Unfortunately, such a table cannot be easily constructed for every hypothesis that Amos can be used to test. However, this much can be said about any such table: moving from top to bottom, the numbers in the .05 column would approach .05, and the numbers in the .01 column would approach .01. This very property is what is meant by an *asymptotically correct* hypothesis tests.

	Nominal Significance Level	
Sample Size	**.05**	**.01**
3	.250	.122
4	.150	.056
5	.115	.038
10	.073	.018
20	.060	.013
30	.056	.012
40	.055	.012
50	.054	.011
100	.052	.011
150	.051	.010
200	.051	.010
≥500	.050	.010

Table 3.1: Realized Type I rejection rates when using Amos to test the hypothesis that two variables are uncorrelated.

Example 4: Conventional Linear Regression

Purpose

- Demonstrate a conventional regression analysis, predicting a single observed variable as a linear combination of three other observed variables.

- Introduce the concept of *identifiability*.

The data

Warren, White and Fuller (1974) studied 98 managers of farm cooperatives. Four of the measurements made on each manager were:

test	explanation
performance	A 24-item test of performance related to "planning, organization, controlling, coordinating and directing."
knowledge	A 26-item test of knowledge of "economic phases of management directed toward profit-making ... and product knowledge."
value	A 30-item test of "tendency to rationally evaluate means to an economic end."
satisfaction	An 11-item test of "gratification obtained ... from performing the managerial role."

A fifth measure, *past training*, was reported, but will not be employed in this example.

In this example, we are using the Excel worksheet **Warren5v** in **UserGuide.xls** found in Amos's Examples subdirectory: **C:\Program Files\Amos 4\Examples**.

These are the sample variances and covariances in a table format:

rowtype_	varname_	performance	knowledge	value	satisfaction	past_training
n		98	98	98	98	98
cov	performance	0.0209				
cov	knowledge	0.0177	0.052			
cov	value	0.0245	0.028	0.1212		
cov	satisfaction	0.0046	0.0044	-0.0063	0.0901	
cov	past_training	0.0187	0.0192	0.0353	-0.0066	0.0946
mean		0.0589	1.3796	2.8773	2.4613	2.1174

Warren5v also contains the sample means. Raw data are not available, but they are not needed in Amos for most analyses as long as the sample moments (*i.e.*, means, variances and covariances) are provided. In fact, only sample variances and covariances are required in this example. We will not need the sample means in **Warren5v** for the time being, and Amos will ignore them.

Analysis of the data

Suppose you would like to use scores on **knowledge**, **value** and **satisfaction** to predict **performance**. More specifically, suppose you think that **performance** scores can be approximated by a *linear combination* of **knowledge**, **value** and **satisfaction**. The prediction will not be perfect however, and the model should thus include an *error term*.

Here is the initial path diagram for this relationship:

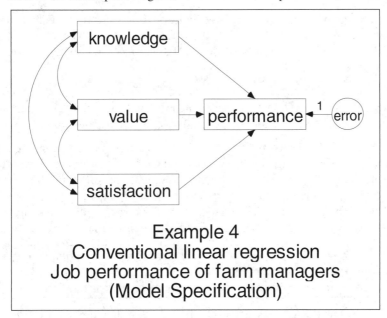

Example 4
Conventional linear regression
Job performance of farm managers
(Model Specification)

The single-headed arrows represent linear dependencies. For example, the arrow leading from **knowledge** to **performance** indicates that **performance** scores depend, in part, on **knowledge**. The variable **error** is enclosed in a circle because it is not directly observed. **Error** represents much more than random fluctuations in **performance** scores due to measurement error. **Error** also represents a composite of age, socioeconomic status, verbal ability, and anything else on which **performance** may depend, but which was not measured in this study. This variable is essential because the path diagram is supposed to show *all* variables that affect **performance** scores. Without the circle, the path diagram would make the implausible claim that **performance** is an *exact* linear combination of **knowledge**, **value** and **satisfaction**.

The double-headed arrows in the path diagram connect variables that may be correlated with each other. They include the predictor variables **knowledge**, **value** and **satisfaction.** The absence of a double-headed arrow connecting **error** with any other variable indicates that **error** is assumed to be uncorrelated with every other predictor variable — a fundamental assumption in linear regression. **Performance** is also not connected to any other variable by a double-headed arrow, but this is for a different reason. Since **performance** *depends* on the other variables, it goes without saying that it might be correlated with them.

Modeling in Amos Graphics

You will need to be familiar with three icons or commands to draw the path diagram for this example. The first is the **Draw unobserved variable** (ellipse) icon, or the equivalent command from the **Diagram** menu. Use this command to draw a circle or ellipse for the **error** variable.

If you wish to change the shape or size of the **error** variable, select the **Change the shape of objects** icon (four two-headed arrows), and then drag the object into its desired shape. Then, name and if needed, move the unobserved variable.

The third icon is the **Draw paths** (single-headed arrow) button. Simply click on it, so that it becomes highlighted. Then click on an *exogenous* or predictor variable (**knowledge, value, satisfaction,** or **error**) and, with the left mouse button still pressed, drag out a path with the mouse to the *endogenous* or response variable (**performance**) and release the mouse button. The arrow points to the object you drew *to*. Repeat this step for the other three exogenous variables.

> *Endogenous variables have at least one single-headed path pointing towards them. Exogenous variables, in contrast, only* send out *single-headed paths, but do not receive any.*

If you have done this part correctly, all of the arrows should point towards **performance**, like this:

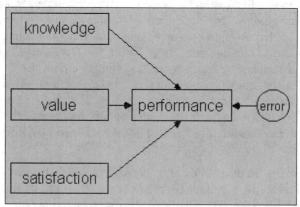

To finish the path diagram, draw in three covariance paths between the observed predictor variables. Use the **Draw covariances** icon to connect the observed exogenous variables (**knowledge, satisfaction,** and **value**), allowing them to be freely correlated.

Forgetting to do so would generate the warning message:

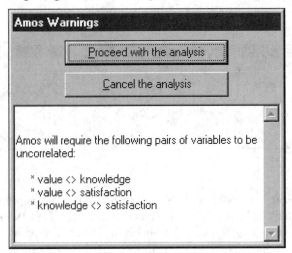

The diagram now looks complete:

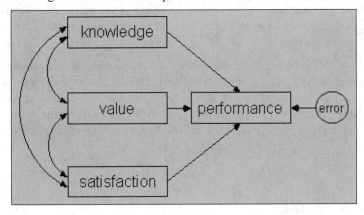

However, when you ask for parameter estimates by pressing the **Calculate estimates** icon, you may be in for a shock. Amos will produce an error dialog box message that reads:

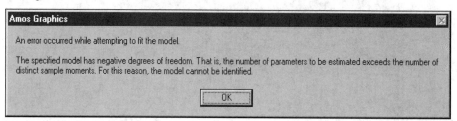

Identification

The error message indicates a modeling problem known as *nonidentifiability*. Identifiability (or the lack of it) is a difficult subject. However, it is too important to simply make it a footnote that you would probably skip over. The problem in this example is that it is impossible to estimate the regression weight for the regression of **performance** on error, and the variance of **error** at the same time. It is like having someone tell you, "I bought $5 worth of widgets," and attempting to determine both the price of each widget and the number purchased. There is just not enough information.

You can solve this problem by *fixing* either the path coefficient from **error** to **performance**, or the variance of the **error** variable itself, at an arbitrary, non-zero value. We will discuss trade-offs between the two options later with the Amos output for this example. For the time being, we will choose to fix the path coefficient at unity. This will yield the same estimates as conventional linear regression.

To implement the identification constraint, double-click on the path between **error** and **performance**. The **Object Properties** dialog box will appear. Click on the **Parameters** tab and enter the value "1" in the **Regression weight** field:

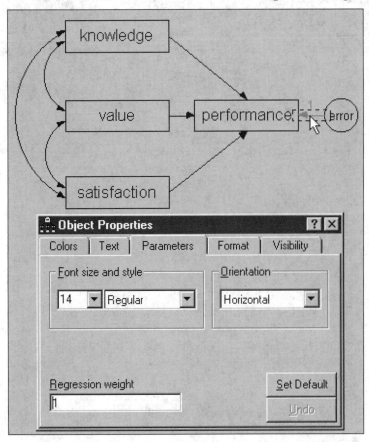

Remembering to constrain every path between an error and another parameter can become tedious. Fortunately, **Amos Graphics** provides a default solution that works well in most cases. You can simply select the **Add a unique variable** icon (circle connected to rectangle). Then, when you click on an endogenous variable, **Amos Graphics** will automatically attach a latent exogenous variable to it, complete with a fixed path coefficient of "1". Clicking on the observed variable repeatedly will change the position of the error variable. Your final path diagram will look like the initial path diagram found on page .

Modeling in Amos Basic

This example represents a single linear regression equation, as there is only one endogenous variable. Each single-headed arrow corresponds to a regression weight. These are the regression weights that need to be estimated. Here is an **Amos Basic** input file that will do the job:

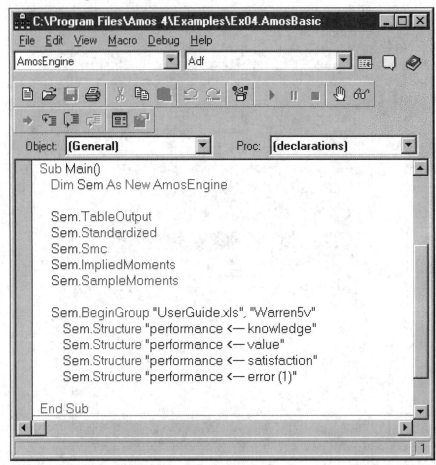

The four lines that come after the Sem.BeginGroup statement represent the single-headed arrows in the **Amos Graphics** path diagram. You can also use dashes when drawing arrows (*i.e.*, <---) if your default font more easily produces dashes. The *identification* constraint appears as the "(1)" symbol in the last line to fix the path coefficient from error to **performance** at unity.

Defaults for correlations among the exogenous variables

The **Amos Basic** program uses certain default correlation (or covariance) structures of the exogenous variables in the model that are not incorporated in **Amos Graphics**. These defaults simplify the specifications for many types of models with **Amos Basic** statements, especially with models containing many parameters. The differences between **Amos Graphics** and **Amos Basic** are as follows:

1. **Amos Graphics** has no defaults whatsoever for correlation or covariance structures. The program is entirely WYSIWYG (What You See Is What You Get). If you draw a two-headed path (with no constraints) between two variables (latent or observed), **Amos Graphics** will attempt to estimate the associated correlation or covariance term. Alternatively, if the path is missing, then **Amos Graphics** will not estimate the associated terms.

2. The **Amos Basic** default rules for correlation/covariance structures are:

   a. *Unique latent* variables (*e.g.*, error terms or structural residuals) are uncorrelated with each other and with all other exogenous variables.

   b. All *observed* exogenous and *non-unique* latent exogenous variables are correlated with each other. Non-unique latent variables (factors) are introduced in Example 5.

The **Amos Basic** defaults reflect the standard assumptions of conventional linear regression analysis. That is, we assume the predictor variables **knowledge**, **value**, and **satisfaction** are correlated. Further, the unique latent variable **error** is treated as being independent of the other exogenous variables.

Alternative equation input

As a further option, **Amos Basic** permits model specification in equation format rather than by the pseudo-paths previously shown. For instance, the following Sem.Structure statement describes the path model as a single linear regression equation, where **performance** depends on the three other observed variables and an error term. You will find this statement in the **Amos Basic** Program files under `Amos 4\Examples\Ex04-eq.AmosBasic`:

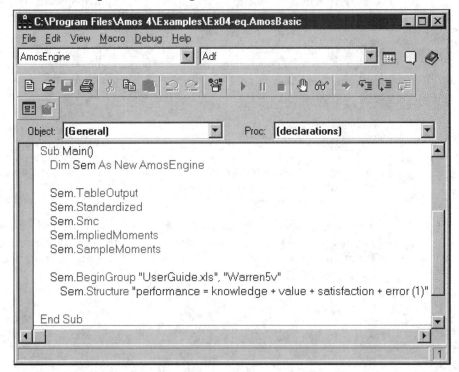

Note that in the preceding Sem.Structure statement, each predictor variable (on the right side of the equation) is associated with a regression weight to be estimated. We could note these regression parameters explicitly indicating their places by empty parentheses such as:

Sem.Structure "performance = () knowledge + () value + () satisfaction + error (1)"

You do not need the empty parentheses because **Amos Basic** assumes free path coefficients by default and will estimate a regression weight for each predictor. Ultimately, your text output will be the same, whether you created the input file in **Amos Graphics** or **Amos Basic**. Which version to use is a matter of personal preference.

Results of the analysis

Table output

Amos Basic displays the maximum likelihood estimates:

Regression Weights			Estimate	S.E.	c.r.
performance	<--	knowledge	0.26	0.05	4.82
performance	<--	value	0.15	0.04	4.14
performance	<--	satisfaction	0.05	0.04	1.27
Covariances					
			Estimate	S.E.	c.r.
knowledge	<-->	value	0.03	0.01	3.28
knowledge	<-->	satisfaction	0.00	0.01	0.63
value	<-->	satisfaction	-0.01	0.01	-0.59
Variances					
			Estimate	S.E.	c.r.
		knowledge	0.05	0.01	6.96
		value	0.12	0.02	6.96
		satisfaction	0.09	0.01	6.96
		error	0.01	0.00	6.96

Amos does not display the path **performance <--- error** because its value is fixed at the default "1". You may wonder how much the other estimates would be affected if a different identification constant had been chosen. It turns out that only the variance estimate for **error** is subject to any changes. All other estimates would remain constant.

Table 4.1 gives the resulting variance estimates for various choices of fixing the path coefficient **performance <--- error.**

Path Constraint	Variance of **error**
0.5	0.050
0.707	0.025
1.0	0.0125
1.414	0.00625
2.0	0.00313

Table 4.1: Variance Estimate as a Function of the Identification Constraint

Suppose you fixed the path coefficient at 2 instead of 1. Then the variance estimate would essentially have to be divided by a factor of 4. You can extrapolate the rule that multiplying the path coefficient by a fixed factor goes along with dividing the error variance by the square of the same factor. Extending this, the product of the *squared* regression weight and the error variance is always a constant. This is what we mean when we say the regression weight (together with the error variance) is unidentified. If you assign a value to one of them, the other can be estimated, but they cannot both be estimated at the same time.

The identifiability problem just discussed arises from the fact that the variance of a variable, and any regression weights associated with it, depend on the units in which the variable is measured. Since **error** is an unobserved variable, there is no natural way to specify a measurement unit for it. Assigning an arbitrary value to a regression weight associated with **error** can be thought of as a way of indirectly choosing a unit of measurement for **error**. Every unobserved variable presents this identifiability problem, which must be resolved by imposing some constraint that will determine its unit of measurement.

Changing the scale unit of the unobserved **error** variable does not change the overall model fit. In all the analyses you still get:

```
Chi-square =      0.000
Degrees of freedom =    0
Probability level cannot be computed
```

There are four sample variances and six sample covariances, for a total of ten sample moments. There are three regression paths, four model variances, and three model covariances, for a total of ten parameters that must be estimated. Hence, the model has zero degrees of freedom. Such a model is often called *saturated* or *just-identified*.

The *standardized* coefficient estimates are:

```
Standardized Regression Weights:        Estimate
-------------------------------         --------

    performance <-------- knowledge       0.407
    performance <----------- value        0.349
    performance <----- satisfaction       0.101


Correlations:                           Estimate
------------                            --------

    knowledge <------> satisfaction       0.064
    value <----------> satisfaction      -0.060
    knowledge <-------------> value       0.353
```

These estimates are also displayed in the path diagram output at the end of this example. The standardized regression weights and the correlations are independent of the units in which all variables are measured. Therefore, they will not be affected by the choice of identification constraints.

The optional **Sem.Smc** statement displays the squared multiple correlation, a useful statistic that is also independent of all units of measurement:

```
Squared Multiple Correlations:          Estimate
-----------------------------           --------

                  performance           0.399
```

Amos will display a squared multiple correlation for each endogenous variable.

> *A variable's squared multiple correlation is the proportion of its variance that is accounted for by its predictors.*

In the present example, **knowledge**, **value** and **satisfaction** account for 39.9 percent of the variance of **performance**.

Graphics output

The path diagram output, for both unstandardized and standardized model solutions, follows below. Here is the diagram with unstandardized values:

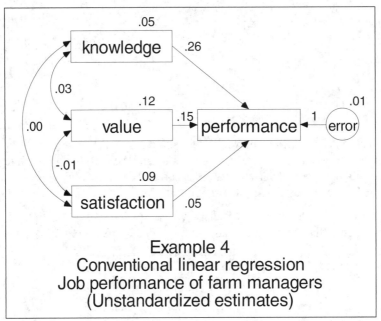

Example 4
Conventional linear regression
Job performance of farm managers
(Unstandardized estimates)

The standardized solution is:

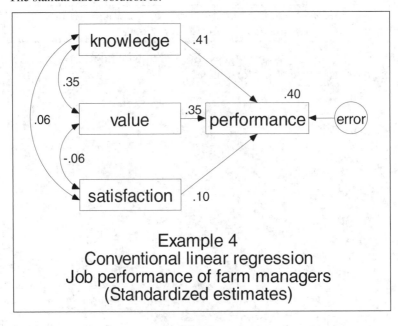

Example 4
Conventional linear regression
Job performance of farm managers
(Standardized estimates)

Note that the estimates are displayed in relatively fixed locations in the path diagrams. Their positions are assigned according to the rules in Table 4.2.

Location	Unstandardized Estimates	Standardized Estimates
Near Single-Headed Arrows	Regression weights	Standardized regression weights
Near Double-Headed Arrows	Covariances	Correlations
Near Endogenous Variables	Intercepts[1]	Squared multiple correlations
Near Exogenous Variables	Means[1] and variances	————

Table 4.2: Location of Parameter Estimates in the Path Diagram Output

Additional output

Diagnostic information about the model appears at the beginning of the Amos text output. For instance, the following portion of the output file shows each variable in the model and its status:

```
Your model contains the following variables

        performance                    observed   endogenous

        knowledge                      observed   exogenous
        value                          observed   exogenous
        satisfaction                   observed   exogenous

        error                          unobserved exogenous

              Number of variables in your model:    5
              Number of observed variables:         4
              Number of unobserved variables:       1
              Number of exogenous variables:        4
              Number of endogenous variables:       1
```

Again, *endogenous* variables are those that have single-headed arrows pointing to them in the path diagram, and depend on other variables. *Exogenous* variables are those that do not have arrows pointing at them; they do not depend on other variables in a regression setting.

---

[1] Only when mean structures are analyzed. See Examples 13 through 16.

Inspecting the preceding list will help you catch the most common (and insidious) errors in an input file: typing errors. If you try to type `performance` twice, but unintentionally misspell it as `performence` one of those times, both versions will appear on the list.

The following message indicates that there are no *loops* in the path diagram:

```
The model is recursive.
```

Later you will see path diagrams where you can pick a variable and, by tracing along the single-headed arrows, follow a path that leads again to the same variable.

> *Path diagrams that have feedback loops are called nonrecursive.*
> *Those that do not are called recursive (from the Latin "recurso,"*
> *meaning, "I return").*

When we step backwards through the paths of a recursive model, we are forced to return to the exogenous variables in a finite number of steps.

Because the model is saturated, there are zero degrees of freedom (as explained previously), and the estimated variances and covariances obtained with the Sem.Impliedmoments statement are identical to the sample values:

```
Implied Covariances

            satisfact value     knowledge performan
            --------- --------- --------- ---------
satisfacti   0.08918
value       -0.00624   0.11996
knowledge    0.00436   0.02771   0.05147
performanc   0.00455   0.02425   0.01752   0.02069
```

Example 5: Unobserved Variables

Purpose

- Demonstrate a regression analysis with unobserved variables, as a means of considering the unreliability of the observed variables.

The data

When we use variables, such as **performance** and **satisfaction** in the previous example, we expect the variable values to be *reliable* measures of "true" manager performance and satisfaction. But the Example 4 variables were based on psychological *tests* and could easily be unreliable. For example, the researchers could have replaced some test items, or administered tests on different days. These changes would have resulted in numerically different measurements.

The fact that the reliability of **performance** is unknown presents a minor problem when it comes to interpreting the fact that the predictors only account for 39.9 percent of the variance of **performance**. If the test were extremely unreliable, that fact in itself would explain why the **performance** score would not be predicted accurately. Unreliability of the *predictors*, on the other hand, presents a more serious problem because it frequently leads to biased regression estimates. Thus, there may be several reasons for the lack of predictive power of the regression model:

- **performance** is an unreliable measure of "true" performance. Measurement error in the dependent variable deflates the squared multiple correlation and increases the standard error of the estimated regression weights.

- **knowledge**, **value**, and/or **satisfaction** may also be unreliable measures. Error in predictor variables tends to bias both the estimates of the regression weights and the squared multiple correlation (Bollen, 1989, *pp.* 151-176; Rigdon, 1994).

- Omitted variables: All measures may be reliable, but one or more important exogenous variables for predicting job performance of farm managers are left out of the model. In this instance, both regression estimates and squared multiple correlation are often biased (Draper and Smith, 1981, *pp.* 117-121).

None of these situations can be compensated for by an increase in sample size, however large.

The present example, based on Rock, *et al.* (1977), will assess the reliabilities of the four tests included in the previous analysis. It will also obtain estimates of regression weights for perfectly reliable, hypothetical versions of the four tests. Rock, *et al.* re-examined the data of Warren, White and Fuller (1974) that were discussed in the previous example. This time, each test was randomly split into two halves, and each half was scored separately. Names of the split-half subtests are composed of the name of the respective measured attribute (**performance**, **knowledge**, **value**, and **satisfaction**), preceded by a number (**1** or **2**) to identify the subscale.

Here is a list of the input variables and an explanation of their content:

test	explanation
1performance	12-item subtest of Role Performance
2performance	12-item subtest of Role Performance
1knowledge	13-item subtest of Knowledge
2knowledge	13-item subtest of Knowledge
1value	15-item subtest of Value Orientation
2value	15-item subtest of Value Orientation
1satisfaction	5-item subtest of Role Satisfaction
2satisfaction	6-item subtest of Role Satisfaction
past_training	degree of formal education

For this example, we will use a Lotus data file **Warren9v.wk1** to obtain the sample variances and covariances of these subtests. The sample means that appear in the file will not be used in this example. Statistics on formal education (**past_training**) are present in the file, but they also will not enter the present analysis.

Amos will display the data input in a table format. Here is a portion of the table's contents:

rowtype_	varname_	1performance	2performance
n		98	98
cov	1performance	0.0271	
cov	2performance	0.0172	0.0222
cov	1knowledge	0.0219	0.0193
cov	2knowledge	0.0164	0.013
cov	1value	0.0284	0.0294
cov	2value	0.0217	0.0185

Model A

This path diagram presents a model for the eight subtests:

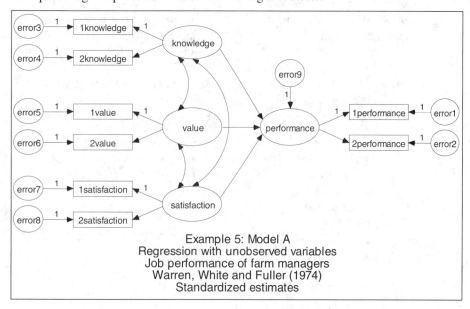

Example 5: Model A
Regression with unobserved variables
Job performance of farm managers
Warren, White and Fuller (1974)
Standardized estimates

Four ellipses in the figure are labeled **knowledge**, **value**, **satisfaction** and **performance**. They represent the unobserved variables that are indirectly measured by the eight split-half tests.

Measurement model

The set of connections between the observed and unobserved variables is often called the measurement model. The current problem has four distinct measurement submodels:

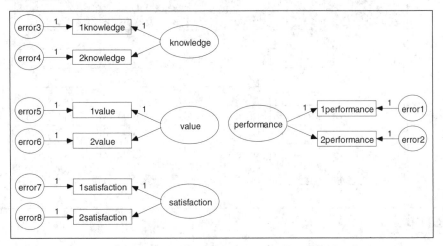

Consider, for instance, the **knowledge** submodel: the scores of the two split-half subtests, **1knowledge** and **2knowledge**, are thought to depend on the single underlying, but not directly observed variable **knowledge**. The two observed scores are not expected to be identical, though, due to the influence of **error3** and **error4** — the respective measurement error components of the two subtests. The measurement model for **knowledge** forms a pattern that is repeated three more times in the above path diagram.

> *Two or more observed variables each depend on a common unobserved variable and on a specific error or unique variable. The observed variables in such a pattern may be regarded as imperfect observable measures, or indicators, of the common unobserved variable. The unobserved common variable in such a measurement model is often referred to as a factor or latent construct.*

Structural model

The model component connecting the unobserved variables to each other is often called the structural model:

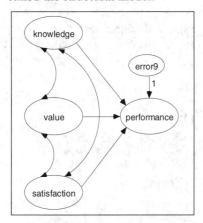

The relationship between these four variables is identical to the regression model used in Example 4, except with *unobserved* variables in place of the observed ones. Examples 4 and 5 differ in the measurement model.

Identification

With thirteen unobserved variables in this model, it is certainly not identified. It will be necessary to fix the unit of measurement of each unobserved variable by suitable constraints on the parameters. Do this by repeating the trick that was used for the single unobserved variable in the previous example, only this time; you will need to repeat the following procedure thirteen times.

Find a single-headed arrow leading away from each unobserved variable in the path diagram, and fix the corresponding regression weight to unity. If there is more than one single-headed arrow leading away from an unobserved variable, any one of them will usually do, although in some cases, you will obtain better parameter estimates when you choose the most reliable indicator variable. In this example, all paths from unobserved variables towards the indicator variables whose names start with the numeral "1" (such as between **knowledge** and **1knowledge**), will be constrained. All paths connecting the (unique) error components will also be set to unity.

Modeling in Amos Graphics

Because the diagram will be a long horizontal, you will need to change the drawing area so the diagram fits. Nothing should be drawn beyond the drawing boundaries, or otherwise that portion of your work will not be printed or copied to the clipboard. **Amos Graphics** uses the page size and orientation of your printer setup by default. However, if you change the **Orientation** in **Page Layout**, Amos will automatically change your printer's page orientation for that particular job.

To change the orientation of the drawing area, click on the menu: **View/Set** → **Interface Properties**. Next, click on the **Page Layout** tab, change the **Orientation** to **Landscape** and click **Apply**:

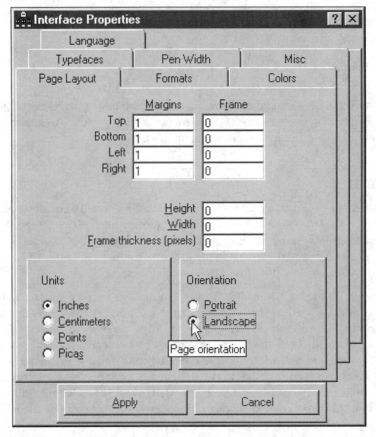

Now you are ready to set up the model as specified in the path diagram on page 145. This can be done in a number of ways. Several drawing and editing tools make it more efficient to start with the measurement model first. Here, we demonstrate how to construct the measurement model for one of the variables, **knowledge**, say, and use it as a stencil for the remaining three.

First, draw the ellipse for the unobserved variable **knowledge**:

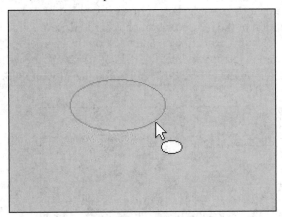

 As a shortcut for drawing the indicator variables, complete with their paths and unique error components, **Amos Graphics** provides the **Draw indicator variable** (circle/square branch) icon. To add the two indicator branches for the **knowledge** variable, select the **Draw indicator variable** icon. Your arrow will transform into a replica of the icon. Move the icon replica over to the ellipse and click twice inside it.

Amos Graphics will instantly create the branches for the two split-half tests:

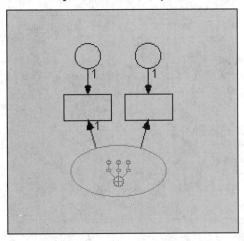

With the **Draw indicator variable** icon selected, you can click multiple times on an unobserved variable to create all its indicator branches. **Amos Graphics** maintains suitable spacing among the indicators and inserts the required identification constraints.

Now you have all of the variables you need for the **knowledge** structure, except that the structure points upwards from the large ellipse instead of to its left. One tool to change the orientation of the indicator branches is the **Rotate** (circle with red arrow) icon. Simply select the **Rotate** icon and click on the large ellipse. Each time you click on the common latent variable, all its indicator branches will be rotated 90° clockwise. Click on the ellipse three times and the structure will look like this:

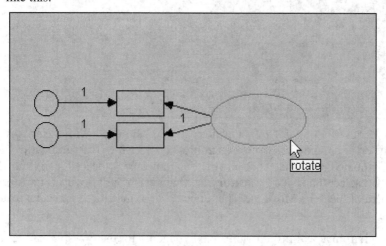

The next step is to make two duplicate measurement models for the **value** and **satisfaction** structures. Do this by clicking on the **Select all objects** (hand with fingers extended) icon and highlight the entire measurement model (it will turn blue). Select the **Duplicate objects** (copy) icon and click on the highlight the model. With the mouse button depressed, drag out a duplicate model. Repeat this procedure, so you have created two more models:

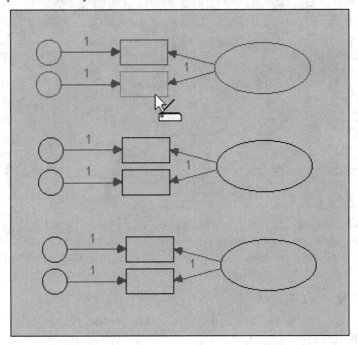

Next, copy one more model structure for **performance**. After dragging the unobserved variable model into position, click on the **Reflect** icon while the ellipse is highlighted, so its observed variables face the opposite direction from the others:

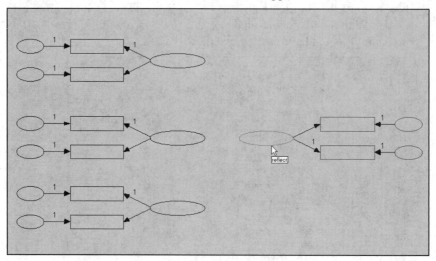

As in earlier examples, enter the variable names in all objects by double clicking on the object and entering the appropriate information in the **Text** tab of the **Object Properties** dialog box. Alternatively, you can click on the **List Variables in data set** icon and drag-and-drop the variable names from the displayed list.

There are only a few things left to do to complete the structural model:

1. Draw in the three covariance paths between **knowledge**, **value**, and **satisfaction**.

2. Draw the single-headed paths from each of the unobserved predictors, **knowledge**, **value**, and **satisfaction**, to the latent dependent variable, **performance**.

3. Add the unobserved variable **error9** to **performance** (use the **Add a unique variable** icon).

The path diagram should now look like the full specification on page 125. The **Amos Graphics** input file is `Ex05-a.amw`.

Modeling in Amos Basic

Here are the lines of code to input in **Amos Basic** to achieve the same model with the same identification constraints:

```
Sub Main( )
    Dim Sem As New AmosEngine

    Sem.TextOutput
    Sem.Standardized
    Sem.Smc

    Sem.BeginGroup "Warren9v.wk1"
        Sem.Structure "1performance <--- performance (1)"
        Sem.Structure "2performance <--- performance"
        Sem.Structure "1knowledge <--- knowledge (1)"
        Sem.Structure "2knowledge <--- knowledge"
        Sem.Structure "1value <--- value (1)"
        Sem.Structure "2value <--- value"
        Sem.Structure "1satisfaction <--- satisfaction (1)"
        Sem.Structure "2satisfaction <--- satisfaction"

        Sem.Structure "1performance <--- error1 (1)"
        Sem.Structure "2performance <--- error2 (1)"
        Sem.Structure "1knowledge <--- error3 (1)"
        Sem.Structure "2knowledge <--- error4 (1)"
        Sem.Structure "1value <--- error5 (1)"
        Sem.Structure "2value <--- error6 (1)"
        Sem.Structure "1satisfaction <--- error7 (1)"
        Sem.Structure "2satisfaction <--- error8 (1)"

        Sem.Structure "performance <--- knowledge"
        Sem.Structure "performance <--- satisfaction"
        Sem.Structure "performance <--- value"
        Sem.Structure "performance <--- error9 (1)"

End Sub
```

Because of the **Amos Basic** default assumptions about the correlations among exogenous variables (discussed in Example 4), you do not need to indicate that **knowledge**, **value** and **satisfaction** may be correlated. It is also not necessary to specify that **error1**, **error2**, ... **error9** are uncorrelated among themselves and with every other exogenous variable.

Results for Model A

As an exercise, you might want to confirm the following degrees of freedom calculation in **Amos Basic**:

```
Computation of Degrees of Freedom

              Number of distinct sample moments:    36
     Number of distinct parameters to be estimated: 22
                                               --------------------------
                                   Degrees of freedom:   14
```

The chi-square test shows that Model A is reasonable:

```
Chi-square =      10.335
Degrees of freedom =    14
Probability level =      0.737
```

The parameter estimates are to be interpreted relative to the identification constraints:

```
Regression Weights:                    Estimate     S.E.      C.R.
-------------------                    --------    -------   -------

    performance <---------- knowledge    0.337      0.125     2.697
    performance <------- satisfaction    0.061      0.054     1.127
    performance <------------- value     0.176      0.079     2.225
    1performance <------- performance    1.000
    2performance <------- performance    0.867      0.116     7.450
    1knowledge <----------- knowledge    1.000
    2knowledge <----------- knowledge    0.683      0.161     4.252
    1value <------------------- value    1.000
    2value <------------------- value    0.763      0.185     4.128
    1satisfaction <----- satisfaction    1.000
    2satisfaction <----- satisfaction    0.792      0.438     1.806


Covariances:                           Estimate     S.E.      C.R.
------------                           --------    -------   -------

    knowledge <--------------> value     0.037      0.012     3.036
    knowledge <---------> satisfaction   0.004      0.009     0.462
    value <------------> satisfaction   -0.008      0.013    -0.610


Variances:                             Estimate     S.E.      C.R.
----------                             --------    -------   -------

                         knowledge      0.046      0.015     3.138
                             value      0.100      0.032     3.147
                       satisfaction     0.090      0.052     1.745
                            error9      0.007      0.003     2.577
                            error1      0.007      0.002     3.110
                            error2      0.007      0.002     3.871
                            error3      0.041      0.011     3.611
                            error4      0.035      0.007     5.167
                            error5      0.080      0.025     3.249
                            error6      0.087      0.018     4.891
                            error7      0.022      0.049     0.451
                            error8      0.045      0.032     1.420
```

Note that the parameter estimates would have been different if different constraints had been imposed. Results produced by the **Sem.Standardized** statement, on the other hand, are not affected by the identification constraints:

```
Standardized Regression Weights:          Estimate
--------------------------------          --------

   performance <---------- knowledge        0.516
   performance <------- satisfaction        0.130
   performance <-------------- value        0.398
   1performance <------- performance        0.856
   2performance <------- performance        0.819
   1knowledge <---------- knowledge         0.728
   2knowledge <---------- knowledge         0.618
   1value <------------------ value         0.745
   2value <------------------ value         0.633
   1satisfaction <----- satisfaction        0.896
   2satisfaction <----- satisfaction        0.747


Correlations:                             Estimate
-------------                             --------

   knowledge <---------------> value        0.542
   knowledge <--------> satisfaction        0.064
   value <-----------> satisfaction        -0.084
```

Amos Graphics output

The path diagram with standardized parameter estimates inserted is:

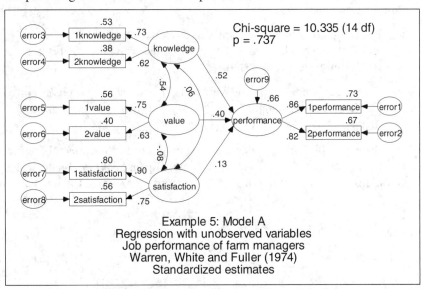

Example 5: Model A
Regression with unobserved variables
Job performance of farm managers
Warren, White and Fuller (1974)
Standardized estimates

The value above the **performance** object indicates that "pure" **knowledge**, **value** and **satisfaction** account for 66 percent of the variance of the hypothetical "pure" **performance** construct. The values printed over the observed variables are the reliability estimates for the eight individual subtests. You will find a formula to compute the reliability of the original tests (before they were split in half) in Rock *et al.* (1977) or any book on mental test theory.

Model B

If Model A is correct (and we see no evidence to the contrary), then you can consider the additional hypothesis that **1knowledge** and **2knowledge** are parallel tests. In other words, they are two tests with same-sized common variance components and equal-sized error variances. Under the parallel test hypothesis, the regression of **1knowledge** on **knowledge** should be the same as the regression of **2knowledge** on **knowledge**. Furthermore, the "error" variables associated with **1knowledge** and **2knowledge** should have identical variances. Similar consequences flow from the assumption that **1value** and **2value** are parallel tests, as well as **1performance** and **2performance**. But it is not altogether reasonable to assume that **1satisfaction** and **2satisfaction** are parallel. One of the subtests is slightly longer than the other because the original test had an odd number of items, and could not be split exactly in half. Therefore, **2satisfaction** is 20 percent longer than **1satisfaction**. Assuming that the tests differ only in length leads to the following conclusions:

- The weight for regressing **2satisfaction** on the unobserved **satisfaction** variable should be 1.2 times the weight for regressing **1satisfaction** on **satisfaction**.

- Given equal variances for **error7** and **error8**, the (fixed) regression weight for **error8** should be $\sqrt{1.2} = 1.095445$ times as large as the (fixed) regression weight for **error7**.

Whichever method of input you use, you do not need to completely re-enter the input file or redraw the path diagram. Simply open the **Amos Basic** or **Amos Graphics** file you created for Model A, modify it, and save the input as a new file.

The following are the model specifications in the **Amos Basic** form. The input file supplies all constraints for the regression weight and error variance parameters:

```
Sub Main( )
  Dim Sem As New AmosEngine

  Sem.TextOutput
  Sem.Standardized
  Sem.Smc

  Sem.BeginGroup "Warren9v.wk1"
    Sem.Structure "1performance <--- performance (1)"
    Sem.Structure "2performance <--- performance (1)"
    Sem.Structure "1knowledge <--- knowledge (1)"
    Sem.Structure "2knowledge <--- knowledge (1)"
    Sem.Structure "1value <--- value (1)"
    Sem.Structure "2value <--- value (1)"
    Sem.Structure "1satisfaction <--- satisfaction (1)"
    Sem.Structure "2satisfaction <--- satisfaction (1.2)"

    Sem.Structure "performance <--- knowledge"
    Sem.Structure "performance <--- value"
    Sem.Structure "performance <--- satisfaction"
    Sem.Structure "performance <--- error9 (1)"

    Sem.Structure "1performance <--- error1 (1)"
    Sem.Structure "2performance <--- error2 (1)"
    Sem.Structure "1knowledge <--- error3 (1)"
    Sem.Structure "2knowledge <--- error4 (1)"
    Sem.Structure "1value <--- error5 (1)"
    Sem.Structure "2value <--- error6 (1)"
    Sem.Structure "1satisfaction <--- error7 (1)"
    Sem.Structure "2satisfaction <--- error8 (1.095445)"

    Sem.Structure "error1 (alpha)"
    Sem.Structure "error2 (alpha)"
    Sem.Structure "error8 (delta)"
    Sem.Structure "error7 (delta)"
    Sem.Structure "error6 (gamma)"
    Sem.Structure "error5 (gamma)"
    Sem.Structure "error4 (beta)"
    Sem.Structure "error3 (beta)"

End Sub
```

The corresponding **Amos Graphics** model specification is:

Example 5: Model B
Parallel tests regression
Job performance of farm managers
Warren, White and Fuller (1974)
Model Specification

Results for Model B

The additional parameter constraints of Model B have resulted in increased degrees of freedom for the model:

```
Computation of Degrees of Freedom

                    Number of distinct sample moments:    36
        Number of distinct parameters to be estimated:    14
                    --------------------------
                                Degrees of freedom:    22
```

The chi-square statistic has also increased, but not by much. There is still no indication that Model B might be particularly bad:

```
Chi-square =      26.967
Degrees of freedom =    22
Probability level =     0.212
```

Assuming Model B is correct, you will want to use these associated parameter estimates instead of those obtained under Model A. The raw parameter estimates are too affected by the choice of identification constraints to even bother presenting. However, here are the standardized estimates and squared multiple correlations in **Amos Basic** output:

```
Standardized Regression Weights:              Estimate
-------------------------------               --------

    performance <---------- knowledge           0.529
    performance <------------- value            0.382
    performance <------- satisfaction           0.114
    1performance <------- performance           0.835
    2performance <------- performance           0.835
    1knowledge <----------- knowledge           0.663
    2knowledge <----------- knowledge           0.663
    1value <------------------ value            0.685
    2value <------------------ value            0.685
    1satisfaction <----- satisfaction           0.790
    2satisfaction <----- satisfaction           0.816
    2satisfaction <----------- error8           0.578


Correlations:                                 Estimate
-------------                                  --------

    knowledge <---------------> value           0.565
    knowledge <--------> satisfaction           0.094
    value <------------> satisfaction          -0.085


Squared Multiple Correlations:                Estimate
------------------------------                --------

                      performance              0,671
                     2satisfaction             0.666
                     1satisfaction             0.625
                           2value              0.469
                           1value              0.469
                       2knowledge              0.439
                       1knowledge              0.439
                      2performance             0.698
                      1performance             0.698
```

Now, here are the corresponding standardized estimates and squared multiple correlations in **Amos Graphics** output:

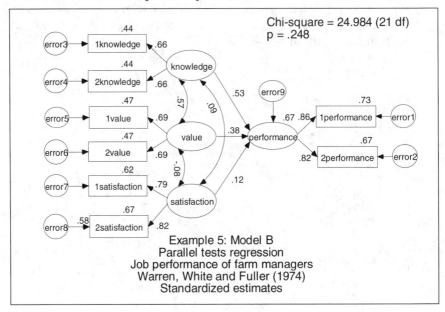

Chi-square = 24.984 (21 df)
p = .248

Example 5: Model B
Parallel tests regression
Job performance of farm managers
Warren, White and Fuller (1974)
Standardized estimates

Testing Model B against Model A

Sometimes you may have two alternative models for the same set of data, and you would like to know which model fits the data better. You can perform a direct comparison whenever one of the models can be obtained by placing additional constraints on the parameters of the other. We have such a case here. We obtained Model B by imposing *eight* additional constraints on the parameters of Model A. Let us say that Model B is the stronger of the two models, in the sense that it represents the strongest hypothesis about the population parameters (Model A would, consequently, be the weaker model). In a case like this, the stronger model will necessarily have both larger degrees of freedom and a larger chi-square statistic.

A test of the stronger model (Model B here) against the weaker one (Model A) can be obtained by subtracting the smaller chi-square statistic from the larger one. In this example, the new statistic is 16.632 (*i.e.*, 26.967 – 10.335). If the stronger model (Model B) is correctly specified, this statistic will have an approximate chi-square distribution with degrees of freedom equal to the difference between the degrees of freedom of the competing models. In this example, the difference in degrees of freedom is 8 (*i.e.*, 22 – 14). That is, Model B imposes all of the parameter constraints of Model A, plus an additional 8.

In summary, if Model B is correct, the value 16.632 comes from a chi-square distribution with 8 degrees of freedom. If only the weaker model (Model A) is correct, but the additional constraints of Model B are not supported by the data, then the new statistic will tend to be large. Hence, the stronger model (Model B) is to be rejected in favor of the weaker model (Model A) when the new chi-square statistic is unusually large. With 8 degrees of freedom, chi-square values greater than 15.507 are significant at the .05 level. Based on this test, we reject Model B.

This seems like a paradoxical decision. How can we now *reject* the more restrictive Model B, if we already accepted it based on its chi-square fit statistic of 26.967 (22 df, p=.212)? The disagreement between the two conclusions can be explained by noting that the two tests differ in their baseline assumptions. The test we just calculated, based on 8 df, evaluates the likelihood of Model B under the assumption that Model A is correct. The initial test based on 22 degrees of freedom makes no such assumptions about Model A. It should be used if Model A was never considered an interesting alternative (and therefore never tested). If you are quite sure that Model A is correct, you should use the test comparing Model B against Model A. On the other hand, if Model A had been found to be unrealistic, then there would have been no reason to consider the more constrained (thus even less realistic) Model B.

Example 6: Exploratory Analysis

Purpose

- Introduce structural modeling of time-dependent latent variables.

- Use modification indices and critical ratios to explore autocorrelations among error terms.

- Show how to specify multiple, related models in a single file, as a technique for efficient model comparisons.

- Demonstrate computation of fitted moments, factor score weights, total effects and indirect effects.

The data

Wheaton *et al.* (1977) report a longitudinal study of 932 persons over the four-year period from 1966 to 1971. One aim of the study was to determine reliability and stability of alienation, a social psychological variable measured by attitude scales. Jöreskog and Sörbom (1984), and others since, have used the Wheaton data to demonstrate analysis of moment structures.

We will use six of Wheaton's measures for this example:

measure	explanation
anomia67	1967 score on the *anomia* scale
anomia71	1971 *anomia* score
powles67	1967 score on the *powerlessness* scale
powles71	1971 *powerlessness* score
education	Years of schooling recorded in 1966
SEI	Duncan's Socioeconomic Index administered in 1966

Take a look at the sample means, standard deviations and correlations for these six measures. You will find the following table in the SPSS file, **Wheaton.sav**. After reading the data, Amos converts the standard deviations and correlations into variances and covariances, as needed for the analysis. We will not use the sample means in the analysis.

	rowtype_	varname_	anomia67	powles67	anomia71	powles71	educatio	sei
1	n		932.00	932.00	932.00	932.00	932.00	932.00
2	corr	anomia67	1.00	.	.	.	.	.
3	corr	powles67	.66	1.00	.	.	.	.
4	corr	anomia71	.56	.47	1.00	.	.	.
5	corr	powles71	.44	.52	.67	1.00	.	.
6	corr	educatio	-.36	-.41	-.35	-.37	1.00	.
7	corr	sei	-.30	-.29	-.29	-.28	.54	1.00
8	stddev		3.44	3.06	3.54	3.16	3.10	21.22
9	mean		13.61	14.76	14.13	14.90	10.90	37.49

Model A for the Wheaton data

Jöreskog and Sörbom (1984) proposed the model shown on page 145 for the Wheaton data, referring to it as their Model A. The model asserts that all of the observed variables depend on underlying, unobserved variables. For example, **anomia67** and **powles67** both depend on the unobserved variable **67_alienation**, a hypothetical variable that Jöreskog and Sörbom referred to as alienation. The unobserved variables **eps1** and **eps2** appear to play the same role as the variables **error1** and **error2** did in Example 5. However, their interpretation here is different. In Example 5, **error1** and **error2** had a natural interpretation as errors of measurement. In the present example, since the anomia and powerlessness scales were not designed to measure the exact same construct, it seems reasonable to believe that differences between them will be due to more than mere measurement error. So in this case, **eps1** and **eps2** should be thought of as representing not only errors of measurement in **anomia67** and **powles67**, but every other variable that might affect scores on the two tests besides **67_alienation** (the one variable that affects them both).

Modeling in Amos Graphics

Here is the path diagram for Model A:

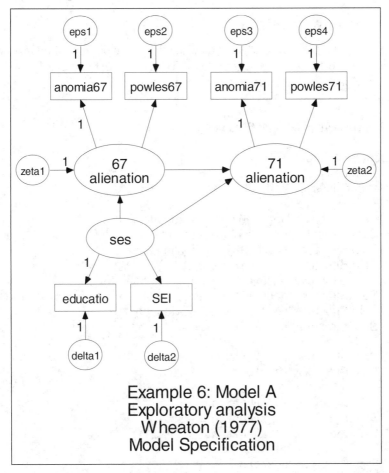

Example 6: Model A
Exploratory analysis
Wheaton (1977)
Model Specification

To specify Model A in **Amos Graphics**, construct the path model shown above, or use the example file **Ex06-a.amw**. In either case, your path model should look like the one above.

Identification

Model A is identified except for the usual problem that the measurement scale of each unobserved variable is indeterminate. The measurement scale of each unobserved variable may be fixed arbitrarily by setting a coefficient to unity (1) in one of the paths that are pointing away from it. The path diagram shows 11 regression weights fixed at unity (1), *i.e.*, one value constraint for each unobserved variable. These constraints are sufficient to make the model identified for **Amos Graphics** input.

Modeling in Amos Basic

If you are working in **Amos Basic**, you can either write out the following input file, or open the Amos example file: **Ex06-a.AmosBasic.** This input file specifies Model A with the same identification constraints:

```
Sub Main( )
   Dim Sem As New AmosEngine

   Sem.TextOutput
   Sem.Mods 4
   Sem.BeginGroup "Wheaton.sav"

     Sem.Structure "anomia67 <--- 67_alienation (1)"
     Sem.Structure "anomia67 <--- eps1 (1)"
     Sem.Structure "powles67 <--- 67_alienation"
     Sem.Structure "powles67 <--- eps2 (1)"
     Sem.Structure "anomia71 <--- 71_alienation (1)"
     Sem.Structure "anomia71 <--- eps3 (1)"
     Sem.Structure "powles71 <--- 71_alienation"
     Sem.Structure "powles71 <--- eps4 (1)"

     Sem.Structure "67_alienation <--- ses"
     Sem.Structure "67_alienation <--- zeta1 (1)"

     Sem.Structure "71_alienation <--- 67_alienation"
     Sem.Structure "71_alienation <--- ses"
     Sem.Structure "71_alienation <--- zeta2 (1)"

     Sem.Structure "educatio <--- ses (1)"
     Sem.Structure "educatio <--- delta1 (1)"
     Sem.Structure "SEI <--- ses"
     Sem.Structure "SEI <--- delta2 (1)"

End Sub
```

Note that SPSS data files truncate the names of observed variables to eight characters. For instance, the observed variable education is called educatio in the SPSS file. In Structure statements, all observed variables have to be typed exactly how they are named in the data files or else Amos will interpret them as unobserved variables.

The eight unique variables delta1, delta2, zeta1, zeta2, and eps1 through eps4 are uncorrelated among themselves, and with the three common factors ses, 67_alienation, and 71_alienation.

Output from the analysis of Model A

The model has 15 parameters to be estimated (6 regression weights and 9 variances). There are 21 sample moments (6 sample variances and 15 covariances). This leaves 6 degrees of freedom:

```
Computation of Degrees of Freedom

                Number of distinct sample moments:    21
    Number of distinct parameters to be estimated:    15
                                          ------------------------
                                Degrees of freedom:     6
```

Model A does not fit the Wheaton data particularly well:

```
Chi-square =      71.544
Degrees of freedom =      6
Probability level =       0.000
```

Dealing with rejection

You have several options when a proposed model has to be rejected on statistical grounds:

- You can point out that statistical hypothesis testing can be a poor tool for choosing a model. Jöreskog (1967) discussed this issue in the context of factor analysis. It is a widely accepted view that a model can be only an approximation at best, and that, fortunately, a model can be useful without being true. This point of view implies that models are never perfectly correct and thus can always be rejected on statistical grounds if tested against a big enough sample. Consequently, rejection of a model on purely statistical grounds (particularly with a large sample) is not necessarily a condemnation.

  While this argument is generally recognized as valid, most published applications of analysis of moment structures do have statistically acceptable fit. Moderately misfitting models can be entertained throughout the research process even though the publication practice of peer-reviewed journals may follow much stricter guidelines.

- You can start from scratch to devise another model to replace the rejected one.

- You can try to modify the rejected model in small ways to improve its fit to the data.

We will demonstrate how to perform the last tactic for this example. The most natural way of modifying a model to make it fit better is to relax some of its assumptions. For example, Model A assumes that **eps1** and **eps3** are uncorrelated. You could relax this restriction by connecting **eps1** and **eps3** with a double-headed arrow. The model also specifies that **anomia67** does not depend directly on **ses**. Remove this assumption by drawing a single-headed arrow from **ses** to **anomia67**. Model A does not happen to constrain any parameters to be equal to other parameters, but if such constraints were present, you might consider removing them in hopes of getting a better fit. Of course, you have to be careful when relaxing the assumptions of a model that you do not turn an identified model into an unidentified one.

Modification indices

You can test various modifications of a model by carrying out a separate analysis for each proposed modification, but this approach is time-consuming and unnecessary. Instead, if you are using **Amos Basic**, just add the statement Sem.Mods 4 to your input file. For **Amos Graphics** follow the path: **View/Set** → **Analysis Properties** → **Output** and check the **Modification Indices** box. For this example, leave the **Threshold of modification indices** set at 4.

Either way, these modifications will allow you to examine all potential modifications in a single analysis. They will produce suggestions for modifications that will likely result in lower chi-square values. Here is the output produced by either of these modifications:

```
Covariances:                                    M.I.      Par Change
                                              ---------   ----------
        eps2 <-------------------> delta1       5.906       -0.424
        eps2 <-------------------> eps4        26.545        0.825
        eps2 <-------------------> eps3        32.070       -0.989
        eps1 <-------------------> delta1       4.608        0.421
        eps1 <-------------------> eps4        35.367       -1.070
        eps1 <-------------------> eps3        40.911        1.254


Variances:                                      M.I.      Par Change
                                              ---------   ----------


Regression Weights:                             M.I.      Par Change
                                              ---------   ----------
    powles71 <------------- powles67            5.458        0.057
    powles71 <------------- anomia67            9.006       -0.065
    anomia71 <------------- powles67            6.775       -0.069
    anomia71 <------------- anomia67           10.353        0.076
    powles67 <------------- powles71            5.613        0.054
    powles67 <------------- anomia71            7.278       -0.054
    anomia67 <------------- powles71            7.706       -0.070
    anomia67 <------------- anomia71            9.065        0.068
```

The column heading M.I. in this table is short for **modification index**. The modification indices produced are those described by Jöreskog and Sörbom (1984). The first modification index listed (5.905) is a conservative estimate of the decrease in chi-square if **eps2** and **delta1** were allowed to correlate. If the additional parameter were indeed added, then the degrees of freedom associated with the new model would be one less. The new chi-square statistic would have 5 (= 6 − 1) degrees of freedom, and would be no greater than 65.639 (*i.e.*, 71.544 − 5.905). The actual decrease of the chi-square statistic might be much larger than 5.905. The column labeled Par change gives approximate estimates of how much the parameter would change if it were relaxed. Amos estimates that the covariance between **eps2** and **delta1** would be –0.424. Based on the small modification index, it does not look as though much would be gained by allowing **eps2** and **delta1** to be correlated. Besides, it would be hard to justify this particular modification on theoretical grounds even if it did produce a numerically acceptable fit.

Notice that the threshold 4 in the **Amos Basic** statement, Sem.Mods 4 specifies that only modification indices greater than 4 should be displayed. The statement Sem.Mods 0 would have displayed all modification indices greater than zero. However, many of these indices would have been small, and thus of little interest.

The largest modification index in Model A is 40.911. It indicates that allowing **eps1** and **eps3** to be correlated will decrease the chi-square statistic by at least

40.911. This is a modification well worth considering, particularly because autocorrelated residuals are frequently encountered in time-structured models.

The substantive reasoning for this is that the term **eps1** represents variability in **anomia67** that is not due to variation in **67_alienation**. Similarly, **eps3** represents variability in **anomia71** that is not due to variation in **71_alienation**. **Anomia67** and **anomia71** are scale scores on the same instrument (at different times). If the anomia scale also reflects some other attitude besides alienation, you would expect to find a nonzero correlation between **eps1** and **eps3**. In fact, you would expect the correlation to be positive, which is consistent with the fact that the number in the Par Change column is positive.

The theoretical reasons for suspecting that **eps1** and **eps3** might be correlated apply to **eps2** and **eps4** as well. The modification indices also suggest allowing **eps2** and **eps4** to be correlated. However, we will ignore this potential modification and proceed immediately to look at the results of modifying Model A by allowing **eps1** and **eps3** to be correlated.

Model B for the Wheaton data

If you are using **Amos Basic**, you can turn Model A into Jöreskog and Sörbom's Model B by adding the following line in the Group 2 section of the program:
Sem.Structure "eps1 <---> eps3"

With **Amos Graphics**, simply draw a covariance path between **eps1** and **eps3** in the input path diagram. If the path goes beyond the bounds of the print area, you can use the **Shape** icon to adjust the curvature of the covariance curve or make it arc in the other direction. The **Move** icon lets you reposition the end points of the covariance path, if needed. The **Amos Graphics** file for this example is **Ex06-b.amw**.

Analysis of Model B

Amos Basic output

The added covariance between **eps1** and **eps3** decreases the degrees of freedom by one:

```
Computation of Degrees of Freedom

                    Number of distinct sample moments:    21
        Number of distinct parameters to be estimated:    16
                                        ------------------
                                    Degrees of freedom:     5
```

The chi-square statistic is reduced by substantially more than the promised 40.911:

```
Chi-square =       6.383
Degrees of freedom =    5
Probability level =    0.271
```

Model B cannot be rejected. Since the fit of Model B is reasonable, we will not pursue the possibility, mentioned earlier, that **eps2** and **eps4** might also be correlated. However, an argument could be made that a nonzero correlation between **eps2** and **eps4** should be allowed in order to achieve a symmetry that is now lacking in the model.

You must be cautious when interpreting the raw parameter estimates since they would have been different if you had imposed different identification constraints. The text output of the parameter estimates is:

```
Regression Weights:                     Estimate   S.E.     C.R.    Label
-------------------                     --------  -------  -------  -------

67_alienation <-------------- ses       -0.550    0.053   -10.294   par-3
71_alienation <----- 67_alienation       0.617    0.050    12.421   par-4
71_alienation <-------------- ses        -0.212    0.049    -4.294   par-5
anomia67 <--------- 67_alienation         1.000
powles67 <--------- 67_alienation         1.027    0.053    19.322   par-1
anomia71 <--------- 71_alienation         1.000
powles71 <--------- 71_alienation         0.971    0.049    19.650   par-2
educatio <------------------- ses         1.000
SEI <----------------------- ses          5.164    0.421    12.255   par-6


Covariances:                            Estimate   S.E.     C.R.    Label
------------                            --------  -------  -------  -------

eps1 <--------------------> eps3          1.886    0.240    7.866    par-7


Variances:                              Estimate   S.E.     C.R.    Label
----------                              --------  -------  -------  -------

                           ses            6.872    0.657   10.458   par-8
                          zeta1           4.700    0.433   10.864   par-9
                          zeta2           3.862    0.343   11.257   par-10
                          eps1            5.059    0.371   13.650   par-11
                          eps2            2.211    0.317    6.968   par-12
                          eps3            4.806    0.395   12.173   par-13
                          eps4            2.681    0.329    8.137   par-14
                         delta1           2.728    0.516    5.292   par-15
                         delta2         266.567   18.173   14.668   par-16
```

Note the large critical ratio associated with the new covariance path. The covariance parameter between **eps1** and **eps3** is clearly different from zero. This explains the poor fit of Model A, which fixed this covariance at zero.

Amos Graphics output

The following path diagram displays the standardized estimates (near the paths) and squared multiple correlations (near the endogenous variables):

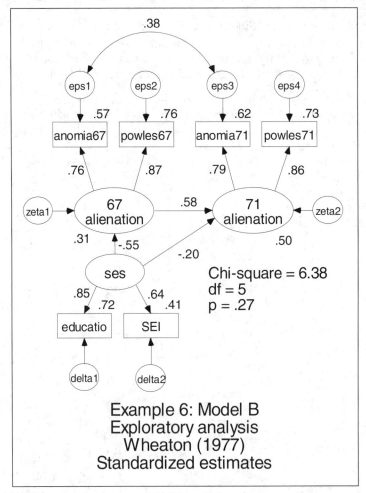

Because the error variables in the model represent more than just measurement error, the squared multiple correlations cannot be interpreted as estimates of reliabilities. Rather, each squared multiple correlation may serve as a lower-bound estimate of the corresponding reliability. Take **education**, for instance. **ses** accounts for 72 percent of its variance. Therefore, you would estimate that its reliability to be at least 0.72. Considering that **education** is measured in years of schooling, the reliability of this variable ought to be closer to 1.

Misuse of modification indices

In trying to improve upon a model, you should not be guided exclusively by the modification indices.

> *A modification must only be considered if it makes theoretical or common sense.*

Without such a limitation, slavish reliance on modification indices will amount to sorting through a very large number of potential modifications in search of one that provides a big improvement in fit. Such a strategy is, through capitalization on chance, prone to producing incorrect models in the sense that their low chi-square values will not likely be replicated by cross-validation. There is also the danger that the structure and the parameter estimates of the resulting model could be fairly absurd. These issues are discussed by MacCallum (1986) and by MacCallum, Roznowski and Necowitz (1992).

Improving a model by adding new constraints

Modification indices suggest ways of improving a model by increasing the number of parameters, so that the chi-square statistic decreases faster than the degrees of freedom. While subject to abuse, this device still has a legitimate place in exploratory studies. There is another trick you can use to produce a model with a more acceptable chi-square value. This technique introduces additional constraints that produce a relatively large increase in degrees of freedom with only a small increase in the chi-square statistic. Many such modifications can be roughly evaluated by looking at the critical ratios in the C.R. column. We have already seen in Example 1 how a single critical ratio can be used to test the hypothesis that a single population parameter equals zero.

If two parameter estimates turned out to be nearly equal, you might be able to improve the chi-square test of fit by postulating a new model where those two parameters are assumed to be exactly equal. Amos provides a powerful exploratory tool for separating promising from unlikely candidates for equality constraints. The Crdiff method in **Amos Basic** produces a listing of critical ratios for the pairwise differences among all parameter estimates.

Likewise, in **Amos Graphics**, you can request this listing by following the path: **View/Set** → **Analysis Properties** → **Output** and checking the **Critical ratios for differences** box.

Either way, this method changes the Amos output in two ways. First, it attaches unique labels to the parameter estimates. These will be the labels supplied by the model specification, plus simple default labels for all other estimated parameters, such as the par-*nn* labels in this output listing:

```
Regression Weights:                      Estimate   S.E.     C.R.    Label
-------------------                      --------  -------  -------  ------

67_alienation <-------------- ses         -0.550    0.053  -10.294  par-6
71_alienation <----- 67_alienation         0.617    0.050   12.421  par-4
71_alienation <------------- ses          -0.212    0.049   -4.294  par-5
powles71 <--------- 71_alienation          0.971    0.049   19.650  par-1
anomia71 <--------- 71_alienation          1.000
powles67 <--------- 67_alienation          1.027    0.053   19.322  par-2
anomia67 <--------- 67_alienation          1.000
educatio <------------------- ses          1.000
SEI <----------------------- ses           5.164    0.421   12.255  par-3


Covariances:                             Estimate   S.E.     C.R.    Label
------------                             --------  -------  -------  ------

eps1 <--------------------> eps3           1.888    0.240    7.866  par-7


Variances:                               Estimate   S.E.     C.R.    Label
----------                               --------  -------  -------  ------

                              ses          6.879    0.658   10.458  par-8
                            zeta1          4.705    0.433   10.864  par-9
                            zeta2          3.866    0.343   11.257  par-10
                             eps1          5.065    0.371   13.650  par-11
                             eps2          2.213    0.318    6.969  par-12
                             eps3          4.811    0.395   12.173  par-13
                             eps4          2.684    0.330    8.138  par-14
                           delta1          2.731    0.516    5.292  par-15
                           delta2        266.852   18.193   14.668  par-16
```

Secondly, the parameter labels are used to identify the critical ratio statistics in the following table:

```
Critical Ratios for Differences between Parameters

          par-1     par-2     par-3     par-4     par-5     par-6     par-7
        --------  --------  --------  --------  --------  --------  --------
par-1     0.000
par-2     0.877     0.000
par-3     9.883     9.742     0.000
par-4    -4.429    -5.930   -10.579     0.000
par-5   -17.943   -16.634   -12.284   -18.098     0.000
par-6   -22.343   -26.471   -12.661   -17.300    -5.115     0.000
par-7     3.908     3.693    -6.757     5.058     8.490    10.121     0.000
par-8     8.957     8.868     1.713     9.577    10.995    11.796     7.128
par-9     8.367     7.875    -0.706     9.258    11.311    12.046     5.388
par-10    7.785     8.044    -2.353     9.472    11.683    12.628     4.668
par-11   11.108    11.707    -0.177    11.971    14.038    15.429     9.772
par-12    3.829     3.340    -5.592     5.001     7.697     8.252     0.740
par-13   10.427     9.661    -0.612    10.308    12.712    13.573     8.318
par-14    4.700     4.909    -4.635     6.356     8.554     9.601     1.798
par-15    3.396     3.286    -7.264     4.020     5.508     5.974     1.482
par-16   14.615    14.612    14.192    14.637    14.687    14.712    14.563

          par-8     par-9     par-10    par-11    par-12    par-13    par-14
        --------  --------  --------  --------  --------  --------  --------
par-8     0.000
par-9    -2.996     0.000
par-10   -4.112    -1.624     0.000
par-11   -2.402     0.548     2.308     0.000
par-12   -6.387    -5.254    -3.507    -4.727     0.000
par-13   -2.695     0.169     1.553    -0.507     5.042     0.000
par-14   -5.701    -3.909    -2.790    -4.735     0.999    -3.322     0.000
par-15   -3.787    -2.667    -1.799    -3.671     0.855    -3.199     0.077
par-16   14.506    14.440    14.458    14.387    14.544    14.400    14.518

          par-15    par-16
        --------  --------
par-15    0.000
par-16   14.293     0.000
```

Ignoring the zeros down the main diagonal, the table of critical ratios contains 120 entries, one for each pair of parameters. Look at the figure 0.877 near the upper left corner of the table. This critical ratio is the difference between the parameters labeled par-1 and par-2 divided by the estimated standard error of this difference. The two parameters in question are the path coefficients for powles67 <-- 67_alienation and powles71 <-- 71_alienation.

Under the distribution assumptions stated in the technical note at the end of Example 1, the critical ratio statistic can be compared to a table of the standard normal distribution to test whether the two parameters are equal in the population. Since 0.877 is less in magnitude than 1.96, you would not reject, at the .05 level, the hypothesis that the two regression weights are equal in the population. More importantly, you can justify theoretically why these two paths could be equal: the relationship between alienation and powerlessness might well remain constant over the four-year period.

The *square* of the critical ratio for differences between parameters is approximately the amount by which the chi-square statistic would increase if the two parameters were set equal to each other. Since the square of 0.877 is 0.769, modifying Model B so that the two regression weights are estimated at one equal value would yield a chi-square value of about 6.383 + 0.769 = 7.152. The degrees of freedom for the new model would be 6 instead of 5. This would be an improved fit (p = 0.307 *vs.* 0.275 for Model B), but we can do much better than that.

Let us look for the smallest critical ratio to use as an example. The smallest critical ratio in the table is 0.077, for the parameters labeled `par-14` and `par-15`. These two parameters are the variances of **eps4** and **delta1**. The square of 0.077 is 0.006. A modification of Model B that assumes **eps4** and **delta1** to have equal variances will result in a chi-square value that exceeds 6.383 by about 0.006, but with 6 degrees of freedom instead of 5. The associated probability level would be about 0.381. The only problem with this modification is that there is absolutely no justification for it. That is, we cannot think of any *a priori* reason why **eps4** and **delta1** should have equal variances.

We have just been discussing a misuse of the table of critical ratios for differences. However, the table does have legitimate exploratory use in the quick examination of a small number of hypotheses. As an example of the proper use of the table, consider the fact that observations on **anomia67** and **anomia71** were obtained by using the same instrument on two occasions. The same goes for **powles67** and **powles71**. It is plausible that the tests would behave the same way on the two occasions. The critical ratios for differences are consistent with this hypothesis. The variances of **eps1** and **eps3** (`par-11` and `par-13`) differ with a critical ratio of -0.507. The variances of **eps2** and **eps4** (`par-12` and `par-14`) differ with a critical ratio of 0.999. The weights for the regression of powerlessness on alienation (`par-1` and `par-2`) differ with a critical ratio of 0.877. None of these differences, taken individually, is significant at conventional significance levels. This suggests that it may be worthwhile to investigate more carefully a model in which all three differences are constrained to be zero. We will call the new model, Model C, and we are interested in evaluating its fit to the data, above and beyond the fit of the more general Model B.

Model C for the Wheaton data

The **Amos Basic** input for Model C, from file **Ex06-c.AmosBasic**, is:

```
Sub Main ( )
   Dim Sem As New AmosEngine

   Sem.TextOutput
   Sem.Standardized
   Sem.Smc
   Sem.AllImpliedMoments
   Sem.FactorScoreWeights
   Sem.TotalEffects

   Sem.BeginGroup "Wheaton.sav"
      Sem.Structure
"anomia67 <--- 67_alienation (1)"
      Sem.Structure "anomia67 <--- eps1 (1)"
      Sem.Structure "powles67 <--- 67_alienation (path_p)"
      Sem.Structure "powles67 <--- eps2 (1)"
      Sem.Structure "anomia71 <--- 71_alienation (1)"
      Sem.Structure "anomia71 <--- eps3 (1)"
      Sem.Structure "powles71 <--- 71_alienation (path_p)"
      Sem.Structure "powles71 <--- eps4 (1)"
      Sem.Structure "67_alienation <--- ses"
      Sem.Structure "67_alienation <--- zeta1 (1)"
      Sem.Structure "71_alienation <--- 67_alienation"
      Sem.Structure "71_alienation <--- ses"
      Sem.Structure "71_alienation <--- zeta2 (1)"
      Sem.Structure "educatio <--- ses (1)"
      Sem.Structure "educatio <--- delta1 (1)"
      Sem.Structure "SEI <--- ses"
      Sem.Structure "SEI <--- delta2 (1)"
      Sem.Structure "eps3 <--> eps1"
      Sem.Structure "eps1 (var_a)"
      Sem.Structure "eps2 (var_p)"
      Sem.Structure "eps3 (var_a)"
      Sem.Structure "eps4 (var_p)"

End Sub
```

The label `path_p` sets the path coefficients from alienation to powerlessness to the same value at the two measurement occasions. The label `var_a` is used to specify that **eps1** and **eps3** have the same variance. The label `var_p` specifies that **eps2** and **eps4** have the same variance.

The corresponding **Amos Graphics** model specification, from **Ex06-c.amw** is:

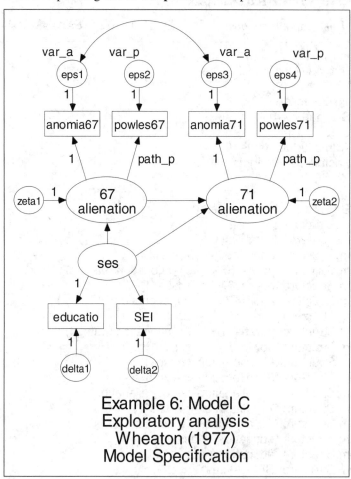

Example 6: Model C
Exploratory analysis
Wheaton (1977)
Model Specification

Output from the analysis of Model C

Model C has 3 more degrees of freedom than Model B:

```
Computation of Degrees of Freedom

                Number of distinct sample moments:     21
      Number of distinct parameters to be estimated:   13
                ------------------------
                              Degrees of freedom:        8
```

Testing Model C

As expected, Model C has an acceptable fit, with a higher probability level than Model B:

```
Chi-square =        7.501
Degrees of freedom =     8
Probability level =     0.484
```

You may test Model C against Model B by examining the difference in chi-square values ($7.501 - 6.383 = 1.118$) and the difference in degrees of freedom ($8 - 5 = 3$). A chi-square value of 1.118 with 3 degrees of freedom is not significant.

Parameter estimates for Model C

The raw parameter estimates for Model C will not be discussed because they are affected by the identification constraints. The standardized estimates are:

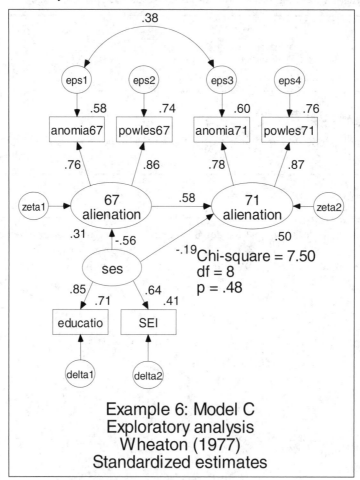

Example 6: Model C
Exploratory analysis
Wheaton (1977)
Standardized estimates

Multiple models in a single file

Both **Amos Graphics** and **Amos Basic** allow for the inclusion of multiple models in a single file. There are two reasons for doing so: not only are all of your results maintained under a single heading, but also several models can be estimated together. In addition, Amos prints the chi-square difference tests between any two nested models, along with the *p* values for these comparisons. Putting all three models in a single file in this example requires a little foresight, for the individual models must be expressed as restricted versions of the most general model considered.

Modeling in Amos Basic

Suppose you took the **Amos Basic** statement file for Model B and added unique labels to get a file section that looks like the following:

```
Sem.TextOutput

Sem.BeginGroup "Wheaton.sav"

    Sem.Structure "anomia67 <--- 67_alienation (1)"
    Sem.Structure "anomia67 <--- eps1 (1)"
    Sem.Structure "powles67 <--- 67_alienation (b_pow67)"
    Sem.Structure "powles67 <--- eps2 (1)"

    Sem.Structure "anomia71 <--- 71_alienation (1)"
    Sem.Structure "anomia71 <--- eps3 (1)"
    Sem.Structure "powles71 <--- 71_alienation (b_pow71)"
    Sem.Structure "powles71 <--- eps4 (1)"

    Sem.Structure "67_alienation <--- ses"
    Sem.Structure "67_alienation <--- zeta1 (1)"
    Sem.Structure "71_alienation <--- 67_alienation"
    Sem.Structure "71_alienation <--- ses"
    Sem.Structure "71_alienation <--- zeta2 (1)"

    Sem.Structure "educatio <--- ses (1)"
    Sem.Structure "educatio <--- delta1 (1)"
    Sem.Structure "SEI <--- ses"
    Sem.Structure "SEI <--- delta2 (1)"

    Sem.Structure "eps3 <--> eps1 (cov1)"

    Sem.Structure "eps1 (var_a67)"
    Sem.Structure "eps2 (var_p67)"
    Sem.Structure "eps3 (var_a71)"
    Sem.Structure "eps4 (var_p71)"
```

All three of the models discussed are manifestations of this new model. Model A did not include a covariance term between **eps1** and **eps3** — this is equivalent to setting `cov1=0`. Model B is the most general model — it imposes no constraints on the parameters. Model C specifies time-invariance measurement relationships for the alienation construct. This is equivalent to setting the three equality constraints:

```
b_pow67 = b_pow71
var_a67 = var_a71
var_p67 = var_p71
```

For completeness sake, a fourth specification (Model D) might be considered that combines the single constraint of Model A with the three constraints of Model C. The models can easily be specified in the **Amos Basic** program by using the Model method. This has been done in the example file **Ex06-all.AmosBasic.** The model definition section of this statement file is:[1]

```
Sem.Model "Model A: No Autocorrelation", "cov1 = 0"
Sem.Model "Model B: Most General", ""
Sem.Model "Model C: Time-Invariance", _
      "b_pow67 = b_pow71;var_a67 = var_a71;var_p67 = var_p71"
Sem.Model "Model D: A and C Combined", _
      "Model A: No Autocorrelation;Model C: Time-Invariance"
```

Each model specification is made up of a Sem.Model statement, a label in double quotes (" ") for the particular model, a comma and a string of model constraints enclosed in double quotes (""). The label is used in the list output to identify the results. The label can also be used as a reference in subsequent model specifications. Remember to use the following syntax:

• Use a comma after the label string

• Constraints are enclosed in double quotes

• Multiple constraints are separated from each other by semicolons

The last model specification (Model D) demonstrates how earlier model specifications can easily be assembled into a more restricted, combined model. To enter all constraints used by a previous model, the label of that model may be used as a reference. This back-referencing facility makes systematic model comparisons quite easy.

---

[1] To make this Amos Basic model statements fit on this page, we had to break some lines of code. You will not need to do this. However, the model will still run because we followed Amos Basic (and Visual Basic) syntax for breaking lines of code. Notice that we ended the first section of the longer line with the label string, and comma, and added a trailing underscore (_). Then we simply entered the string of constraints on the following line. We also indented the continuation line so you could spot them more easily.

Modeling in Amos Graphics

Entering multiple models into a path diagram input file is done in much the same way as under **Amos Basic**. First, add unique parameter labels to the path diagram. In this example, we have added seven:

var_a67
var_p67
var_a71
var_p71
b_pow67
b_pow71
cov1

Add these labels by double clicking on each parameter and entering a label in the **Variance** field of the **Object Properties** dialog box.

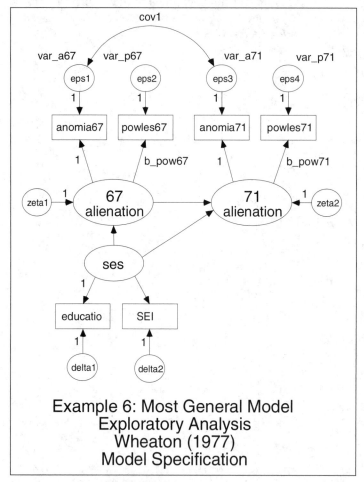

Example 6: Most General Model
Exploratory Analysis
Wheaton (1977)
Model Specification

Next, double-click on the Default Model in the **Models** box.

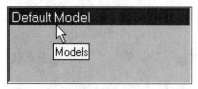

The **Manage Models** dialog box appears. In the **Model Name** text box, change Default Model to:

Model A: No Autocorrelation

Here is what the dialog box will look like:

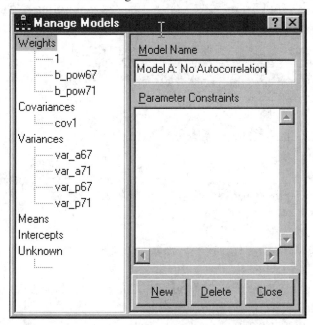

Then, double-click on the cov1 parameter in the left panel. You will notice that cov1 is copied into the **Parameter Contraints** panel. Type in = 0 to finish up the constraint to cov1 = 0.

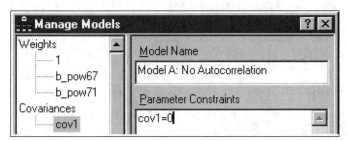

When you are finished specifying Model A, click on the **New** button in the **Manage Models** dialog box for the next model. Change Model Number 2 to Model B: Most General in the **Model Name** field.

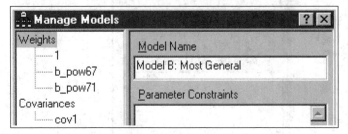

Because there are no constraints, you can speedily move to Model C by again clicking on the **New** button. Change Model Number 3 to Model C: Time-Invariance and add the constraints:

    b_pow67 = b_pow71
    var_a67 = var_a71
    var_p67 = var_p71

Similarly, Change Model Number 4 to Model D: A and C Combined and add these constraints:

    Model A: No Autocorrelation
    Model C: Time-Invariance

Now we have set up the parameter constraints for all four models. The next step is to calculate the estimates and view the output.

Output from multiple models

Amos Graphics output

When you are running multiple models, use the **Models** panel to display the diagrams from different models. This panel is always open on the upper left portion of the screen. To display a model, simply scroll to the label of the model you wish to view and click on it:

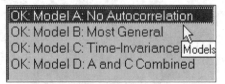

To view the fit statistics for all the models, click on the **Table Output** icon and then the **Fit Measures 2** display option. Amos 4.0 displays the fit statistics for all the models with one line for each model:

	A	B	C	D
1	Fit Measures			
2		cmin	df	p
3	Model A: No Autocorrelation	71.54	6	0.00
4	Model B: Most General	6.38	5	0.27
5	Model C: Time-Invariance	7.50	8	0.48
6	Model D: A and C Combined	73.08	9	0.00
7	Saturated	0.00	0	
8	Independence	2131.79	15	0.00

If you wish to see **All Implied Moments**, **Factor Score Weights**, **Total Effects**, and other types of output in **Amos Graphics**, simply follow the path: **View/Set** → **Analysis Properties** → **Output** and check the appropriate boxes on the **Output** tab:

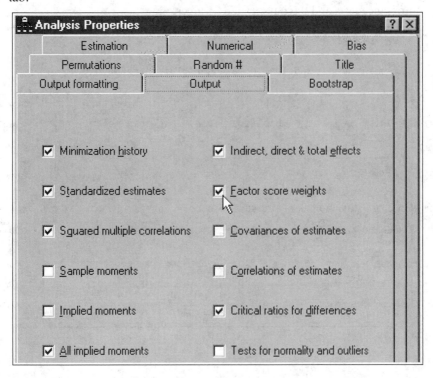

Amos Basic output

When you have specified multiple models, Amos computes and prints the estimates and related output for each model in turn. In addition, Amos summarizes various fit statistics for the models near the end of the list output file:

```
Summary of models
-----------------

              Model  NPAR       CMIN   DF          P    CMIN/DF
-----------------   ----  ---------   --  ---------  ---------
Model A: No Autocorr    15     71.544    6      0.000     11.924
Model B: Most Genera    16      6.383    5      0.271      1.277
Model C: Time-Invari    13      7.501    8      0.484      0.938
Model D: A and C Com    12     73.077    9      0.000      8.120
      Saturated model    21      0.000    0
    Independence model     6   2131.790   15      0.000    142.119
```

With maximum likelihood estimation (default), the column labeled CMIN contains the usual chi-square fit statistics. The column labeled *p* contains the corresponding upper tail probabilities for testing the null hypothesis. At the very end of the list output file, Amos provides tables of model comparisons, complete with chi-square difference tests and their associated *p* values:

```
Model Comparisons
-----------------

Assuming model Model A: No Autocorrelation to be correct:

                                     NFI      IFI     RFI      TLI
                  DF   CMIN     P  Delta-1  Delta-2  rho-1    rho-2
                  --  ----- -----  -------  -------  -----    -----
Model D: A and C Comb 3  1.533 0.675    0.001    0.001  -0.027   -0.027


Assuming model Model B: Most General to be correct:

                                     NFI      IFI     RFI      TLI
                  DF   CMIN     P  Delta-1  Delta-2  rho-1    rho-2
                  --  ----- -----  -------  -------  -----    -----
Model A: No Autocorre 1 65.160 0.000    0.031    0.031   0.075    0.075
Model C: Time-Invaria 3  1.117 0.773    0.001    0.001  -0.002   -0.002
Model D: A and C Comb 4 66.693 0.000    0.031    0.031   0.048    0.048


Assuming model Model C: Time-Invariance to be correct:

                                     NFI      IFI     RFI      TLI
                  DF   CMIN     P  Delta-1  Delta-2  rho-1    rho-2
                  --  ----- -----  -------  -------  -----    -----
Model D: A and C Comb 1 65.576 0.000    0.031    0.031   0.051    0.051
```

Because the four models in this example follow a two-by-two factorial design, the chi-square comparisons for relative model fit can be arranged more compactly in Table 6.1.

	Measurement of alienation		
	varying	time-invariant	Chi-square difference
`cov1` estimated	Model B: $\chi_5^2 = 6.38$	Model C: $\chi_8^2 = 7.50$	$\chi_3^2 = 1.12$
`cov1` = 0	Model A: $\chi_6^2 = 71.54$	Model D: $\chi_9^2 = 73.08$	$\chi_3^2 = 1.53$
Chi-square difference	$\chi_1^2 = 65.16$	$\chi_1^2 = 65.58$	

Table 6.1 : χ^2 Fit Statistics of Models A through D, and χ^2–Differences

The chi-square difference statistics in the bottom margin of the table do not support the hypothesis that the autocorrelation parameter `cov1` equals zero, no matter which of the two measurement models for alienation is chosen. The chi-square values in the right margin of the table indicate that the time-invariant measurement model performs as well as the more general (varying) model, no matter whether the parameter `cov1` is estimated or fixed at zero. According to this table, Model C wins the competition for the simplest model to fit the Wheaton *et al.* (1977) data.

Other optional output

The variances and covariances among the observed variables under Model C can be deduced from the parameter estimates, by using the Moments method. The implied variances and covariances of the *unobserved* common variables may be obtained with the Allimpliedmoments method.

For Model C, this method gives the following output:

```
Implied (for all variables) Covariances

            ses       67_alien 71_alien SEI      educatio powles71 anomia71
          --------  -------- -------- -------- -------- -------- --------
ses          6.858
67_aliena   -3.838     6.914
71_aliena   -3.720     4.977     7.565
SEI         35.484   -19.858   -19.246  449.805
educatio     6.858    -3.838    -3.720   35.484    9.600
powles71    -3.717     4.973     7.559  -19.231   -3.717     9.989
anomia71    -3.720     4.977     7.565  -19.246   -3.720     7.559   12.515
powles67    -3.835     6.909     4.973  -19.842   -3.835     4.969    4.973
anomia67    -3.838     6.914     4.977  -19.858   -3.838     4.973    6.865

          powles67 anomia67
          -------- --------
powles67     9.339
anomia67     6.909    11.864
```

As you can see, the moments for the observed variables are not the same as the
sample variances and covariances. As estimates of the corresponding population
values, the variances and covariances displayed by Allimpliedmoments are more
efficient than the sample variances and covariances (assuming that Model C is
correct). When both the Standardized and Allimpliedmoments methods are
specified, Amos will also list the implied *correlation* matrix of all variables.

You can use the variances and covariances produced by the Allimpliedmoments
method to estimate the scores of the unobserved variables, based on the values of
the observed variables. The Factorscores method produces the required
regression weights based on the implied covariance matrix:

```
Factor Score Weights

            SEI      educatio powles71 anomia71 powles67 anomia67
          -------- -------- -------- -------- -------- --------
ses          0.0289    0.5418   -0.0547   -0.0164   -0.0686   -0.0275
67_aliena   -0.0033   -0.0610    0.1338   -0.0265    0.4715    0.2423
71_aliena   -0.0026   -0.0486    0.4907    0.2534    0.1338   -0.0308
```

The table of factor score weights has a separate row for each unobserved variable,
and a separate column for each observed variable. Here is an example of how you
would use the table. Suppose you wanted to estimate the **ses** score of an individual.
You would compute a weighted sum of the individual's observed scores using the
weights found in the **ses** row of the table.

The coefficients associated with the single-headed arrows in a path diagram are often called the *direct effects* among the variables. In Model C, for example, **ses** has a direct effect on **71_alienation**. **71_alienation**, in turn, has a direct effect on **powles71**. **ses** is then said to have an *indirect* effect (through the intermediary of **71_alienation**) on **powles71**. Tables of direct and indirect effects are produced by the Totaleffects method:

```
Total Effects

              ses     67_alien  71_alien
           --------  --------  --------
67_aliena   -0.560     0.000     0.000
71_aliena   -0.542     0.607     0.000
SEI          5.174     0.000     0.000
educatio     1.000     0.000     0.000
powles71    -0.542     0.607     0.999
anomia71    -0.542     0.607     1.000
powles67    -0.559     0.999     0.000
anomia67    -0.560     1.000     0.000
```

The first row indicates that **67_alienation** depends, directly or indirectly, on **ses** only. The *total effect* of **ses** on **67_alienation** is -0.560. The fact that the effect is negative means that (all other things being equal), relatively high **ses** scores are associated with relatively low **67_alienation** scores. Looking in the fifth row of the table, **powles71** depends, directly or indirectly, on **ses**, **67_alienation**, and **71_alienation**. Low scores on **ses**, high scores on **67_alienation**, and high scores on **71_alienation** are associated with high scores on **powles71**. Consult Fox (1980) for more help in interpreting direct, indirect, and total effects.

Example 7:
A Nonrecursive Model

Purpose

- Demonstrate structural equation modeling with a nonrecursive model.

- Investigate a model with two structural equations where the dependent variable of each equation appears as a predictor variable in the other equation.

The data

Felson and Bohrnstedt (1979) studied 209 girls from sixth through eighth grade. They recorded the variables shown:

variable	explanation
academic	Perceived academic ability, a sociometric measure based on the item *Name who you think are your three smartest classmates*
attract	Perceived attractiveness, a sociometric measure based on the item *Name the three girls in the classroom who you think are the most good-looking (excluding yourself)*
GPA	Grade point average
height	Deviation of height from the mean height for a subject's grade and sex
weight	Weight, adjusted for height
rating	Ratings of physical attractiveness obtained by having children from another city rate photographs of the subjects

Sample correlations, means and standard deviations for these six variables are contained in the SPSS file **Fels_fem.sav**. The following is an excerpt of that table output. The sample means are not used in this example.

	rowtype_	varname_	academic	athletic	attract	gpa	height	weight	rating
1	n		209.00	209.00	209.0	209.0	209.0	209.0	209.0
2	corr	academic	1.00	.	.	.	.	.	.
3	corr	athletic	.43	1.00	.	.	.	.	.
4	corr	attract	.50	.48	1.00	.	.	.	.
5	corr	GPA	.49	.22	.32	1.00	.	.	.
6	corr	height	.10	-.04	-.03	.18	1.00	.	.
7	corr	weight	.04	.02	-.16	-.10	.34	1.00	.
8	corr	rating	.09	.14	.43	.15	-.16	-.27	1.00
9	stddev		.16	.07	.49	3.49	2.91	19.32	1.01
10	mean		.12	.05	.42	10.34	.00	94.13	2.65

Felson and Bohrnstedt's model

Felson and Bohrnstedt proposed the model shown on page. Perceived **academic** performance is modeled as a function of **GPA** and perceived attractiveness (**attract**). Perceived attractiveness, in turn, is modeled as a function of perceived **academic** performance, **height**, **weight**, and the **rating** of attractiveness by children from another city. Particularly noteworthy in this model is that perceived academic ability depends on perceived attractiveness, and *vice versa*. A model with these feedback loops is called *nonrecursive* (the terms *recursive* and *nonrecursive* were defined earlier in Example 4). The current model is *nonrecursive* because we can trace the path from attract to academic and back *infinitely* many times, and never be forced to return to the exogenous variables.

Modeling in Amos Graphics

The Felson and Bohrnstedt model can be specified in **Amos Graphics** as:

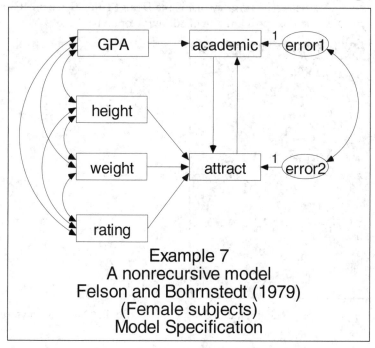

Example 7
A nonrecursive model
Felson and Bohrnstedt (1979)
(Female subjects)
Model Specification

Making a second path in between **academic** and **attract** is no more difficult than making the first. Just remember that the object you drew *towards* in making the first path is the object you draw *away from* in making the second. The **Amos Graphics** file for this example is **Ex07.amw**.

Drawing functions

Remember that **Amos Graphics** features several drawing functions to make the path diagram look neat. The primary one is the **Drag Properties** icon. Clicking on it gives you a dialog box, providing many drawing options:

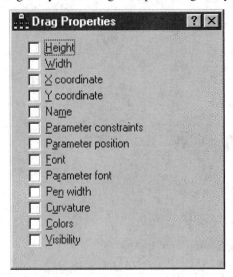

Check the properties to be copied and drag them from the source to the target object(s).

The **Preserve Symmetries** icon helps to maintain proper spacing in selected groups of objects. Suppose that you want to move the **height** object, but simultaneously wish to move the **rating** object so that **height**, **weight** and **rating** remain equidistant. Select the three objects and click on the **Preserve Symmetries** icon. Then when you move one of the outer two objects up or down, the opposite object will also move, maintaining the same distance from **weight**.

Model identification

We need to establish measurement units for the two unobserved variables, **error1** and **error2** for identification purposes. The figure on page shows two regression weights fixed at unity (1). These two constraints are enough to make the model identified.

Modeling in Amos Basic

You can find the **Amos Basic** model specification in `Ex07.AmosBasic`:

```
Sub Main()
    Dim Sem As New AmosEngine

    Sem.TextOutput
    Sem.Standardized
    Sem.Smc
    Sem.BeginGroup "Fels_fem.sav"
        Sem.Structure "academic <--- GPA"
        Sem.Structure "academic <--- attract"
        Sem.Structure "academic <--- error1 (1)"

        Sem.Structure "attract <--- height"
        Sem.Structure "attract <--- weight"
        Sem.Structure "attract <--- rating"
        Sem.Structure "attract <--- academic"
        Sem.Structure "attract <--- error2 (1)"

        Sem.Structure "error2 <--> error1"

End Sub
```

We need to include a line asking for an estimate of the covariance of **error1** and **error2**, because Felson and Bohrnstedt's model permits the residual terms to be correlated. Ordinarily, Amos assumes that *error* variables are uncorrelated.

You can also use this equation format in **Amos Basic** to specify the model. The following input file is a straightforward transcription of the path notation shown before, with a separate line for each endogenous variable:[1]

```
Sem.BeginGroup "Fels_fem.sav"
     Sem.Structure "academic = GPA + attract + error1 (1)"
     Sem.Structure "attract  = height + weight + rating + " _
        & "academic + error2 (1)"
     Sem.Structure "error2 <--> error1"
```

[1] To make our **Amos Basic** model fit on this page, we have had to break lines of code. You will not have to do this. Our Visual Basic method of breaking the code is slightly different than the one in Example 6. Here, we ended the first section of the longer lines with a quote mark (") and an underscore (_). Then, we began the second section of the line with an ampersand (&), followed by the rest of the string enclosed in double quotes. We also indented the second section of these longer lines so you could spot them more easily.

Output from the analysis

The resulting model has two degrees of freedom, and there is no significant evidence that the model is wrong.

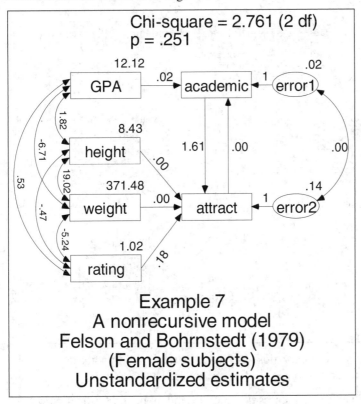

Chi-square = 2.761 (2 df)
p = .251

Example 7
A nonrecursive model
Felson and Bohrnstedt (1979)
(Female subjects)
Unstandardized estimates

There is, however, some evidence that the model is unnecessarily complicated, as indicated by the low critical ratios in **Amos Graphics**' text output:

```
Regression Weights:                        Estimate      S.E.       C.R.
-------------------                        --------      ------     -------

          academic <--------- GPA            0.023       0.004       6.241
          attract <------- height            0.000       0.010       0.050
          attract <------- weight           -0.002       0.001      -1.321
          attract <------- rating            0.176       0.027       6.444
          attract <----- academic            1.607       0.349       4.599
          academic <----- attract           -0.002       0.051      -0.039


Covariances:                               Estimate      S.E.     . C.R.
------------                               --------      ------     -------

       GPA <----------> rating              0.526       0.246       2.139
       height <-------> rating             -0.468       0.205      -2.279
       GPA <----------> weight             -6.710       4.676      -1.435
       GPA <----------> height              1.819       0.712       2.555
       height <-------> weight             19.024       4.098       4.643
       weight <-------> rating             -5.243       1.395      -3.759
       error1 <-------> error2             -0.004       0.010      -0.382


Variances:                                 Estimate      S.E.       C.R.
----------                                 --------      ------     -------

                        GPA               12.122       1.189      10.198
                     height                8.428       0.826      10.198
                     weight              371.476      36.426      10.198
                     rating                1.015       0.100      10.198
                     error1                0.019       0.003       5.747
                     error2                0.143       0.014       9.974
```

Judging by the critical ratios, each of these three null hypotheses would be accepted at conventional significance levels:

- Perceived attractiveness does not depend on height (critical ratio = 0.050).

- Perceived academic ability does not depend on perceived attractiveness (critical ratio = −.039). However, there is some evidence that girls who are perceived as academically able are perceived as more attractive than others (critical ratio = 4.599).

- The residual terms **error1** and **error2** are uncorrelated (critical ratio = −.382).

Strictly speaking, you cannot use the critical ratios to test all three hypotheses at once. Instead, you would have to construct a model that incorporates all three constraints simultaneously. However, we will not pursue further modifications of this model.

The raw parameter estimates reported above are not affected by the identification constraints (except for the variances of **error1** and **error2**). They are, of course, affected by the units in which the observed variables are measured. As usual, the standardized estimates produced by the Sem.Standardized statement are independent of the unit of measurement:

```
Standardized Regression Weights:            Estimate
-------------------------------             --------

        academic <--------- GPA               0.492
        attract <------- height                0.003
        attract <------- weight               -0.078
        attract <------- rating                0.363
        attract <----- academic                0.525
        academic <----- attract               -0.006


Correlations:                               Estimate
-------------                               --------

        GPA <----------> rating               0.150
        height <-------> rating               -0.160
        GPA <----------> weight               -0.100
        GPA <----------> height                0.180
        height <-------> weight                0.340
        weight <-------> rating                -0.270
        error1 <-------> error2                -0.076
```

You can see that the regression weights and the correlation that we judged earlier to be statistically insignificant, are also (speaking descriptively) negligible.

The squared multiple correlations produced by Sem.Smc are also independent of the unit of measurement:

```
Squared Multiple Correlations:              Estimate
-----------------------------               --------

                        attract             0.402
                        academic            0.236
```

The two endogenous variables in this model are not predicted very accurately by the other variables in the model. This demonstrates that the chi-square test of fit is *not* a measure of accuracy of prediction. Here is the path diagram output with standardized estimates and squared multiple correlations as produced by **Amos Graphics**:

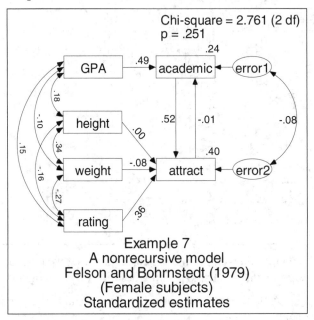

Chi-square = 2.761 (2 df)
p = .251

Example 7
A nonrecursive model
Felson and Bohrnstedt (1979)
(Female subjects)
Standardized estimates

Stability index

The existence of feedback loops in a *nonrecursive* model permits certain problems to arise that cannot occur in recursive models. In the present model, attractiveness depends on perceived academic ability, which in turn depends on attractiveness, which depends on perceived academic ability, and so on. This appears to be an infinite regress — and it is. You may be wondering whether this infinite sequence of linear dependencies can actually result in well defined relationships among attractiveness, academic ability and the other variables of the model. The answer is that they might — or they might not — depending on the regression weights. For some values of the regression weights, the infinite sequence of linear dependencies will converge to a set of well-defined relationships. In this case, the system of linear dependencies is called *stable*. Otherwise, it is called *unstable*.

> *You cannot tell whether a linear system is stable by looking at the path diagram. You need to know the regression weights.*

Amos cannot know what the regression weights are in the population, but it estimates them, and from the estimates it computes a **stability index** (Fox, 1980; Bentler and Freeman, 1983).

If the stability index falls between −1 and +1, the system is stable. Otherwise, it is unstable. In the present example, the system is stable:

```
Stability index for the following variables is      0.003


            attract
            academic
```

An unstable system (with a stability index equal to, or greater than, one) is *impossible*, in the same sense that, say, a negative variance is impossible. If you do obtain a stability index of one (or greater than one), this implies that your model is wrong or that your sample size is too small to provide accurate estimates of the regression weights. If there are several loops in a path diagram, Amos will compute a stability index for each one. If any one of the stability indices equals or exceeds one, the linear system is unstable and should not be modeled in its current form.

Example 8:
Factor Analysis

Purpose

- Demonstrate confirmatory common factor analysis.

The data

Holzinger and Swineford (1939) administered twenty-six psychological tests to 301 seventh- and eighth-grade students in two Chicago schools. In the present example, we use scores obtained by the 73 girls from a single school (the Grant-White school). Here is a summary of the tests we will use in this example:

test	explanation
visperc	Visual perception score
cubes	Test of spatial visualization
lozenges	Test of spatial orientation
paragraph	Paragraph comprehension score
sentence	Sentence completion score
wordmean	Word meaning test score

The file, **Grnt_fem.sav** contains their scores on the following six tests:

	visperc	cubes	lozenges	paragrap	sentence	wordmean
1	33.00	22.00	17.00	8.00	17.00	10.00
2	30.00	25.00	20.00	10.00	23.00	18.00
3	36.00	33.00	36.00	17.00	25.00	41.00
4	28.00	25.00	9.00	10.00	18.00	11.00
5	30.00	25.00	11.00	11.00	21.00	8.00
6	20.00	25.00	6.00	9.00	21.00	16.00
7	17.00	21.00	6.00	5.00	10.00	10.00
8	33.00	31.00	30.00	11.00	23.00	18.00

A common factor model

Consider the following model for the six tests:

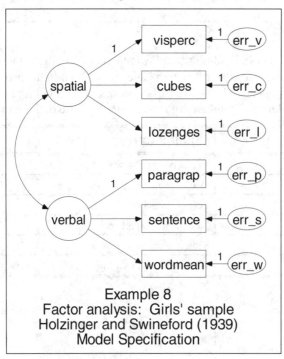

Example 8
Factor analysis: Girls' sample
Holzinger and Swineford (1939)
Model Specification

This model supposes the first three tests depend on an unobserved variable called **spatial**. We are viewing **spatial** as an underlying (spatial) ability that is not directly observed. According to the model, performance on the first three tests depends on this ability. In addition, performance on each of these tests may depend on something other than spatial ability as well. In the case of **visperc,** for example, the unique variable **err_v** is also involved. **err_v** represents any and all influences on **visperc** that are not shown elsewhere in the path diagram. **err_v** represents error of measurement in **visperc**, certainly, but also components of knowledge, ability and/or aptitude that might specifically affect the **visperc** scores.

The model under consideration is a common *factor analysis* model. In the lingo of common factor analysis, the unobserved variable **spatial** is called a *common factor* and the three unobserved variables, **err_v**, **err_c** and **err_l**, are called *unique factors*. This path diagram also shows another common factor, **verbal**, on which the last three tests depend. The diagram also shows three more unique factors, **err_p**, **err_s** and **err_w**. The two common factors, **spatial** and **verbal**, are allowed to be correlated. However, the unique factors are assumed to be uncorrelated with each other and with the common factors. The path coefficients leading from the common factors to the observed variables are often called *factor weights* or *factor loadings*.

Identification

This model is identified except that (as usual) the measurement scale of each unobserved variable is indeterminate. The measurement scale of each unobserved variable may be fixed arbitrarily by setting its regression weight to one (1) in some regression equation. These constraints are sufficient to make the model identified, and have been included in the preceding path diagram.

The proposed model is a particularly simple version of the common factor analysis model, because each observed variable depends on just one common factor. In other applications of common factor analysis, an observed variable can depend on many common factors at the same time. In the general case, it can be very difficult to decide whether a common factor analysis model is identified or not (Davis, 1993; Jöreskog, 1969, 1979). The treatment of identifiability given in this and earlier examples made the issue appear simpler than it actually is. Do not get the idea that lack of a unit of measurement for unobserved variables might be the sole cause of nonidentification. It *is* true that lack of a unit of measurement for unobserved variables is an ever-present cause of nonidentification. Fortunately, this situation is easy to fix, as we have done repeatedly.

But other kinds of underidentification can occur where there are no such corresponding sets of remedies. Conditions for identifiability have to be established separately for individual models. Jöreskog and Sörbom (1984) show how to achieve identification of many models by imposing equality constraints on their parameters. In the case of the factor analysis model, and many others, figuring out what must be done to make the model identified requires a pretty deep understanding of the model. If you are unable to tell whether a model is identified, you can try using the model in order to see whether Amos reports that it is unidentified. In practice, this empirical approach works quite well, although there are objections to it in principle (McDonald and Krane, 1979). Further, it is no substitute for an *a priori* awareness of the identification status of a model. Bollen (1989) discusses causes and treatments of many types of nonidentification in his excellent textbook.

Model input

Modeling in Amos Graphics

Amos Graphics analyzes the model directly from the preceding path diagram. Notice that the model can conceptually be separated into **spatial** and **verbal** branches. You can use the structural similarity of the two branches to accelerate drawing the model. After you have drawn the first branch to your liking, simply click on the **Select all objects** icon to highlight the entire branch. Then, click on the **Duplicate objects** (copy) icon and click/drag out a second branch. Notice that you must connect the **spatial** and **verbal** objects with a two-headed arrow. Otherwise, **Amos Graphics** would assume that the two common factors are uncorrelated. The **Amos Graphics** file for this example is **Ex08.amw**.

Modeling in Amos Basic

The following input file specifies the factor model for the Holzinger and Swineford data in **Amos Basic** equation format:

```
Sub Main()
    Dim Sem As New AmosEngine

    Sem.TextOutput
    Sem.Standardized
    Sem.Smc

    Sem.BeginGroup "Grnt_fem.sav"
        Sem.Structure "visperc  = (1) spatial + (1) err_v"
        Sem.Structure "cubes    =     spatial + (1) err_c"
        Sem.Structure "lozenges =     spatial + (1) err_l"

        Sem.Structure "paragrap = (1) verbal  + (1) err_p"
        Sem.Structure "sentence =     verbal  + (1) err_s"
        Sem.Structure "wordmean =     verbal  + (1) err_w"

End Sub
```

You do not need to specify explicitly that the common factors, **spatial** and **verbal**, may be correlated. Nor is it necessary to specify that the unique factors are uncorrelated with each other and the two common factors. This is because of **Amos Basic**'s default correlation assumptions for common factors and unique factor components.

Results of the analysis

Here are the unstandardized results of the analysis. As shown at the upper right corner of the figure, the model fits the data quite well.

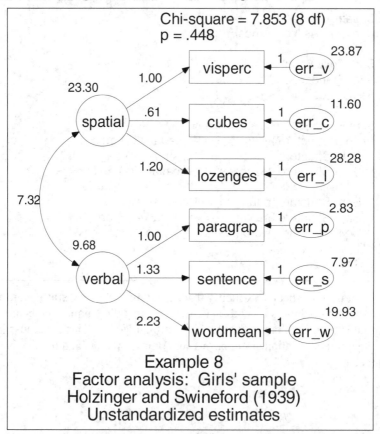

Chi-square = 7.853 (8 df)
p = .448

Example 8
Factor analysis: Girls' sample
Holzinger and Swineford (1939)
Unstandardized estimates

As an exercise, you may wish to confirm the computation of degrees of freedom:

```
Computation of Degrees of Freedom

              Number of distinct sample moments:    21
    Number of distinct parameters to be estimated:  13
                                        ------------------------
                            Degrees of freedom:     8
```

The model estimates, both in their original scale and standardized form, are shown below. As you would expect, the weights are positive, as is the correlation between the **spatial** and **verbal** common factors.

```
Regression Weights:                  Estimate    S.E.     C.R.
-------------------                  --------  -------  -------

      visperc <------ spatial          1.000
      cubes <-------- spatial          0.610    0.143    4.250
      lozenges <----- spatial          1.198    0.272    4.405
      paragrap <------ verbal          1.000
      sentence <------ verbal          1.334    0.160    8.322
      wordmean <------ verbal          2.234    0.263    8.482


Standardized Regression Weights:     Estimate
--------------------------------     --------

      visperc <------ spatial          0.703
      cubes <-------- spatial          0.654
      lozenges <----- spatial          0.736
      paragrap <------ verbal          0.880
      sentence <------ verbal          0.827
      wordmean <------ verbal          0.841


Covariances:                         Estimate    S.E.     C.R.
------------                         --------  -------  -------

      spatial <------> verbal          7.315    2.571    2.846


Correlations:                        Estimate
-------------                        --------

      spatial <------> verbal          0.487


Variances:                           Estimate    S.E.     C.R.
----------                           --------  -------  -------

                       spatial       23.302    8.123    2.868
                        verbal        9.682    2.159    4.485
                         err_v       23.873    5.986    3.988
                         err_c       11.602    2.584    4.490
                         err_l       28.275    7.892    3.583
                         err_p        2.834    0.868    3.263
                         err_s        7.967    1.869    4.263
                         err_w       19.925    4.951    4.024
```

Here are the squared multiple correlations displayed by the Sem.Smc statement.

```
Squared Multiple Correlations:       Estimate
------------------------------       --------

                      wordmean        0.708
                      sentence        0.684
                      paragrap        0.774
                      lozenges        0.542
                         cubes        0.428
                       visperc        0.494
```

The standardized estimates can be displayed in **Amos Graphics** by following the path: **View/Set** → **Analysis Properties** → **Output** and selecting **Standardized estimates**. Here is the path diagram with standardized estimates:

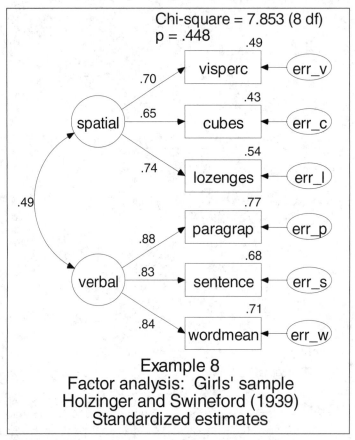

Chi-square = 7.853 (8 df)
p = .448

Example 8
Factor analysis: Girls' sample
Holzinger and Swineford (1939)
Standardized estimates

In this example, the squared multiple correlations can be interpreted as follows. For example, 71% of the variance of **wordmean** is accounted for by the variance in verbal ability. The remaining 29% of the variance of **wordmean** cannot be explained by this model, and is thus attributed to the unique factor **err_w**. If **err_w** represented measurement error only, we could say that the estimated *reliability* of **wordmean** would be 0.71. As it is, however, the term **err_w** may comprise systematic unique variance components in addition to random error. Thus, the figure 0.71 has to be regarded as a lower-bound estimate of the reliability.

The Holzinger and Swineford data have been analyzed repeatedly in textbooks and other demonstrations of modern factor analysis. The six tests discussed in this example are taken from a larger subset of nine tests used in a similar example by Jöreskog and Sörbom (1984). The factor analysis model employed here is also adapted from theirs. Because of the long history of exploring the Holzinger and Swineford data by factor analytic methods, it is no accident that our factor model fits the data very well. Even more than usual, the results presented here require confirmation on a fresh set of data.

Example 9: An Alternative to Analysis of Covariance

Purpose

- Demonstrate a simple alternative to an analysis of covariance that does not require perfectly reliable covariates. A more exact (but also more complicated) alternative will be discussed in Example 16.

Introduction

Before introducing alternatives, we will review *analysis of covariance (ANCOVA)*. ANCOVA is a technique frequently used in experimental and quasi-experimental studies to reduce the error variance due to pre-existing differences within treatment groups. When random assignment to treatment groups has eliminated the possibility of systematic pretreatment differences among groups, analysis of covariance can pay off in evaluating treatment effects with higher precision. Alternatively, when random assignment is not employed, analysis of covariance will lead to *conditional* inferences, for treatment and control cases with equal values of the covariate(s).

The usefulness of the analysis of covariance is closely tied to the assumption that each covariate be measured *without error*. The method makes other assumptions as well, but authors (*e.g.*, Cook and Campbell, 1979) have zeroed in on this assumption of perfectly reliable covariates. They point out that the effects of violating this assumption can be disastrous. Using unreliable covariates can lead to the erroneous conclusion that a treatment has an effect when it really does not, or *vice versa*. Really unreliable covariates can make a treatment appear to be harmful when it is actually beneficial. At the same time, (unfortunately) the assumption of perfectly reliable covariates is almost impossible to meet.

The present example demonstrates an alternative to analysis of covariance, allowing measurement error in the covariates. Bentler and Woodward (1979) and others have employed this method. We will demonstrate Sörbom's (1978) more general (and somewhat more complex) approach in Example 16. But simplicity is a virtue, so we begin with this less complicated example. We will closely scrutinize its method's liabilities and the assumptions it makes in Example 16.

The present example employs two treatment groups and a single covariate. It may be generalized to any number of treatment groups and any number of covariates. Sörbom (1978) used the data that we will be using in this example and Example 16. The analysis closely follows Sörbom's example.

The data

Olsson (1973) administered a battery of eight tests to 213 11-year-old students on two occasions. We will employ two of the eight tests, *Synonyms* and *Opposites*, in this example. Between the two administrations of the test battery, 108 of the students (the experimental group) received training that was intended to improve performance on the tests. The other 105 students (the control group) did not receive any special training. As a result of taking two tests on two occasions, each of the 213 students obtained four scores:

scores	explanation
pre_syn	Pretest scores on the Synonyms test
pre_opp	Pretest scores on the Opposites test
post_syn	Post-test scores on the Opposites test
post_opp	Post-test scores on the Synonyms test
treatment	A dichotomous variable taking on the value 1 for students who received the special training, and 0 for those who did not. This variable was created especially for the analyses in this example.

Correlations and standard deviations on these five measures for the entire group of 213 students are contained in the Microsoft Excel workbook **UserGuide.xls**, file **Olss_all**. Here is the data set:

rowtype_	varname_	pre_syn	pre_opp	post_syn	post_opp	treatment
n		213	213	213	213	213
corr	pre_syn	1				
corr	pre_opp	0.78255618	1			
corr	post_syn	0.78207295	0.69286541	1		
corr	post_opp	0.70438031	0.77390019	0.77567354	1	
corr	treatment	0.16261758	0.07784579	0.37887943	0.32533034	1
stddev		6.68680566	6.49938562	6.95007062	6.95685347	0.4999504

There are positive correlations between **treatment** and each of the post-tests, which indicates that the trained students did better on the post-tests than the untrained students. The correlations between **treatment** and each of the pretests are positive, but relatively small. This indicates that the control and experimental groups did about equally well on the pretests. You would expect this, since students were randomly assigned to the control and experimental groups.

Analysis of covariance

Analysis of covariance (ANCOVA) is a traditional method for evaluating the effect of training on performance. In an analysis of covariance of two-wave data, one of the post-tests is often used as the response variable while the corresponding pretest is treated as a covariate. In order for this analysis to be appropriate, the selected pretest, either the *Synonym* test or the *Opposites* test, would have to be perfectly reliable.

Model A for the Olsson data

Consider the model for the Olsson data shown in the path diagram below. The model asserts that **pre_syn** and **pre_opp** are both imperfect measures of an unobserved ability called **pre_verbal** that might be thought of as verbal ability at the time of the pretest. The *unique* variables **eps1** and **eps2** represent errors of measurement in **pre_syn** and **pre_opp**, as well as any other influences on the two tests not represented elsewhere in the path diagram.

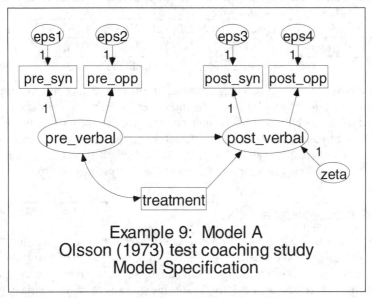

Example 9: Model A
Olsson (1973) test coaching study
Model Specification

Similarly, the model asserts **post_syn** and **post_opp** to be imperfect measures of an unobserved ability called **post_verbal**, that might be thought of as verbal ability at the time of the post-test. **eps3** and **eps4** represent errors of measurement and other sources of variation not shown elsewhere in the path diagram.

The model shows two variables that may be useful in accounting for verbal ability at the time of the post-test. One such predictor is verbal ability at the time of the pretest. You would expect that verbal ability at the time of the post-test depends on verbal ability at the time of the pretest. Because past performance is often an excellent predictor of future performance (despite the disclaimers found in U.S. investment advertisements), the model uses the latent variable **pre_verbal** as a covariate. However, our primary interest lies in the second predictor, **treatment**. We are mostly interested in the regression weight associated with the arrow pointing from **treatment** to **post_verbal**, and whether it is significantly different from zero. In other words, we will eventually want to know whether the model shown above could be accepted as correct under the additional hypothesis that the particular regression weight is zero. But first, we had better ask whether Model A can be accepted as it stands.

Identification

The units of measurement of the seven unobserved variables are indeterminate. This indeterminacy can be remedied by finding one single-headed arrow pointing away from each unobserved variable in the above figure, and fixing the corresponding regression weight to unity. The seven ones (1) shown in the path diagram above indicate a satisfactory choice of identification constraints.

Input file for Model A

To set up Model A in **Amos Graphics**, enter a path diagram that emulates the figure on page. Include the Excel workbook **UserGuide** and the worksheet **Olss_all.xls** by following the path: **File → Data Files...** and selecting the worksheet. The name of the **Amos Graphics** input file is **Ex09-a.amw**.

For **Amos Basic**, the specification of Model A is given in the file **Ex09-a.AmosBasic**. This is what it looks like:

```
Sub Main()
    Dim Sem As New AmosEngine

    Sem.TextOutput
    Sem.Mods 4
    Sem.Standardized
    Sem.Smc

    Sem.BeginGroup "UserGuide.xls", "Olss_all"
        Sem.Structure "pre_syn    = (1) pre_verbal  + (1) eps1"
        Sem.Structure "pre_opp    =     pre_verbal  + (1) eps2"

        Sem.Structure "post_syn   = (1) post_verbal + (1) eps3"
        Sem.Structure "post_opp   =     post_verbal + (1) eps4"

        Sem.Structure "post_verbal = pre_verbal + treatment + (1) zeta"

End Sub
```

Testing Model A

There is considerable empirical evidence *against* Model A:

```
Chi-square =      33.215
Degrees of freedom =    3
Probability level =     0.000
```

This makes life difficult. If we had been able to accept Model A for Olsson's data, examining and testing the path coefficient going from **treatment** to **post_verbal** would have been the logical next step. But there is no point in doing that now. We have to start with a model that we believe is correct before using it as a basis for a stronger version of the model to test the hypothesis of "no treatment effect".

Searching for a better model

We can possibly modify Model A to improve its fit to the Olsson data. Some suggestions for suitable modification can be obtained from modification indices computed by Amos. To request modification indices in **Amos Graphics**, open **View/Set** → **Analysis Properties**→ **Output** tab. Then check the **Modification indices** option and enter a suitable **Threshold** in the field to its right (or leave the threshold at its default value, 4):

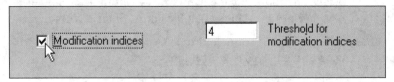

Adding a Sem.Mods statement (in this case, Sem.Mods 4) in the **Amos Basic** input file achieves the same result. Either way produces the following additional output:

```
Modification Indices
--------------------

Covariances:                              M.I.      Par Change
                                        ---------   ----------
       eps2 <-----------------> eps4     13.161       3.249
       eps2 <-----------------> eps3     10.813      -2.822
       eps1 <-----------------> eps4     11.968      -3.228
       eps1 <-----------------> eps3      9.788       2.798
```

According to the first modification index in the M.I. column, the chi-square statistic will decrease by at least 13.161 when the *unique* terms **eps2** and **eps4** are allowed to correlate (the actual decrease may be greater). This fit improvement would cost one degree of freedom for the extra parameter to be estimated. Since 13.161 is the largest modification index, we should consider it first, and ask whether it is reasonable to think that **eps2** and **eps4** might be correlated.

Since **eps2** and **eps4** represent the *unique* terms of the same *Opposites* test at two different measurement occasions—terms not shared with the *Synonyms* reasoning test—it may indeed be reasonable to assume that **eps2** and **eps4** are correlated over time. Furthermore, the expected parameter change (the number in the Par Change column) associated with the covariance between **eps2** and **eps4** is positive, as one would expect when stable systematic components correlate over time.

Notice that the same reasoning which suggests allowing **eps2** and **eps4** to be correlated applies almost as well to **eps1** and **eps3**, whose covariance also has a fairly large modification index. For now, however, we will add only one parameter to Model A: the covariance between **eps2** and **eps4**. We call this new specification *Model B*.

Model B for the Olsson data

The following is the path diagram for Model B. The model can be specified either by adding the line eps2 <---> eps4 to the Sem.Structure section in the **Amos Basic** statements, or by adding a covariance path between the **eps2** and **eps4** objects in the **Amos Graphics** path diagram input. The resulting **Amos Basic** input file is **Ex09-b.AmosBasic**, the path diagram input is located in the file **Ex09-b.amw**.

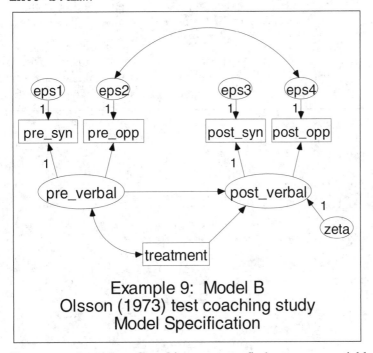

Example 9: Model B
Olsson (1973) test coaching study
Model Specification

 If you are using **Amos Graphics**, you may find your error variables already positioned against the top drawing boundary, with nowhere to draw the covariance path. Alleviate this problem by using the **Resize** (page with arrows) icon. The command is also under the **Edit** menu. Just draw your path out of bounds and then activate this command. Amos will shrink your path diagram to fit within the page boundary, although text elements will not. If you find that your variable names are too long for the objects they now occupy, you can just change the font size of one variable object by double-clicking on the object to reveal the **Object Properties** dialog box. Click on the **Text** tab and reduce the font size in the **Font size** field.

Results for Model B

Allowing **eps2** and **eps4** to be correlated results in a dramatic reduction of the chi-square statistic:

```
Chi-square =      2.684
Degrees of freedom =    2
Probability level =     0.261
```

You may recall from the results of Model A that the modification index for the covariance between **eps1** and **eps3** was 9.788. Clearly, freeing that covariance in addition to the **eps2–eps4** covariance would not have produced an additional drop in the chi-square statistic of 9.788, since this would imply a negative chi-square statistic. Thus, the modification indices represent the minimal drop in the chi-square statistic if the corresponding constraint — and *only* that constraint — is removed.

The raw parameter estimates are to be interpreted relative to the identification constraints. In particular, the unobserved variables **preverbal** and **post_verbal** have been set to the same scale as the synonyms tests at the two occasions:

```
Regression Weights:                        Estimate    S.E.      C.R.
-------------------                        --------   -------   -------

     post_verbal <----- pre_verbal          0.889     0.053    16.900
     post_verbal <------ treatment          3.640     0.477     7.625
     pre_syn <--------- pre_verbal          1.000
     pre_opp <--------- pre_verbal          0.881     0.053    16.606
     post_syn <------- post_verbal          1.000
     post_opp <------- post_verbal          0.906     0.053    16.948


Covariances:                               Estimate    S.E.      C.R.
------------                               --------   -------   -------

     pre_verbal <------> treatment          0.467     0.226     2.066
     eps2 <----------------> eps4           6.797     1.344     5.058


Variances:                                 Estimate    S.E.      C.R.
----------                                 --------   -------   -------

                         pre_verbal        38.491     4.501     8.552
                          treatment         0.249     0.024    10.296
                               zeta         4.824     1.331     3.624
                               eps1         6.013     1.502     4.004
                               eps2        12.255     1.603     7.646
                               eps3         6.546     1.501     4.360
                               eps4        14.685     1.812     8.102
```

The covariance between **eps2** and **eps4** is positive, as expected. The most interesting result that appears along with the parameter estimates is the critical ratio for the effect of **treatment** on **post_verbal**. This critical ratio shows that **treatment** has a highly significant effect on **post_verbal**. We will shortly obtain a better test of the significance of this effect by modifying Model B so that this regression weight is fixed at zero.

In the meantime, here are the standardized results displayed by **Amos Graphics**, as well as the squared multiple correlations:

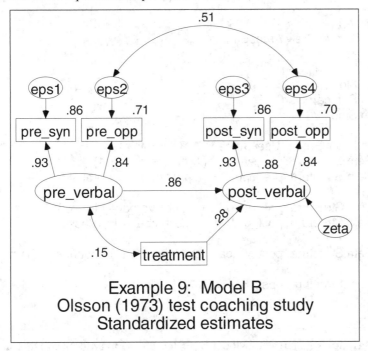

Example 9: Model B
Olsson (1973) test coaching study
Standardized estimates

Note that in this example, we are primarily concerned with testing a particular hypothesis, and not so much with parameter estimation. However, even when the parameter estimates themselves are not of primary interest, it is a good idea to look at them anyway to see if they are *reasonable*. Here, for instance, you may not care exactly what the correlation between **eps2** and **eps4** is, but you would expect it to be positive. Similarly, you would be surprised to find any negative estimates for regression weights in this model. In any model, you know that variables cannot have negative variances, and so a negative variance estimate would always be an unreasonable estimate. If estimates cannot pass a gross sanity check (particularly with a reasonably large sample size), you have to question the correctness of the model — no matter how "good" the chi-square or any other fit statistic may be.

Model C for the Olsson data

Now that we have a model (Model B) that we can reasonably believe is correct, let us see how it fares if we add the constraint that **post_verbal** does not depend on **treatment**. In other words, we will test a new model (Model C) that is just like

Model B with one exception. Model C specifies that **post_verbal** has a zero regression weight on **treatment**.

Here is the **Amos Basic** input file (`Ex09-c.AmosBasic`) that describes this model:

```
Sub Main()
    Dim Sem As New AmosEngine

    Sem.TextOutput
    Sem.Mods 4
    Sem.Standardized
    Sem.Smc

    Sem.BeginGroup "UserGuide.xls", "Olss_all"
        Sem.Structure "pre_syn    = (1) pre_verbal  + (1) eps1"
        Sem.Structure "pre_opp    =     pre_verbal  + (1) eps2"

        Sem.Structure "post_syn   = (1) post_verbal + (1) eps3"
        Sem.Structure "post_opp   =     post_verbal + (1) eps4"

        Sem.Structure "post_verbal = pre_verbal + (0) treatment + (1) zeta"

        Sem.Structure "eps2 <---> eps4"

End Sub
```

In **Amos Graphics**, start with Model B, then use the **Parameter constraints** button to constrain the path treatment ---> post_verbal to zero (0). The path diagram specification is located in `Ex09-c.amw`.

Multiple model input

The following **Amos Basic** input file (`Ex09-all.AmosBasic`) specifies all three models (A through C) at once:

```
Sub Main()
  Dim Sem As New AmosEngine

  Sem.TextOutput
  Sem.Mods 4
  Sem.Standardized
  Sem.Smc

  Sem.BeginGroup "UserGuide.xls", "Olss_all"
    Sem.Structure "pre_syn    = (1) pre_verbal  + (1) eps1"
    Sem.Structure "pre_opp    =     pre_verbal  + (1) eps2"

    Sem.Structure "post_syn   = (1) post_verbal + (1) eps3"
    Sem.Structure "post_opp   =     post_verbal + (1) eps4"

    Sem.Structure "post_verbal = pre_verbal + (effect) treatment + (1) zeta"

    Sem.Structure "eps2 <---> eps4 (cov2_4)"


  Sem.Model "Model_A", "cov2_4 = 0"
  Sem.Model "Model_B"
  Sem.Model "Model_C", "effect = 0"

End Sub
```

If you are using **Amos Graphics**, open Model B (**Ex09-b.amw**). Label the covariance between **eps2** and **eps4** as **cov2_4** and the regression path pointing from **treatment** to **post_verbal** as **effect**. The combined model specification will look like this:

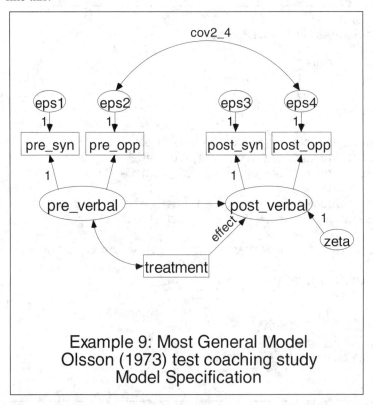

Example 9: Most General Model
Olsson (1973) test coaching study
Model Specification

Then, double click on the **Models** panel to open up the **Manage Models** dialog box:

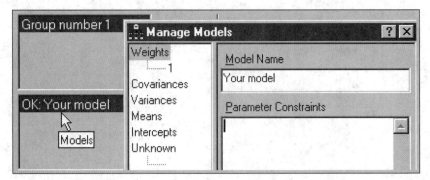

Set up the three models by first giving the first model a name in the **Model Name** field (*i.e.*, Model A) and then entering its constraint(s) in the **Parameter**

Constraints field. Click on **New**, and repeat the procedure for the other models. (See Example 6 for a more complete explanation of this procedure). When finished, the three models should be defined this way:

- Model A has constraint cov2_4 = 0
- Model B is unconstrained
- Model C has constraint effect = 0

In **Amos Basic**, simply add the .Model statements after the block of .Structure specification:

```
Sem.Model "Model_A", "cov2_4 = 0"
Sem.Model "Model_B"
Sem.Model "Model_C", "effect = 0"
```

Results for Model C

Model C has to be rejected at any conventional significance level:

```
Chi-square =      55.396
Degrees of freedom =    3
Probability level =     0.000
```

If you assume that Model B is correct, and that only the correctness of Model C is in doubt, then there is a better test for Model C by using the following procedure. In changing from Model B to Model C, the chi-square statistic increased by 52.712 (= 55.396 – 2.684), while the number of degrees of freedom increased by 1 (= 3 – 2). If Model C is correct, 52.712 is an observation on a random variable that has an approximate chi-square distribution with 1 degree of freedom (with multiple model input, this value is calculated near the end of the text output). The probability of such a random variable exceeding 52.712 is vanishingly small. Thus Model C is rejected in favor of Model B: **treatment** has a significant effect on **post_verbal**.

Example 10: Simultaneous Analysis of Several Groups

Purpose

- Demonstrate how to fit a model to two sets of data at once. Amos is capable of modeling data from multiple groups (or samples) simultaneously. This multigroup facility allows for many additional types of analyses, as illustrated in the next several examples.

Introduction

We will return once again to Attig's (1983) data on young and old subjects, as introduced and analyzed in Examples 1 through 3. In this example, we will compare the results from the two groups to see how similar they are. However, we will not compare the groups by performing separate analyses for old people and young people. Instead, we will demonstrate how to perform a single analysis that will estimate parameters and test hypotheses about both groups *at once*. This method has two advantages over doing separate analyses for the young and old groups. First, it provides a test for the significance of *any* differences found between young and old people. Second, if it can be concluded that there is no difference between young and old people, or if the group differences concern only a few model parameters, multigroup analysis provides *more efficient* parameter estimates than either of the two single-group models.

The data

We will use Attig's data on spatial memory from both young and old subjects. The following is a partial listing of the data file for the old subjects from the Microsoft Excel worksheet **Attg_old** contained in the **UserGuide.xls** workbook.

subject	age	education	sex	recall1	recall2	cued1	cued2
1	65	16	1	5	11	5	11
2	68	18	0	12	16	14	16
3	64	17	1	11	11	10	11
4	77	16	0	3	3	3	4
5	72	12	0	8	9	11	9
6	75	12	1	10	9	10	10
7	69	12	0	8	7	10	8
8	74	12	0	7	6	8	9
9	66	12	0	8	12	9	13
10	77	12	0	8	11	10	13

This file is identical to the worksheet for the young subjects, **Attg_yng**, except for the numbers themselves. In this example, we will only use the measures **recall1** and **cued1**.

Data for multigroup analysis can be organized in a variety of ways. One option is to separate the data into different files, with one file for each group (as we have done in this example). A second possibility is to keep all data in one big file and include a group membership variable.

Model A

We will begin with a truly trivial model (Model A) for the two variables, **recall1** and **cued1**. The model simply says that, for young subjects as well as old subjects, **recall1** and **cued1** are two variables that have some unspecified variances and some unspecified covariance. The variances and covariance terms can be different for young and old people.

Modeling in Amos Basic

Here is an **Amos Basic** input file (**Ex10-a.AmosBasic**) that directs Amos to estimate the variances and the covariance for both populations:

```
Sub Main()
    Dim Sem As New AmosEngine
    Sem.TextOutput

    Sem.BeginGroup "Userguide.xls", "Attg_yng"
        Sem.GroupName "young subjects"
        Sem.Structure "recall1"
        Sem.Structure "cued1"

    Sem.BeginGroup "Userguide.xls", "Attg_old"
        Sem.GroupName "old subjects"
        Sem.Structure "recall1"
        Sem.Structure "cued1"

End Sub
```

Repeating the Sem.BeginGroup statement for "Attg_old" splits the file into two parts. Each half of the file contains a model for the subjects together with a file reference for their data. This trivial model simply says that **recall1** and **cued1** are two variables with unspecified variances and an unspecified covariance. The Sem.GroupName statement, while truly optional in single-group analyses, becomes an important part of multisample input files, structuring both input and result files with meaningful headings.

Modeling in Amos Graphics

Model specification in **Amos Graphics** is somewhat different from **Amos Basic**. In particular, **Amos Graphics** has several specific *default rules* for multigroup analyses:

- All groups in the analysis will have the *identical* path diagram *structure*, unless explicitly declared otherwise. To specify Model A, for instance, the model structure only needs to be drawn for the first group (young subjects). All other groups will have the same model structure by default.

- Unnamed parameters may (and generally will) take on different values in the different groups. Thus, the default multigroup model under **Amos Graphics** uses the *same model structure*, but allows *different parameter values*.

- Parameters in different groups can be constrained to the same value by giving them the same label (this will be demonstrated in Model B, later in this example).

To set up the model for the first group, begin by opening a new path diagram by clicking on **File → New**. Then click on **File → Data Files....** Attach the Excel workbook **UserGuide**. Click on **File Name** and select the **Attg_yng** worksheet:

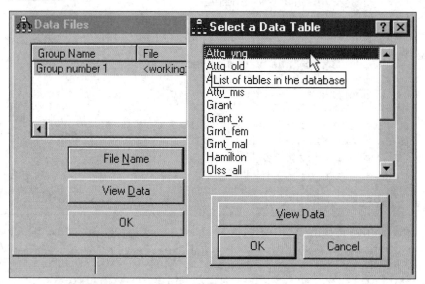

 Click on the **Variables in data set** icon and drag observed variables **recall1** and **cued1** to the diagram:

Connect the two variables with a two-headed arrow.

Next, click on the **Title** icon and add a title with at least these two statements:

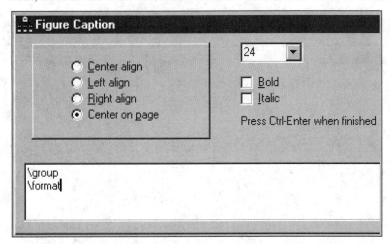

Then, to set up the two-group model, begin by double clicking on the line **Group number 1** in the **Groups** panel. Amos will display the **Manage Groups** dialog box. Change the name in the **Group Name** field to **young subjects**:

Next, click **New** and change the label from **Group number 2** to **old subjects**. Finally, click the **Close** button.

Run **File** → **Data Files...** once again. In the **Data Files** dialog box, connect the **old subjects** group to the **Attg_old** worksheet in the Excel **UserGuide** workbook:

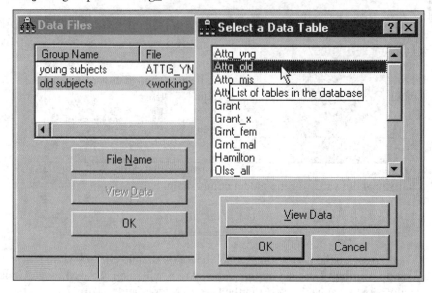

The file **Ex10-a.amw** contains the full **Amos Graphics** specification for Model A:

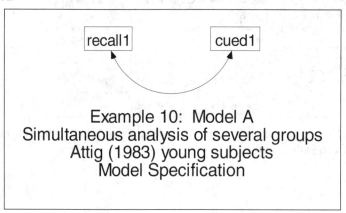

Example 10: Model A
Simultaneous analysis of several groups
Attig (1983) young subjects
Model Specification

Output from Model A

As should be expected, Model A has zero degrees of freedom:

```
Computation of Degrees of Freedom

               Number of distinct sample moments:    6
    Number of distinct parameters to be estimated:   6
               ----------------------------------
                             Degrees of freedom:    0
```

Amos computed the number of distinct sample moments this way: the young subjects have two sample variances and one sample covariance, which makes three sample moments. The old subjects also have three sample moments, making a total of six sample moments. The parameters to be estimated are the population moments, and there are six of them as well.

Since there are zero degrees of freedom, we cannot test this model for goodness of fit:

```
Chi-square =      0.000
Degrees of freedom =    0
Probability level cannot be computed
```

The unstandardized parameter estimates for the young subjects are:

Covariances:		Estimate	S.E.	C.R.
recall1 <-----> cued1		3.225	0.944	3.416

Variances:	Estimate	S.E.	C.R.
recall1	5.788	1.311	4.416
cued1	4.210	0.953	4.416

And for the old subjects:

Covariances:		Estimate	S.E.	C.R.
recall1 <-----> cued1		4.887	1.252	3.902

Variances:	Estimate	S.E.	C.R.
recall1	5.569	1.261	4.416
cued1	6.694	1.516	4.416

Notice how the open panels on the left side of the screen provide a variety of viewing options. Click on either the **View Input** or **View Output** icon to see an input or output path diagram. Select either the young or old subject in the **Groups** panel. Or toggle between standardized and unstandardized estimates of either group in the **Parameter Formats** panel:

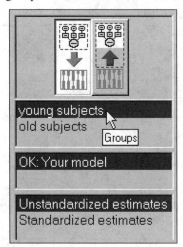

Here are the unstandardized **Amos Graphics** outputs for the two groups:

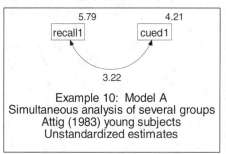

Example 10: Model A
Simultaneous analysis of several groups
Attig (1983) young subjects
Unstandardized estimates

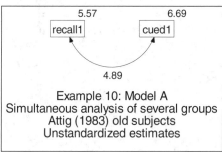

Example 10: Model A
Simultaneous analysis of several groups
Attig (1983) old subjects
Unstandardized estimates

Model B

It is easy to see that the parameter estimates are different for the two groups. But are the differences significant or still within the margin of sampling error? One way to find out is to repeat the analysis, but this time requiring that each parameter in the young population be equal to the corresponding parameter in the old population. The resulting model will be called Model B.

Modeling in Amos Basic

The **Amos Basic** input file for Model B is `Ex10-b.AmosBasic`. Here is the file listing:

```
Sub Main()
    Dim Sem As New AmosEngine

    Sem.Standardized
    Sem.TextOutput

    Sem.BeginGroup "UserGuide.xls", "Attg_yng"
        Sem.GroupName "young subjects"
        Sem.Structure "recall1        (var_rec)"
        Sem.Structure "cued1          (var_cue)"
        Sem.Structure "recall1 <> cued1  (cov_rc)"

    Sem.BeginGroup "UserGuide.xls", "Attg_old"
        Sem.GroupName "old subjects"
        Sem.Structure "recall1        (var_rec)"
        Sem.Structure "cued1          (var_cue)"
        Sem.Structure "recall1 <> cued1  (cov_rc)"

End Sub
```

The names var_rec, var_cue and cov_rc (appearing in parentheses), specify that the model parameters are the same for old and young people. The name var_rec specifies that **recall1** has the same variance in the two populations. Similarly, the name var_cue specifies that **cued1** has the same variance in the two populations. The name cov_rc specifies that **recall1** and **cued1** have the same covariance in the two populations.

Modeling in Amos Graphics

To set up Model B in **Amos Graphics**, you can enter the three parameter labels in each of the two groups' path diagram. For simple path diagrams (like this one), it is probably the easiest procedure. But for more complex diagrams, there is another way of entering parameter labels that may save time using the **View/Set** → **Matrix Representation** commands.

Here is how it is done. To begin, select the first group by clicking on **young subjects** in the **Groups** panel:

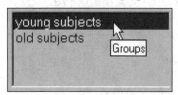

Next, follow the path **View/Set → Matrix Representation**. The **Matrix Representation** spreadsheet appears. Click on **Matrix → New Covariance Matrix**. This will activate the Sigma 1 spreadsheet.

Drag the **Drag exogeneous variables** icon to field A2 and then once again to B1:

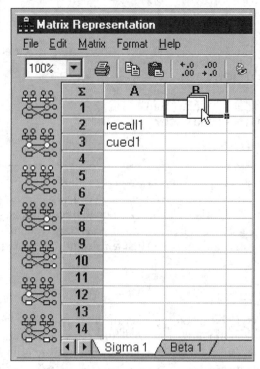

You will see the four cells 2B, 2C, 3B and 3C now contain stars, indicating free variance parameters:

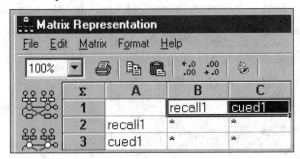

Change diagonal cell 2B to var_rec and diagonal cell 3C to var_cue. Label off-diagonal cell 2C to cov_rc. The second off-diagonal cell 3B will change to cov_rc automatically:

Σ	A	B	C
1		recall1	cued1
2	recall1	var_rec	cov_rc
3	cued1	cov_rc	var_cue

Drag the **Matrix Representation** spreadsheet off to the side momentarily to verify that the three parameter labels appeared in the right places:

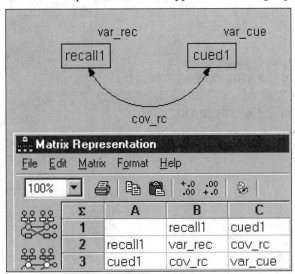

Now, click and drag on the entire matrix (columns A-C/rows 1-3) so that it is highlighted. Then copy the matrix to the Windows clipboard by clicking **Edit** → **Copy**.

Set up the second group by selecting **old subjects** from the **Groups** panel. This will automatically give you an empty matrix. Highlight nine cells (three across, three down) and select **Edit → Paste** to paste the old matrix into the new one.

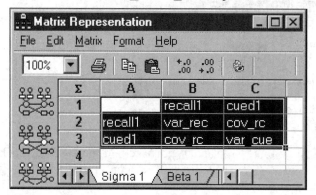

Finally, label the new model (Model B) and save it. The resulting **Amos Graphics** model specification appears in the file **Ex10-b.amw**:

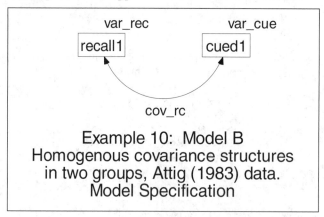

Example 10: Model B
Homogenous covariance structures
in two groups, Attig (1983) data.
Model Specification

Multiple model input

In **Amos Basic**, the multiple models input is similar to single models. Here is the **Amos Basic** file (**Ex10-all.AmosBasic**) that specifies both Models A and B at once:[1]

```
Sub Main()
    Dim Sem As New AmosEngine

    Sem.Standardized
    Sem.TextOutput

    Sem.BeginGroup "UserGuide.xls", "Attg_yng"
        Sem.GroupName "young subjects"
        Sem.Structure "recall1        (yng_rec)"
        Sem.Structure "cued1          (yng_cue)"
        Sem.Structure "recall1 <> cued1  (yng_rc)"

    Sem.BeginGroup "UserGuide.xls", "Attg_old"
        Sem.GroupName "old subjects"
        Sem.Structure "recall1        (old_rec)"
        Sem.Structure "cued1          (old_cue)"
        Sem.Structure "recall1 <> cued1  (old_rc)"

    Sem.Model "Model_A"
    Sem.Model "Model_B", "yng_rec=old_rec", "yng_cue=old_cue", _
        "yng_rc=old_rc"

End Sub
```

The Sem.Model statements should appear immediately after the .Structure specifications for the last group. It does not matter which .Model statement is given first.

You specify multiple models in the same **Amos Graphics** file much like you would in **Amos Basic**. Insert the parameter names yng_rec, yng_cue, and yng_rc in the path diagram for the **young subjects'** data, and the names old_rec, old_cue, and old_rc in the diagram for the **old subjects'** data. When you name these

---

[1] You may recall that in Example 6, file **Ex06-all.AmosBasic**, all model constraints were written in a single string, separated by semicolons. Here in **Ex10-all.AmosBasic**, we have given each constraint its own string, and all strings are separated by commas. Both syntax forms are admissible and produce the same results. Also, to make our **Amos Basic** model fit on this page, we have had to once again break lines of code. You will not have to do this. Our Visual Basic method of breaking the code here is to end the first section of the longer line with a comma and adding a trailing underscore (_). Then we simply completed the constraints on the following line. We indented the continuation line so you could easily spot it.

parameters, make sure the **All groups** option on <u>V</u>iew/Set → <u>O</u>bject Properties →**Parameters** is *not* checked:

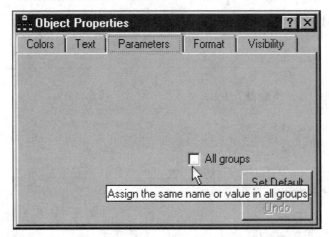

Afterwards, **Amos Graphics** understands all these parameter names, no matter which group is currently in the foreground.

Thus, in the Amos **Model Manager**, you can specify multiple models using the parameter labels from both groups much in the same way as the single-group specifications of **Ex06-all.amw** and **Ex09-all.amw**. Set up **Model A** without any constraint and **Model B** with the three constraints:

    yng_rec = old_rec
    yng_cue = old_cue
    yng_rc = old_rc

After calculating the estimates for multiple model specifications with **Amos Graphics,** click on **Manage Models** and **Manage Groups** to select the model and group for which the estimates (unstandardized or standardized) should be displayed in the output path diagram.

Output from Model B

Basic output

Because of the constraints imposed in Model B, only three distinct parameters are estimated instead of six. As a result, the number of degrees of freedom has increased from zero to three.

```
Computation of Degrees of Freedom

                    Number of distinct sample moments:    6
        Number of distinct parameters to be estimated:    3
                                       ------------------------
                                   Degrees of freedom:    3
```

Model B is acceptable at conventional significance levels.

```
Chi-square  =       4.588
Degrees of freedom =    3
Probability level =     0.205
```

Here are the parameter estimates obtained under Model B for the young subjects:

Covariances:	Estimate	S.E.	C.R.	Label
recall1 <----> cued1	4.056	0.780	5.202	yng_rc

Variances:	Estimate	S.E.	C.R.	Label
recall1	5.678	0.909	6.245	yng_rec
cued1	5.452	0.873	6.245	yng_cue

The parameter estimates and standard errors are, of course, the same in both groups. You can see that the standard error estimates obtained under Model B are smaller (for the young subjects, 0.780, 0.909, and 0.873) than the corresponding estimates obtained under Model A (0.944, 1.311, and 0.953). This is exactly what is meant by the term *more efficient*, applied to parameter estimates. The Model B estimates are to be preferred over the ones from Model A as long as you believe that Model B is correct. And at a probability level of .205, there is not much evidence to the contrary.

The following is the **Amos Graphics** output with standardized estimates from Model B:

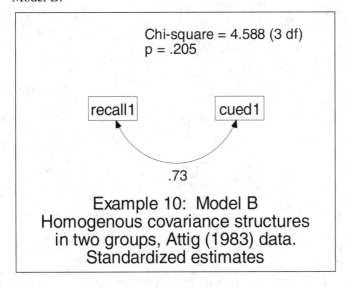

Chi-square = 4.588 (3 df)
p = .205

recall1   cued1

.73

Example 10: Model B
Homogenous covariance structures
in two groups, Attig (1983) data.
Standardized estimates

Example 11: Felson and Bohrnstedt's Girls and Boys

Purpose

- Demonstrate how to fit a simultaneous equations model to two sets of data at once.

Introduction

Example 7 tested Felson and Bohrnstedt's (1979) model for perceived attractiveness and perceived academic ability using a sample of 209 girls. Here, we take their model and attempt to apply it simultaneously to the Example 7 data and data from a sample of 207 boys. We will examine the question of whether attractiveness and academic ability follow the same dynamics in boys as in girls. If they do not follow the same dynamics, we will also explore the source of difference between the two sexes.

The data

The Felson and Bohrnstedt (1979) data for girls were described in Example 7. Here is a table of the boys' data from the SPSS file **Fels_mal.sav**:

	rowtype_	varname_	academic	athletic	attract	gpa	skills	height	weight	rating
1	n		207.00	207.00	207.00	207.00	207.00	207.00	207.00	207.00
2	corr	academic	1.00							
3	corr	athletic	.47	1.00						
4	corr	attract	.49	.72	1.00					
5	corr	GPA	.58	.27	.30	1.00				
6	corr	skills	.35	.65	.44	.35	1.00			
7	corr	height	-.02	.15	.04	-.11	.12	1.00		
8	corr	weight	-.11	-.01	-.19	-.16	-.05	.51	1.00	
9	corr	rating	.11	.24	.28	.13	.38	.06	-.18	1.00
10	stddev		.16	.21	.49	4.04	.74	3.41	24.32	.97
11	mean		.10	.17	.44	8.63	2.93	.00	101.91	2.59

Notice that there are eight variables in the boys' data file, but only seven in the girls'. Amos can accommodate modeling situations where the measured variables differ between groups. However, in the present example the added variable **skills** is not mentioned in any model. Amos therefore skips this variable, like any other variable not entered in a model.

Model A for girls and boys

Modeling in Amos Graphics

Consider extending the Felson and Bohrnstedt model of perceived attractiveness and academic ability to boys as well as girls. To do this we will start with the girls-only model specification from Example 7 and expand it using **Amos Graphics**. If you have already made the path diagram for Example 7, just retrieve your diagram from Example 7. No additional drawing is needed.

You might also want to consider changing the path diagram's title so that it will adapt to a multisample structure. In particular, change the string Female subjects to \group' data:

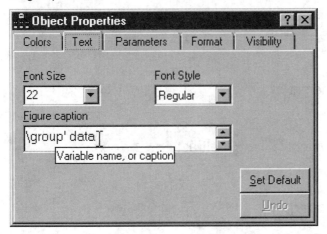

The text macro \group will display the name of the current group.

Since in Example 7 you were only working with one group, having Group number 1 in the **Groups** box sufficed. But with two groups, you now need to double click on Group number 1 and rename it girls. Do this by deleting the existing text and typing in girls. Next, to add the model specification for the boys' group, click on **New** and insert the name boys in the **Group Name** field. Then click on **Close**.

Next select **File** → **Data Files** and attach the appropriate data files, **Fels_fem.sav** for the girls group and **Fels_mal.sav** for the boys group.

The input file for this model is **Ex11-a.amw**. The path diagram specification for the boy's sample is:

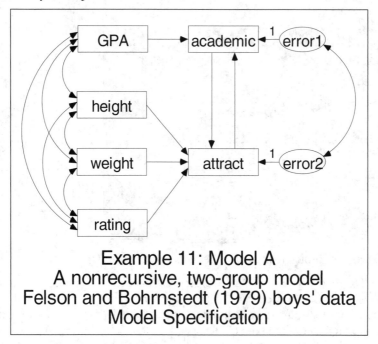

Example 11: Model A
A nonrecursive, two-group model
Felson and Bohrnstedt (1979) boys' data
Model Specification

Modeling in Amos Basic

The following **Amos Basic** input file gives the equivalent model for the two groups. The input file for this model is **Ex11-a.AmosBasic**:[1]

```
Sub Main()
  Dim Sem As New AmosEngine

  Sem.TextOutput

  Sem.BeginGroup "Fels_fem.sav"
    Sem.GroupName "girls"
    Sem.Structure "academic = GPA + attract + error1 (1)"
    Sem.Structure "attract  = height + weight + rating + academic " _
        & "+ error2 (1)"
    Sem.Structure "error2 <--> error1"

  Sem.BeginGroup "Fels_mal.sav"
    Sem.GroupName "boys"
    Sem.Structure "academic = GPA + attract + error1 (1)"
    Sem.Structure "attract  = height + weight + rating + academic " _
        & "+ error2 (1)"
    Sem.Structure "error2 <--> error1"

End Sub
```

Notice that, while the same model structure is specified for girls and boys, there is no restriction that the parameters must have the same values in the two groups. This means that the regression weights, covariance paths, and variances may all be different for boys and girls.

---

[1] As in past examples, to make our **Amos Basic** model fit on this page, we have had to break lines of code. You will not need to do this. The Visual Basic syntax for breaking lines string constraints we used was to end the first section of the longer string with a quote mark (") and an underscore (_). Then, we began the continuation line with an ampersand (&), followed by the rest of the string enclosed in double quotes.

Output from Model A

With two groups instead of one (as opposed to Example 7), there are twice as many sample moments and twice as many parameters to estimate. Therefore, you have twice as many degrees of freedom as there were in Example 7.

```
Computation of Degrees of Freedom

                    Number of distinct sample moments:    42
        Number of distinct parameters to be estimated:    38
                                                       ------------------------
                                      Degrees of freedom:     4
```

The model fits the data from both groups quite well:

```
Chi-square =       3.183
Degrees of freedom =     4
Probability level =      0.528
```

We accept the hypothesis that the Felson and Bohrnstedt model is correct for both boys and girls. The next thing to look at is the parameter estimates. We will be interested in how the girls' estimates compare to the boys' estimates.

First, here are the girls' parameter estimates:

Regression Weights:	Estimate	S.E.	C.R.
academic <--------- GPA	0.023	0.004	6.241
attract <------- height	0.000	0.010	0.050
attract <------- weight	-0.002	0.001	-1.321
attract <------- rating	0.176	0.027	6.444
attract <----- academic	1.607	0.350	4.599
academic <----- attract	-0.002	0.051	-0.039

Covariances:	Estimate	S.E.	C.R.
GPA <----------> rating	0.526	0.246	2.139
height <-------> rating	-0.468	0.205	-2.279
GPA <----------> weight	-6.710	4.676	-1.435
GPA <----------> height	1.819	0.712	2.555
height <-------> weight	19.024	4.098	4.642
weight <-------> rating	-5.243	1.395	-3.759
error1 <-------> error2	-0.004	0.010	-0.382

Variances:	Estimate	S.E.	C.R.
GPA	12.122	1.189	10.198
height	8.428	0.826	10.198
weight	371.476	36.427	10.198
rating	1.015	0.100	10.198
error1	0.019	0.003	5.747
error2	0.143	0.014	9.974

These parameter estimates are exactly the same as those reported in Example 7, as we would expect them to be. The standard errors and critical ratios are also the same in this case.

Next are the unstandardized estimates for the boys' sample:

```
Regression Weights:                      Estimate    S.E.      C.R.
-------------------                      --------  -------   -------

        academic <--------- GPA           0.021    0.003     6.927
        attract <------- height           0.019    0.010     1.967
        attract <------- weight          -0.003    0.001    -2.484
        attract <------- rating           0.095    0.030     3.150
        attract <----- academic           1.386    0.315     4.398
        academic <----- attract           0.063    0.059     1.071


Covariances:                             Estimate    S.E.      C.R.
------------                             --------  -------   -------

        GPA <----------> rating           0.507    0.274     1.850
        height <-------> rating           0.198    0.230     0.860
        GPA <----------> weight         -15.645    6.899    -2.268
        GPA <----------> height          -1.508    0.961    -1.569
        height <-------> weight          42.091    6.455     6.521
        weight <-------> rating          -4.226    1.662    -2.543
        error1 <-------> error2          -0.010    0.011    -0.898


Variances:                               Estimate    S.E.      C.R.
----------                               --------  -------   -------

                    GPA                   16.243    1.600    10.149
                 height                   11.572    1.140    10.149
                 weight                  588.605   57.996    10.149
                 rating                    0.936    0.092    10.149
                 error1                    0.015    0.002     7.571
                 error2                    0.164    0.016    10.149
```

The girls' parameter estimates in path diagram format are:

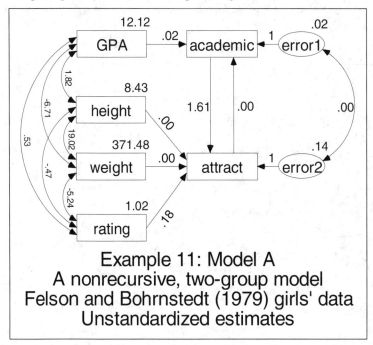

Example 11: Model A
A nonrecursive, two-group model
Felson and Bohrnstedt (1979) girls' data
Unstandardized estimates

And here is the path diagram with the boys' estimates:

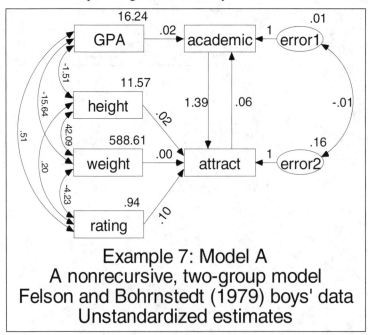

Example 7: Model A
A nonrecursive, two-group model
Felson and Bohrnstedt (1979) boys' data
Unstandardized estimates

You can visually inspect the girls' and boys' estimates in Model A, looking for differences between them. By a rough inspection, the regression paths appear relatively similar, with the exception of **attract <--- rating** (path difference 0.081, pooled s.e. 0.040). To find out if girls and boys differ significantly with respect to any single parameter, you could have Amos compute a table of critical ratios of differences among all pairs of free parameters. For instance, in **Amos Graphics**, follow the path: **View/Set → Analysis Properties → Output** tab and check the **Critical ratios for differences** option:

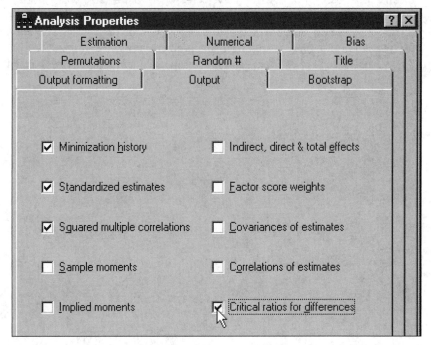

However, we are now proposing you use the following (somewhat more structured) approach.

Model B for girls and boys

Suppose we are mainly interested with the regression weights, and we hypothesize (Model B) that the girls and boys have the same regression weights. Under this model, the variances and covariances of the exogenous variables would still be allowed to differ between the groups while the regression weights are group-invariant.

Models that restrict only the regression weights across groups appear in a number of statistical techniques. In analysis of variance, it is called a *main-effects* model. In analysis of covariance, *homogeneity of within-group regressions* is an important model assumption (Huitema, 1980; Winer, 1971). Examples 12 and 15 will demonstrate multigroup factor analysis models with *group-invariant factor patterns*.

What is the motivation for the group-invariant regression weights proposed in Model B? It is likely that perceived height and weight have different variances and covariances among boys and girls. We might also want to permit the other exogenous variables in the model to take on different variances and covariances across groups. Under Model B, however, we evaluate whether a fixed unit change on an exogenous variable will always correspond to the same change of the endogenous variable(s). This is independent of whether the respondent is male or female. If Model B is confirmed by the data, the same regression weights can be used for all groups, which simplifies the prediction of the endogenous variables. Another advantage to Model B is that the regression weights themselves will be estimated more efficiently.

Modeling in Amos Basic

Here is the **Amos Basic** input file for Model B, using parameter labels p1–p6 to impose equality constraints across groups. The input file for this model is `Ex11-b.AmosBasic`:[2]

```
Sub Main()
    Dim Sem As New AmosEngine
    Sem.TextOutput

    Sem.BeginGroup "Fels_fem.sav"
        Sem.GroupName "girls"
        Sem.Structure "academic = (p1) GPA + (p2) attract + (1) error1"
        Sem.Structure "attract  = (p3) height + (p4) weight + (p5) rating " _
            & "+ (p6) academic + (1) error2"
        Sem.Structure "error2 <--> error1"

    Sem.BeginGroup "Fels_mal.sav"
        Sem.GroupName "boys"
        Sem.Structure "academic = (p1) GPA + (p2) attract + (1) error1"
        Sem.Structure "attract  = (p3) height + (p4) weight + (p5) rating " _
            & "+ (p6) academic + (1) error2"
        Sem.Structure "error2 <--> error1"

End Sub
```

---

[2] Once again we broke lines of code to make our **Amos Basic** model fit on this page. Refer to `Ex09-all.Amos Basic` in Example 9 for a more complete explanation.

Modeling in Amos Graphics

To set up Model B using path diagram input, you need to constrain twelve paths. To do so, follow these four steps. First, select the girls' group to label its six regression parameters. Click on **View/Set** → **Object Properties** and the **Parameters** tab. Click on the path you want to constrain and enter the label in the **Regression weight** field.

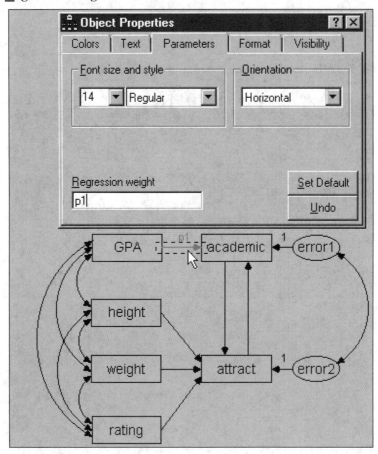

Keep the **Object Properties** dialog box open and click on the next path to be constrained and type in the next label. Continue this procedure until you have constrained all six paths.

Secondly, with the girls' data still selected, open **View/Set → Matrix Representation** to display the parameter labels in a spreadsheet format. Drag the **Drag endogenous variables** icon to field A2:

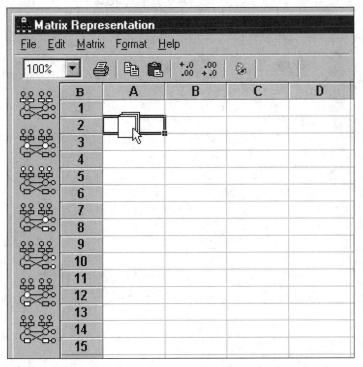

Then drag the **Drag observed variables** icon to field B1. Your matrix view will look like this:

B	A	B	C	D	E	F	G
1		academic	attract	GPA	height	rating	weight
2	academic		p2	p1			
3	attract	p6			p3	p5	p4

Third, select the entire parameter matrix (field A1 through G3) and copy it to the Windows clipboard (select **Edit → Copy**).

Lastly, select the boys' group in the **Group Manager** panel. With the boys' data now selected, open **View/Set → Matrix Representation** to display the parameter labels in a spreadsheet format. Click on field A1 and paste the parameter matrix into it (select **Edit → Paste**).

Afterwards, the path diagram for either of the two samples will look like this:

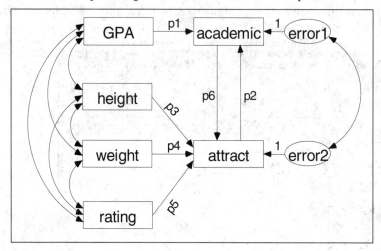

Multiple model input

An **Amos Basic** stacked input file for both Models A and B can be written as:[3]

```
Sub Main()
    Dim Sem As New AmosEngine

    Sem.TextOutput

    Sem.BeginGroup "Fels_fem.sav"
        Sem.GroupName "girls"
        Sem.Structure "academic = (g1) GPA + (g2) attract + (1) error1"
        Sem.Structure "attract  = (g3) height + (g4) weight + (g5) rating" _
            & " + (g6) academic + (1) error2"
        Sem.Structure "error2 <--> error1"

    Sem.BeginGroup "Fels_mal.sav"
        Sem.GroupName "boys"
        Sem.Structure "academic = (b1) GPA + (b2) attract + (1) error1"
        Sem.Structure "attract  = (b3) height + (b4) weight + (b5) rating" _
            & " + (b6) academic + (1) error2"
        Sem.Structure "error2 <--> error1"

    Sem.Model "Model_A"
    Sem.Model "Model_B", "g1=b1", "g2=b2", "g3=b3", "g4=b4", _
        "g5=b5","g6=b6"
End Sub
```

The same, stacked model is easily specified in **Amos Graphics**. You can start from the path diagram for Model A and use the same labeling procedure described earlier in "Modeling in Amos Graphics" on page 236. Assign a total of twelve (12) unique parameter labels to the six (6) path coefficients in the two groups. To be consistent with the previous **Amos Basic** specification, you may want to use the labels g1–g6 in the girls' group and b1–b6 in the boys' group.

---

[3] Once again we broke lines of code to make our **Amos Basic** model fit on this page. Refer to page 229 in this example for a more complete explanation.

Here is the completed **Amos Graphics** multiple-model specification for the girls' group as found in file `Ex11-ab.amw`:

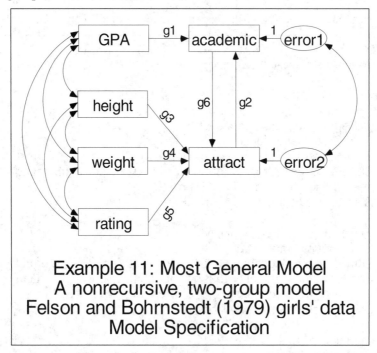

Example 11: Most General Model
A nonrecursive, two-group model
Felson and Bohrnstedt (1979) girls' data
Model Specification

Some of the path diagram *text macros* are worth mentioning. There are three text macros in the Figure caption of `Ex11-ab.amw`. As you can see, the **\format** macro has been replaced by the display format, Model Specification on input. On output, it will change to either Unstandardized Estimates or Standardized Estimates.

Similarly, in the path diagram view, the text macro **\model** is replaced by the model name in view. In the present example, that is, Most General Model on input, and Model A or Model B on output. The **\group' data** macro also changes to the name of the group that is currently displayed:

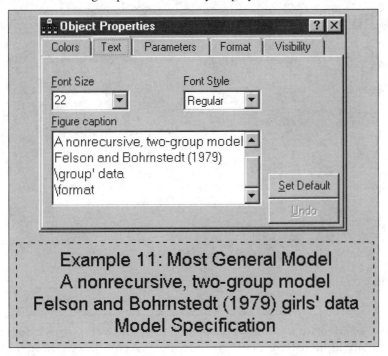

Output from Model B

Amos Basic output

Model B fits the data very well:

```
Chi-square =      9.493
Degrees of freedom =   10
Probability level =    0.486
```

Comparing Model B against Model A gives a nonsignificant chi-square of 9.493 – 3.183 = 6.310 with 10 – 4 = 6 degrees of freedom. Assuming that Model B is indeed correct, the Model B estimates are preferable over the Model A estimates.

The unstandardized parameter estimates for the girls' sample are:

```
Regression Weights:              Estimate    S.E.      C.R.     Label
-------------------              --------   -------   -------   -------

academic <--------- GPA            0.022     0.002     9.475    p1
attract <------- height            0.008     0.007     1.177    p3
attract <------- weight           -0.003     0.001    -2.453    p4
attract <------- rating            0.145     0.020     7.186    p5
academic <----- attract            0.018     0.039     0.469    p2
attract <----- academic            1.448     0.232     6.234    p6


Covariances:                     Estimate    S.E.      C.R.     Label
------------                     --------   -------   -------   -------

GPA <----------> height            1.819     0.712     2.555
GPA <----------> weight           -6.710     4.676    -1.435
height <-------> weight           19.024     4.098     4.642
GPA <----------> rating            0.526     0.246     2.139
height <-------> rating           -0.468     0.205    -2.279
weight <-------> rating           -5.243     1.395    -3.759
error1 <-------> error2           -0.004     0.008    -0.464


Variances:                       Estimate    S.E.      C.R.     Label
----------                       --------   -------   -------   -------

                    GPA          12.122     1.189    10.198
                 height           8.428     0.826    10.198
                 weight         371.476    36.427    10.198
                 rating           1.015     0.100    10.198
                 error1           0.018     0.003     7.111
                 error2           0.144     0.014    10.191
```

Because of Model B's specification, the estimated regression weights for the boys are the same as those for the girls. The variance and covariance estimates for the boys' sample are:

```
Covariances:                     Estimate    S.E.      C.R.     Label
------------                     --------   -------   -------   -------

GPA <----------> height           -1.508     0.961    -1.569
GPA <----------> weight          -15.645     6.899    -2.268
height <-------> weight           42.091     6.455     6.521
GPA <----------> rating            0.507     0.274     1.850
height <-------> rating            0.198     0.230     0.860
weight <-------> rating           -4.226     1.662    -2.543
error1 <-------> error2           -0.004     0.008    -0.466


Variances:                       Estimate    S.E.      C.R.     Label
----------                       --------   -------   -------   -------

                    GPA          16.243     1.600    10.149
                 height          11.572     1.140    10.149
                 weight         588.605    57.996    10.149
                 rating           0.936     0.092    10.149
                 error1           0.016     0.002     7.220
                 error2           0.167     0.016    10.146
```

The output path diagram for the girls is:

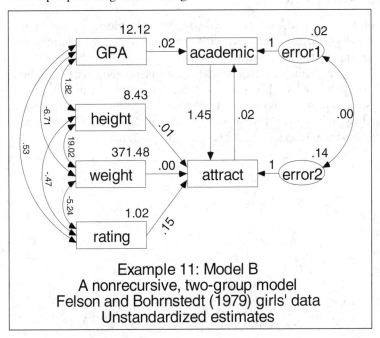

Example 11: Model B
A nonrecursive, two-group model
Felson and Bohrnstedt (1979) girls' data
Unstandardized estimates

And the output for the boys is:

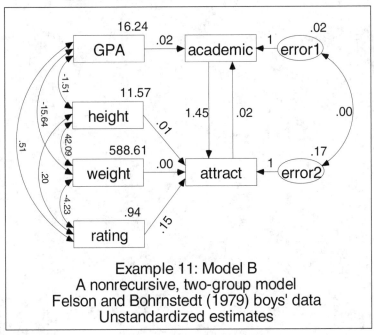

Example 11: Model B
A nonrecursive, two-group model
Felson and Bohrnstedt (1979) boys' data
Unstandardized estimates

Model C for girls and boys

You might consider adding additional constraints to Model B, making *every* parameter the same for boys as for girls. This, of course, would imply that the entire variance/covariance matrix of the observed variables must be the same for boys as for girls, while also requiring that the Felson and Bohrnstedt model be correct for both groups. This is getting too cumbersome. Instead, we will abandon the Felson and Bohrnstedt model and concentrate on the hypothesis that the observed variables have the same variance/covariance matrix for girls and boys. We will construct a model (Model C) that embodies this hypothesis.

Modeling in Amos Basic

Here an input file that describes Model C:

```
Sub Main()
    Dim Sem As New AmosEngine
    Sem.TextOutput

    Sem.BeginGroup "Fels_fem.sav"
        Sem.GroupName "girls"
        Sem.Structure "academic   (a)"
        Sem.Structure "attract    (b)"
        Sem.Structure "GPA        (c)"
        Sem.Structure "height     (d)"
        Sem.Structure "weight     (e)"
        Sem.Structure "rating     (f)"
        Sem.Structure "academic <> attract  (g)"
        Sem.Structure "academic <> GPA      (h)"
        Sem.Structure "academic <> height   (i)"
        Sem.Structure "academic <> weight   (j)"
        Sem.Structure "academic <> rating   (k)"
        Sem.Structure "attract  <> GPA      (l)"
        Sem.Structure "attract  <> height   (m)"
        Sem.Structure "attract  <> weight   (n)"
        Sem.Structure "attract  <> rating   (o)"
        Sem.Structure "GPA      <> height   (p)"
        Sem.Structure "GPA      <> weight   (q)"
        Sem.Structure "GPA      <> rating   (r)"
        Sem.Structure "height   <> weight   (s)"
        Sem.Structure "height   <> rating   (t)"
        Sem.Structure "weight   <> rating   (u)"


    Sem.BeginGroup "Fels_mal.sav"
        Sem.GroupName "boys"
        Sem.Structure "academic   (a)"
        Sem.Structure "attract    (b)"
        Sem.Structure "GPA        (c)"
        Sem.Structure "height     (d)"
        Sem.Structure "weight     (e)"
        Sem.Structure "rating     (f)"
        Sem.Structure "academic <> attract  (g)"
        Sem.Structure "academic <> GPA      (h)"
        Sem.Structure "academic <> height   (i)"
        Sem.Structure "academic <> weight   (j)"
        Sem.Structure "academic <> rating   (k)"
        Sem.Structure "attract  <> GPA      (l)"
        Sem.Structure "attract  <> height   (m)"
        Sem.Structure "attract  <> weight   (n)"
        Sem.Structure "attract  <> rating   (o)"
        Sem.Structure "GPA      <> height   (p)"
        Sem.Structure "GPA      <> weight   (q)"
        Sem.Structure "GPA      <> rating   (r)"
        Sem.Structure "height   <> weight   (s)"
        Sem.Structure "height   <> rating   (t)"
        Sem.Structure "weight   <> rating   (u)"

End Sub
```

Modeling in Amos Graphics

Because each group's model specification has 15 covariance terms, connecting each variable to the other five is starting to become tedious. Fortunately, **Amos 4.0** provides some macro tools that help make this task more automatic:

1. Start with a new path diagram and connect the `Fels_fem.sav` data set to **Group number 1**.

2. Open the **List Variables in Dataset** list and drag the six observed variables onto the path diagram:

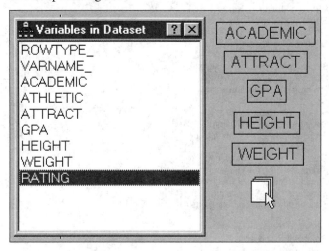

It might be worthwhile at this point to arrange the six variables in a single row or a single column, in order to keep the covariance from going "haywire" in the next step.

3. Note that you can align two variable objects automatically with the **Drag properties** tool. When you click on this icon, the **Drag Properties** dialog box appears. Check the height, width, and either y-coordinate (for alignment in a row) or x-coordinate (for alignment in a column). Then, click on the first variable and drag these properties to the second one. Continue this procedure until all variables are aligned:

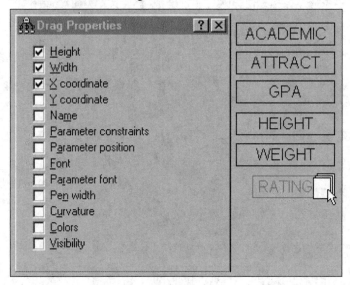

4. To fit in all the covariance paths, you will probably need to space the variables further apart and with even spacing between them. Do this by using the **Move** tool to space variables further apart.

Then use the **Select all objects** icon to highlight all the variable at once. Next, follow the path: **Edit** → **Space Vertically** to *even out the spacing*.

---

5. With all six variables still selected, follow the path: **Tools** → **Macro** → **Macros...** → **Draw Covariances**. **Amos Graphics** draws in all possible covariance paths among the selected variables:

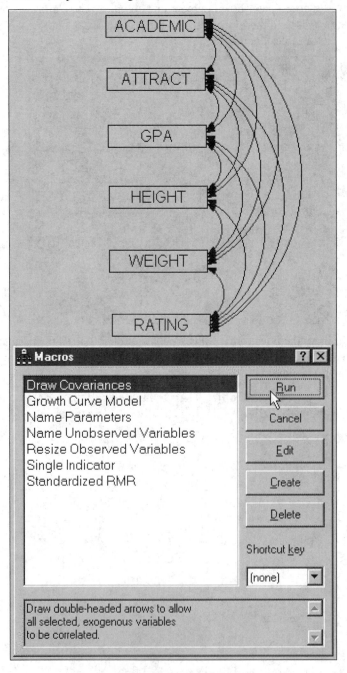

6. Label all variances and covariances with suitable labels, *e.g.*, with letters "a" through "u".

7. Add the second group for the boys and attach the boy's data to it (`Fels_mal.sav`)

The file `Ex11-c.amw` contains the **Amos Graphics** specification for Model C. Here is the group-invariant input path diagram:

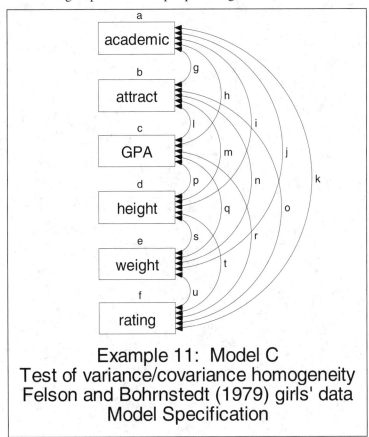

Example 11: Model C
Test of variance/covariance homogeneity
Felson and Bohrnstedt (1979) girls' data
Model Specification

Results for Model C

Model C would have to be rejected at any conventional significance level.

```
Chi-square =     48.977
Degrees of freedom =    21
Probability level =      0.001
```

These results mean that you should not waste time on any model that allows no differences at all between boys and girls. The variances and/or covariances of the exogenous variables are different in the two samples.

Example 12: Simultaneous Factor Analysis for Several Groups

Purpose

- Carry out a factor analysis on data from several populations at once (Jöreskog, 1971).

- Demonstrate how to test whether the same factor model holds for each of several populations (possibly with different parameter values for different populations).

The data

We will use the Holzinger and Swineford (1939) data described in Example 8. This time, however, data from the 72 boys in the Grant-White sample will be analyzed along with data from the 73 girls studied in Example 8. The girls' data are contained in the file, **Grnt_fem.sav**, and are described in Example 8.

Here is a sample of the boys' data as contained in the file, **Grnt_mal.sav**:

	visperc	cubes	lozenges	paragrap	sentence	wordmean
1	23.00	19.00	4.00	10.00	17.00	10.00
2	34.00	24.00	22.00	11.00	19.00	19.00
3	29.00	23.00	9.00	9.00	19.00	11.00
4	16.00	25.00	10.00	8.00	25.00	24.00
5	27.00	26.00	6.00	10.00	16.00	13.00
6	32.00	21.00	8.00	1.00	7.00	11.00
7	38.00	31.00	12.00	10.00	11.00	14.00

Model A for the Holzinger and Swineford boys and girls

Consider the hypothesis that the common factor analysis model of Example 8 (shown next) holds for boys as well as for girls. For **Amos Graphics**, the path diagram associated with Example 8 is again used for this model, and the boys' sample is simply added as a second group. Because **Amos Graphics** automatically assumes that both groups have the same structure, the path diagram need only be created once.

The path diagram file for this model is **Ex12-a.amw**.

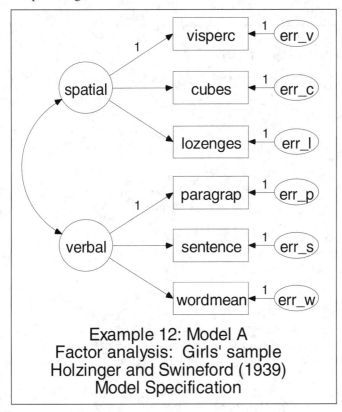

Example 12: Model A
Factor analysis: Girls' sample
Holzinger and Swineford (1939)
Model Specification

Alternatively, the **Amos Basic** input file (`Ex12-a.AmosBasic`) illustrated next, fits this model for both boys and girls.

```
Sub Main()
  Dim Sem As New AmosEngine

  Sem.TextOutput
  Sem.Standardized
  Sem.Smc

  Sem.BeginGroup "Grnt_fem.sav"
    Sem.GroupName "Girls"
    Sem.Structure "visperc  = (1) spatial + (1) err_v"
    Sem.Structure "cubes    =     spatial + (1) err_c"
    Sem.Structure "lozenges =     spatial + (1) err_l"

    Sem.Structure "paragrap = (1) verbal  + (1) err_p"
    Sem.Structure "sentence =     verbal  + (1) err_s"
    Sem.Structure "wordmean =     verbal  + (1) err_w"

  Sem.BeginGroup "Grnt_mal.sav"
    Sem.GroupName "Boys"
    Sem.Structure "visperc  = (1) spatial + (1) err_v"
    Sem.Structure "cubes    =     spatial + (1) err_c"
    Sem.Structure "lozenges =     spatial + (1) err_l"

    Sem.Structure "paragrap = (1) verbal  + (1) err_p"
    Sem.Structure "sentence =     verbal  + (1) err_s"
    Sem.Structure "wordmean =     verbal  + (1) err_w"

End Sub
```

Again, notice that while the same model *structure* is specified for boys and girls, the regression weights are allowed to be different for the two groups. The unique variances may be different too, and so may the variances and the covariance of the common factors.

Results for Model A

In the calculation of degrees of freedom for this model, all of the numbers from Example 8 are exactly doubled:

```
Computation of Degrees of Freedom

                   Number of distinct sample moments:    42
        Number of distinct parameters to be estimated:   26
                                               -------------------------
                                    Degrees of freedom:   16
```

Model A is acceptable at any conventional significance level. If Model A had been rejected, we would have had to make changes in the path diagram for at least one of the two groups:

```
Chi-square  =      16.480
Degrees of freedom =    16
Probability level =      0.420
```

Here are the (unstandardized) parameter estimates for the 73 girls. They are the same estimates that were obtained in Example 8 where the girls alone were studied:

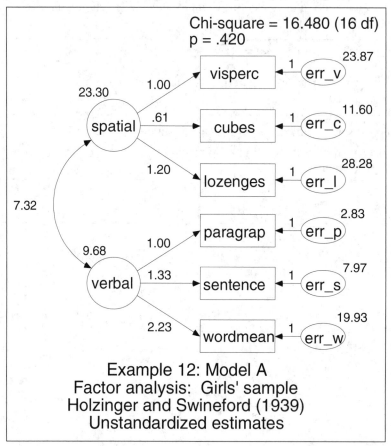

Chi-square = 16.480 (16 df)
p = .420

Example 12: Model A
Factor analysis: Girls' sample
Holzinger and Swineford (1939)
Unstandardized estimates

The corresponding output path diagram for the 72 boys is:

Chi-square = 16.480 (16 df)
p = .420

Example 12: Model A
Factor analysis: Boys' sample
Holzinger and Swineford (1939)
Unstandardized estimates

Notice that the estimated regression weights vary little between the two groups. It is quite plausible that the two groups share the same path values – a hypothesis that we will test in Model B.

Model B for the Holzinger and Swineford boys and girls

We now accept the hypothesis that the same factor analysis model holds for both boys and girls. The next step is to ask whether boys and girls share the same parameter values. The next model (Model B) does not demand that every parameter for the population of boys be equal to the corresponding parameter for the population of girls. What it does require is that the factor loadings (*i.e.*, the regression weights) be the same for both groups. Model B still permits different unique variances for boys and girls. The common factor variances and covariances may also differ in the two groups.

The **Amos Basic** file for Model B is `Ex12-b.AmosBasic`:

```
Sub Main()
  Dim Sem As New AmosEngine

  Sem.TextOutput
  Sem.Standardized
  Sem.Smc

  Sem.BeginGroup "Grnt_fem.sav"
    Sem.GroupName "Girls"
    Sem.Structure "visperc  =      (1) spatial + (1) err_v"
    Sem.Structure "cubes    = (cube_s) spatial + (1) err_c"
    Sem.Structure "lozenges = (lozn_s) spatial + (1) err_l"

    Sem.Structure "paragrap =      (1) verbal  + (1) err_p"
    Sem.Structure "sentence = (sent_v) verbal  + (1) err_s"
    Sem.Structure "wordmean = (word_v) verbal  + (1) err_w"

  Sem.BeginGroup "Grnt_mal.sav"
    Sem.GroupName "Boys"
    Sem.Structure "visperc  =      (1) spatial + (1) err_v"
    Sem.Structure "cubes    = (cube_s) spatial + (1) err_c"
    Sem.Structure "lozenges = (lozn_s) spatial + (1) err_l"

    Sem.Structure "paragrap =      (1) verbal  + (1) err_p"
    Sem.Structure "sentence = (sent_v) verbal  + (1) err_s"
    Sem.Structure "wordmean = (word_v) verbal  + (1) err_w

End Sub
```

Set up Model B in **Amos Graphics** by first entering the parameter names within the corresponding regression paths in the path diagram as shown:

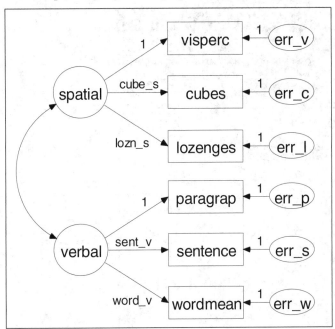

 Run **View/Set** → **Matrix Representation** and make sure that the weight matrix Beta 1 has the foreground. Then, drag the **Drag indicator variables** icon (the first icon) to field 2A.

Next, drag the **Drag latent variables** icon (the second icon) to field 1B. Amos will show the parameter labels in the spreadsheet format like this:

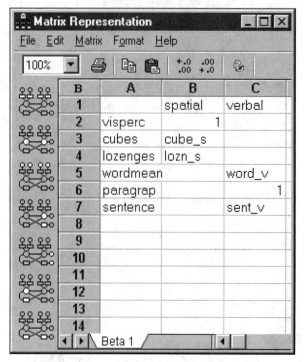

Copy this matrix to the **Boys'** group by highlighting the filled cells in the **Girl's** group, and clicking on **Edit → Copy**. Then click on the **Boys'** group in the **Groups** panel, and highlight the same number of cells in the new matrix. Finally, select **Edit → Paste**. The input file for Model B is **Ex12-b.amw**.

Results for Model B

Because of the additional constraints in Model B, four fewer parameters have to be estimated from the data, increasing the number of degrees of freedom accordingly:

```
Computation of Degrees of Freedom

                  Number of distinct sample moments:    42
    Number of distinct parameters to be estimated:    22
                                  ------------------------
                              Degrees of freedom:    20
```

The chi-square fit statistic is acceptable:

```
Chi-square =     18.292
Degrees of freedom =    20
Probability level =      0.568
```

The chi-square difference between the two models, 18.292 – 16.480 = 1.812, is not significant at any conventional level, either. Thus, Model B, assuming a group-invariant factor pattern, is supported by the Holzinger and Swineford data.

Here are the parameter estimates for the 73 girls:

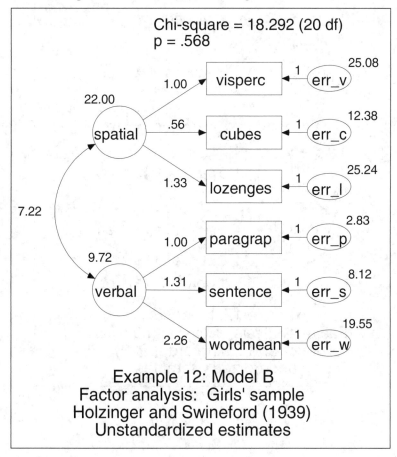

Chi-square = 18.292 (20 df)
p = .568

Example 12: Model B
Factor analysis: Girls' sample
Holzinger and Swineford (1939)
Unstandardized estimates

And the parameter estimates for the 72 boys:

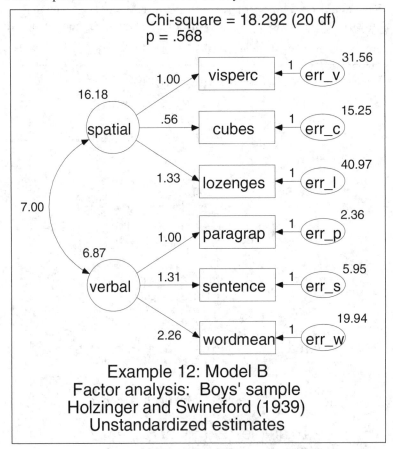

Chi-square = 18.292 (20 df)
p = .568

spatial
16.18
7.00
verbal
6.87

1.00 → visperc ← 1 err_v 31.56
.56 → cubes ← 1 err_c 15.25
1.33 → lozenges ← 1 err_l 40.97
1.00 → paragrap ← 1 err_p 2.36
1.31 → sentence ← 1 err_s 5.95
2.26 → wordmean ← 1 err_w 19.94

Example 12: Model B
Factor analysis: Boys' sample
Holzinger and Swineford (1939)
Unstandardized estimates

Not surprisingly, the Model B parameter estimates are different from the Model A estimates. The following table shows estimates and standard errors for the two models side by side:

Parameter	Model A		Model B	
Girls' sample	**Estimate**	**Standard Error**	**Estimate**	**Standard Error**
g: cubes <--- spatial	0.610	0.143	0.557	0.114
g: lozenges <--- spatial	1.198	0.272	1.327	0.248
g: sentence <--- verbal	1.334	0.160	1.305	0.117
g: wordmean <--- verbal	2.234	0.263	2.260	0.200
g: spatial <---> verbal	7.315	2.571	7.225	2.458
g: var(spatial)	23.302	8.124	22.001	7.078
g: var(verbal)	9.682	2.159	9.723	2.025
g: var(err_v)	23.873	5.986	25.082	5.832
g: var(err_c)	11.602	2.584	12.382	2.481
g: var(err_l)	28.275	7.892	25.244	8.040
g: var(err_p)	2.834	0.869	2.835	0.834
g: var(err_s)	7.967	1.869	8.115	1.816
g: var(err_w)	19.925	4.951	19.550	4.837
Boys' sample	**Estimate**	**Standard Error**	**Estimate**	**Standard Error**
b: cubes <--- spatial	0.450	0.176	*(same as for girls' sample)*	
b: lozenges <--- spatial	1.510	0.461	*(same as for girls' sample)*	
b: sentence <--- verbal	1.275	0.171	*(same as for girls' sample)*	
b: wordmean <--- verbal	2.294	0.308	*(same as for girls' sample)*	
b: spatial <---> verbal	6.840	2.370	6.992	2.090
b: var(spatial)	16.058	7.516	16.183	5.886
b: var(verbal)	6.904	1.622	6.869	1.465
b: var(err_v)	31.571	6.982	31.563	6.681
b: var(err_c)	15.693	2.904	15.245	2.934
b: var(err_l)	36.526	11.532	40.974	9.689
b: var(err_p)	2.364	0.726	2.363	0.681
b: var(err_s)	6.035	1.433	5.954	1.398
b: var(err_w)	19.697	4.658	19.937	4.470

All but two of the estimated standard errors are smaller in Model B, including those for the unconstrained parameters. Therefore, the Model B estimates are somewhat more efficient (assuming the model is correct). In fact, one of the reasons for imposing constraints while estimating the parameters of a model is to get more efficient parameter estimates for the population. The other reason is, of course, to test the hypothesis that the imposed constraints indeed hold in the population.

Example 13: Estimating and Testing Hypotheses about Means

Purpose

- Demonstrate how to estimate means.

- Demonstrate how to test hypotheses about means.

For large samples, this method is equivalent to a multivariate analysis of variance).

Introduction

Amos and similar programs are usually used to estimate models consisting of variances, covariances and regression weights, and to test hypotheses about these parameters. Means are often ignored in these models. Likewise, intercepts are passed over in regression equations. One reason for the relative absence of mean and intercept components in structural equation and factor analysis models is the relative difficulty of specifying these kinds of parameters with existing software.

Amos, however, was designed to make means and intercept modeling easy. This is the first of several examples showing how to specify hypotheses about mean and intercept terms. In this particular example, however, the parameters consist only of variances, covariances and means. The parameters do not involve any regression paths or intercepts.

The data

For this example, we will be using Attig's (1983) spatial memory data as described in Example 1. We will use data from both young and old subjects. The raw data for the two groups are contained in the Microsoft Excel **UserGuide.xls** workbook in the **Attg_yng** and **Attg_old** worksheets. The data were listed in Examples 1 and 10. In this example, we will only be using the measures **recall1** and **cued1**.

Model A for young and old subjects

In the analysis of Model B of Example 10, we concluded that **recall1** and **cued1** have the same variances and covariance for both old and young people — at least, the evidence against that hypothesis was found to be insignificant. The following input file will repeat the analysis of Example 10's Model B with an added twist. This time, the *means* of the two variables, **recall1** and **cued1** will also be estimated.

Mean structure modeling in Amos Graphics

Under **Amos Graphics**, estimating and testing hypotheses involving means is not that much different from analyzing variance and covariance structures. It does, however, require a few additional steps. Suppose you start with the structure of Example 10, Model B, specifying group-invariant variance and covariance terms for the young and old subjects. Restrictions or comparisons of means, however, were not considered in that model. In fact, Example 10 did not use the sample means at all.

Incorporating means and intercepts in **Amos Graphics** is simple: just click on the **Analysis Properties** icon to reveal the **Analysis Properties** dialog box. Then check the **Estimate means and intercepts** box:

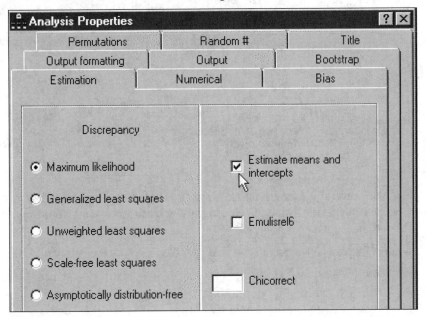

Amos will then automatically add a default mean/intercept structure to the existing path model.

The displayed path diagram changes as well. On the input and unstandardized output diagrams, Amos attaches a "mean, variance" pair of parameters to the *exogenous* variables. Amos displays *endogenous* variables with a single intercept term. The following input diagram shows the labels for variance parameters preceded by commas. These commas imply the presence of yet unlabeled mean parameters.

The new path specification is shown in file **Ex13-a.amw**:

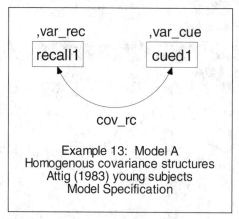

,var_rec   ,var_cue

recall1   cued1

cov_rc

Example 13: Model A
Homogenous covariance structures
Attig (1983) young subjects
Model Specification

Had you constrained the means (to be demonstrated later, in Model B), parameter labels for the means would have been shown to the left of each comma, opposite the variance labels.

Amos Graphics changes in several ways when **Estimate means and intercepts** is selected:

- Mean and intercept fields are shown during input, in addition to variances, covariances and/or regression weights.

- Constraints may be applied to all intercepts, means, regression weights, variances, and covariances in all groups.

- Pressing the **Calculate estimates** icon (while **Estimate means and intercepts** is selected) estimates means and intercepts— subject to constraints, if any.

- The chi-square statistic reflects the model fit to sample mean *and* covariance structures.

If **Estimate means and intercepts** is *not* selected:

- Only fields for variances, covariances and regression weights are displayed during input. Constraints can be placed *only* on these parameters.

- When the **Calculate estimates** icon is pressed, Amos estimates covariance structures, but *not* means or intercepts. Only constraints imposed on variances, covariances and regression weights are used in the estimation. Any (portions of) constraints involving means and/or intercepts remain inactive.

- If you deselect **Estimate means and intercepts** after the means model has *already* been estimated, the output path diagram will continue to show mean and intercept terms. To display the correct output path diagram without means or intercepts, *recalculate* the model estimates with **Estimate means and intercepts** off.

- The chi-square statistic reflects the model fit to sample covariance structures only.

Given these rules, **Estimate mean and intercepts** makes estimating and testing means models as easy as traditional path modeling.

Mean structure modeling in Amos Basic

The **Amos Basic** specification of Model A appears in the file `Ex13-a.AmosBasic`. It maintains the variance and covariance restrictions used by Example 10, Model B, but adds terms for the variable means in the two groups:

```
Sub Main()
   Dim Sem As New AmosEngine

   Sem.TextOutput
   Sem.ModelMeansAndIntercepts

   Sem.BeginGroup "UserGuide.xls", "Attg_yng"
      Sem.GroupName "young_subjects"
      Sem.Structure "recall1        (var_rec)"
      Sem.Structure "cued1          (var_cue)"
      Sem.Structure "recall1 <> cued1  (cov_rc)"
      Sem.Mean "recall1"
      Sem.Mean "cued1"

   Sem.BeginGroup "UserGuide.xls", "Attg_old"
      Sem.GroupName "old_subjects"
      Sem.Structure "recall1        (var_rec)"
      Sem.Structure "cued1          (var_cue)"
      Sem.Structure "recall1 <> cued1  (cov_rc)"
      Sem.Mean "recall1"
      Sem.Mean "cued1"

End Sub
```

The Sem.ModelMeansAndIntercepts statement sets up **Amos Basic** for estimating mean and intercept parameters. Whenever your **Amos Basic** program calls the .ModelMeansAndIntercepts method, the information from both means and (co-)variances is used to estimate the model and test its fit.

The Sem.Mean statements cause the means of **recall1** and **cued1** to be estimated. Except for the use of the Sem.Mean statement (and changes to the comment section at the top), the input file is identical to that of Example 10, Model B. When you use Sem.Mean statements, **Amos Basic** estimates the means of the exogenous variables whose names follow Sem.Mean statements. It assumes that all of the other exogenous variables (*i.e.*, those whose names do not follow a Sem.Mean statement) have *zero means*. It is easy to forget that **Amos Basic** behaves this way when you use Sem.Mean, so you have to keep reminding yourself.

> *If you use the* Sem.ModelMeansAndIntercepts *command anywhere in an* **Amos Basic** *specification, then* Sem.Mean *commands must list all exogenous variables that are allowed to have nonzero means. Any exogenous variable that does not appear in a* Sem.Mean *command is assumed to have a mean of zero (0).*

This is different from **Amos Graphics**, where specifying **Estimate means and intercepts** estimates the means of *all* exogenous variables (subject to constraints, if any). In **Amos Graphics**, if a variable is supposed to have a zero mean, this must be made explicit by a value constraint.

There is more to tell you about modeling mean structures, but we will unfold the full story in Example 14, when we entertain models with regression intercepts.

Output for Model A

Amos Basic output

The number of degrees of freedom for this model is the same as in Example 10, Model B, but we get to it in a different way. This time, the *number of distinct sample moments* includes the sample means as well as the sample variances and covariances. In the young sample, there are two variances, one covariance and two means, for a total of five sample moments. Similarly, there are five sample moments in the old sample. So, taking both samples together, there are ten sample moments. As for the *parameters to be estimated*, there are seven of them, namely var_rec (the common variance of **recall1**), var_cue (the common variance of **cued1**), cov_rc (the common covariance between **recall1** and **cued1**), the means of **recall1** among young and old people (2), and the means of **cued1** among young and old people (2).

The number of degrees of freedom thus works out to be:

```
Computation of Degrees of Freedom

              Number of distinct sample moments:    10
    Number of distinct parameters to be estimated:   7
                                                  -------------------
                              Degrees of freedom:     3
```

The chi-square statistic here is also the same as in Model B of Example 10. The hypothesis that old people and young people share the same variances and covariance would be accepted at any conventional significance level.

```
Chi-square =       4.588
Degrees of freedom =    3
Probability level =     0.205
```

Here are the parameter estimates for the group of 40 young subjects:

Means:		Estimate	S.E.	C.R.	Label
	recall1	10.250	0.382	26.862	
	cued1	11.700	0.374	31.292	
Covariances:		Estimate	S.E.	C.R.	Label
recall1 <-----> cued1		4.056	0.780	5.202	cov_rc
Variances:		Estimate	S.E.	C.R.	Label
	recall1	5.678	0.909	6.245	var_rec
	cued1	5.452	0.873	6.245	var_cue

And here are the estimates for the 40 old subjects:

Means:		Estimate	S.E.	C.R.	Label
	recall1	8.675	0.382	22.735	
	cued1	9.575	0.374	25.609	
Covariances:		Estimate	S.E.	C.R.	Label
recall1 <-----> cued1		4.056	0.780	5.202	cov_rc
Variances:		Estimate	S.E.	C.R.	Label
	recall1	5.678	0.909	6.245	var_rec
	cued1	5.452	0.873	6.245	var_cue

Except for the means, these estimates are the same as those obtained in Example 10, Model B. The estimated standard errors and critical ratios are also the same. This demonstrates that merely estimating means, without placing any constraints on them, has no effect on the estimates of the remaining parameters or their standard errors.

Amos Graphics Output

The path diagram output for the two groups follows. Note that the means are displayed to the left of the variance estimates. For instance, among the young subjects, variable **recall1** has an estimated mean of 10.25 and an estimated variance of 5.68. Mean and variance values, separated by commas, are paired up next to their exogenous variable objects.

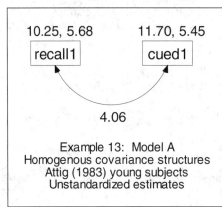

Example 13: Model A
Homogenous covariance structures
Attig (1983) young subjects
Unstandardized estimates

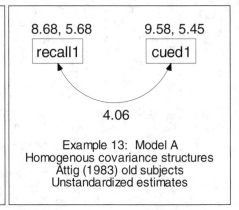

Example 13: Model A
Homogenous covariance structures
Attig (1983) old subjects
Unstandardized estimates

Model B for young and old subjects

We now assume that Model A is correct, and consider the more restrictive hypothesis that the means of the variables **recall1** and **cued1** do not change across the two groups.

Modeling in Amos Graphics

In order to set up Model B in **Amos Graphics**, the means for **recall1** and **cued1** must be constrained in the same way that variances and covariances were constrained in previous examples. To do so, simply double click on the exogenous variable **recall1** to reveal the **Object Properties** dialog box.

Select the Parameters tab:

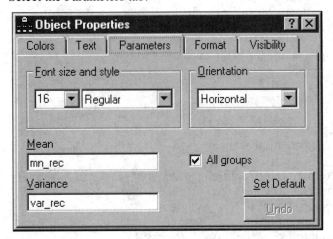

Now you can enter a number or variable name to force the mean of **recall1** to be equal to a value, or to another parameter. We can choose the name mn_rec, for instance. If the **All groups** box remains checked, the parameter name for the mean of **recall1** in the young subjects will carry over to the old subjects. This forces the means to be equal in both groups. Correspondingly, the means of **cued1** for young and old subjects can be constrained to be equal. Double click on **cued1** and constrain the means of the young and old subjects by a common parameter label such as mn_cue.

The path diagram below (from file **Ex13-b.amw**) displays the **Amos Graphics** specification of Model B for the two groups. Notice that the new mean parameter names appear alongside the variance parameter names for each variable object.

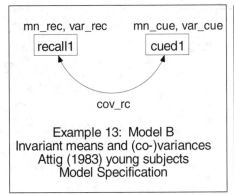

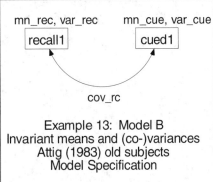

Modeling in Amos Basic

The file **Ex13-b.AmosBasic** specifies the same model for **Amos Basic**. In addition to group-invariant variances and covariances, the means are also restricted to be equal across the two groups:

```
Sub Main()
  Dim Sem As New AmosEngine

  Sem.TextOutput
  Sem.ModelMeansAndIntercepts

  Sem.BeginGroup "UserGuide.xls", "Attg_yng"
    Sem.GroupName "young_subjects"
    Sem.Structure "recall1         (var_rec)"
    Sem.Structure "cued1           (var_cue)"
    Sem.Structure "recall1 <> cued1 (cov_rc)"
    Sem.Mean "recall1", "mn_rec"
    Sem.Mean "cued1", "mn_cue"

  Sem.BeginGroup "UserGuide.xls", "Attg_old"
    Sem.GroupName "old_subjects"
    Sem.Structure "recall1         (var_rec)"
    Sem.Structure "cued1           (var_cue)"
    Sem.Structure "recall1 <> cued1 (cov_rc)"
    Sem.Mean "recall1", "mn_rec"
    Sem.Mean "cued1", "mn_cue"

End Sub
```

Multiple model input

Models A and B can, of course, be specified simultaneously in the same **Amos Graphics** or **Amos Basic** input file, and a good reason for doing so may be the convenience of having the chi-square differences and *p*-values for model comparisons printed near the end of the list output.

```
Sub Main()
   Dim Sem As New AmosEngine

   Sem.TextOutput
   Sem.ModelMeansAndIntercepts

   Sem.BeginGroup "UserGuide.xls", "Attg_yng"
      Sem.GroupName "young subjects"
      Sem.Structure "recall1        (var_rec)"
      Sem.Structure "cued1          (var_cue)"
      Sem.Structure "recall1 <> cued1  (cov_rc)"
      Sem.Mean "recall1", "yng_rec"
      Sem.Mean "cued1", "yng_cue"

   Sem.BeginGroup "UserGuide.xls", "Attg_old"
      Sem.GroupName "old subjects"
      Sem.Structure "recall1        (var_rec)"
      Sem.Structure "cued1          (var_cue)"
      Sem.Structure "recall1 <> cued1  (cov_rc)"
      Sem.Mean "recall1", "old_rec"
      Sem.Mean "cued1", "old_cue"

   Sem.Model "Model_A", ""
   Sem.Model "Model_B", "yng_rec = old_rec", "yng_cue = old_cue"

End Sub
```

In **Amos Graphics**, the multiple-model specification is entered in much the same way. Although not reproduced in this document, the corresponding **Amos Graphics** input file for this example is **Ex13-all.amw**.

Results for Model B

With the new constraints on the means, Model B has five (5) degrees of freedom:

```
Computation of Degrees of Freedom

                    Number of distinct sample moments:    10
            Number of distinct parameters to be estimated:   5
                    ---------------------------------
                            Degrees of freedom:    5
```

Model B has to be rejected at any conventional significance level:

```
Chi-square =     19.267
Degrees of freedom =    5
Probability level =     0.002
```

Comparison of Model B with Model A

If Model A is correct and Model B is wrong (which is at least plausible, since Model A was accepted and Model B was rejected), then the assumption of equal means must be wrong. There is a better test of the hypothesis of equal means under the assumption of equal variances and covariances. When the multiple-model specification is used (*e.g.*, files **Ex13-all.AmosBasic** or **Ex13-all.amw**), the following model comparison appears near the end of either list output file:

```
Model Comparisons
-----------------

Assuming Model_A to be correct:

                    df    chi-2      p
                    --    -----    -----
        ModelNumber2     2    14.679    0.001
```

In comparing Model B with Model A, the difference between the chi-square fit statistics is 14.679, based on two (2) degrees of freedom. Since Model B is obtained by placing additional constraints on Model A, we can say that, if Model B is correct then 14.679 is an observation on a chi-square variable with 2 degrees of freedom. However, the probability of obtaining this large (or a larger) chi-square value is 0.001 — rather unlikely, in other words. Therefore, we reject Model B in favor of Model A: *the two groups have different means*.

Note that this comparison of nested means-level models (given homogenous covariance structures) is as close as Amos can come to conventional multivariate analysis of variance. In fact, Amos's test is equivalent to a conventional MANOVA, except that the chi-square test provided by Amos is only asymptotically correct. However, *F*-tests used by a conventional MANOVA provide are exact, even for small samples.

This example is meant to be a simple demonstration of Amos's mean-level capabilities. In real life, such a problem would be treated by MANOVA, while Amos would be reserved for investigating more complex structural equation models where you would not always know the exact small-sample distribution of the test statistic.

Example 14: Regression with an Explicit Intercept

Purpose

- Demonstrate how to estimate the regression intercept in an ordinary regression analysis.

Introduction

Ordinarily, when you specify that some variable depends linearly on some others, Amos assumes that the linear equation expressing the dependency contains an additive constant, or intercept. For instance, in Example 4, we specified the variable **performance** to depend linearly on three other variables: **knowledge**, **value** and **satisfaction**. Amos assumed that the regression equation was of the following form:

$$\texttt{performance} = a + b_1 \texttt{*knowledge} + b_2 \texttt{*value} + b_3 \texttt{*satisfaction} + \textit{error}$$

where b_1, b_2, and b_3 are the regression weights, and a is the intercept. In Example 4, the regression weights b_1 through b_3 were estimated. The intercept term a, however, was not actually estimated, nor was it mentioned explicitly in the **Amos Graphics** or **Amos Basic** input files. Nevertheless, Amos takes for granted that an intercept is present in the regression equation. You will usually be satisfied with this method of handling intercepts in regression equations. Sometimes, however, you will want to see an estimate of an intercept, or to test a hypothesis about an intercept. You will then need to take the steps demonstrated in this example.

The data

We will once again use the data of Warren, White and Fuller (1974), first used in Example 4. We will use the Excel worksheet **Warren5v** in **UserGuide.xls** found in Amos's Examples subdirectory: `C:\Program Files\Amos 4\Examples`. These are the sample moments (means, variances and covariances in a table format:

rowtype_	varname_	performance	knowledge	value	satisfaction	past_training
n		98	98	98	98	98
cov	performance	0.0209				
cov	knowledge	0.0177	0.052			
cov	value	0.0245	0.028	0.1212		
cov	satisfaction	0.0046	0.0044	-0.0063	0.0901	
cov	past_training	0.0187	0.0192	0.0353	-0.0066	0.0946
mean		0.0589	1.3796	2.8773	2.4613	2.1174

Input file for the regression analysis

Modeling in Amos Graphics

You can set up the regression model as you did in Example 4. In fact, if you have already gone through Example 4, simply copy that input file, click the **Analysis properties** icon, select the **Estimation** tab and check the **Estimate means and intercepts** box before running the analysis. Your diagram (from the **Amos Graphics** input file **Ex14.amw**) will look like this:

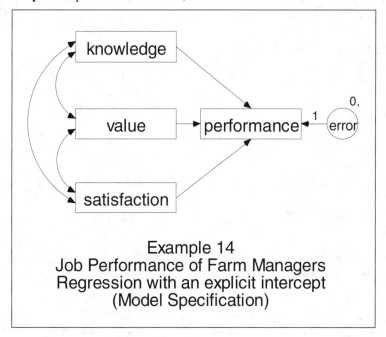

Example 14
Job Performance of Farm Managers
Regression with an explicit intercept
(Model Specification)

An important feature of this path diagram is the string "0," displayed above the **error** object. It indicates that the mean of the residual values is assumed to be zero — a standard assumption in linear regression models. By default, **Amos Graphics** sets the means of regression error terms to zero, so you do not have to worry about using changing the parameter constraints.

Conversely, if you specified the mean of the error term as a parameter to be estimated, rather than being fixed at zero, Amos would produce the error message:

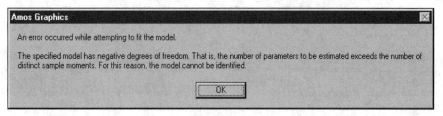

The error would occur because Amos was trying to simultaneously estimate a mean for **error** and an intercept for the dependent variable **performance**. We know from regression theory that the mean of the residual error term *must* be 0 if there is also an intercept. This is another (and more clear) example of unidentification.

In Example 13 we discussed several modeling situations affected by checking **Estimate means and intercepts** box. In the present example, the **Estimate means and intercepts** box must be checked in order to estimate or display the regression intercept (s) and means of the predictor variables. The display of variances, covariances and regression weights will not be affected.

Modeling in Amos Basic

Just as a reminder, here is the **Amos Basic** input file used in Example 4 (equation version):[1]

```
Sub Main()
    Dim Sem As New AmosEngine

    Sem.TextOutput
    Sem.Standardized
    Sem.Smc
    Sem.ImpliedMoments
    Sem.SampleMoments

    Sem.BeginGroup "UserGuide.xls", "Warren5v"
        Sem.Structure "performance = knowledge + value + satisfaction" _
            & " + error (1)"

End Sub
```

---

[1] To make our **Amos Basic** model fit on this page, we had to break a line of code. You will not need to do this. However, the model will still run because we followed **Amos Basic** (and Visual Basic) syntax for breaking lines of code. Notice that we ended the first section of the longer line with a quote mark (") and a trailing underscore (_). Then we began the next line with an ampersand (&) and a quote mark and continued the line. We indented the continuation line so you could spot it more easily.

The **Amos Basic** input (from file **Ex14.AmosBasic**) will produce all the same results, plus the mean and intercept estimates:[2]

```
Sub Main()
    Dim Sem As New AmosEngine

    Sem.TextOutput
    Sem.Standardized
    Sem.Smc
    Sem.ImpliedMoments
    Sem.SampleMoments
    Sem.ModelMeansAndIntercepts

    Sem.BeginGroup "UserGuide.xls", "Warren5v"
        Sem.Structure "performance = () + knowledge + value +" _
            & " satisfaction + error (1)"

        Sem.Mean "knowledge"
        Sem.Mean "value"
        Sem.Mean "satisfaction"

End Sub
```

Note the Sem.ModelMeansAndIntercepts statement that activates Amos's mean-level analysis model. Another set of important differences is an extra pair of empty parentheses and a "plus" sign in the equation statement following the Sem.Structure statement. The extra pair of empty parentheses represents the intercept in the regression equation. One result of the analysis will now be an estimate of that intercept.

The Sem.Mean statements request estimates for the means of **knowledge**, **value** and **satisfaction**. All exogenous variables with means other than zero have to appear on Sem.Mean statements. On the other hand, if the Sem.Mean statements were not given, **Amos Basic** would use the default for mean-level models. In other words, the means of all exogenous variables would be fixed to zero (*cf.*, Example 13).

---

[2] See footnote on page 282.

Intercept parameters can either be specified by an extra pair of parentheses in a Sem.Structure command (as we just showed) or by the Intercept method. For instance, an equivalent syntax for the regression model is:

```
Sem.Structure "performance <--- knowledge"
Sem.Structure "performance <--- value"
Sem.Structure "performance <--- satisfaction"
Sem.Structure "performance <--- error (1)"

Sem.Intercept "performance"
Sem.Mean "knowledge"
Sem.Mean "value"
Sem.Mean "satisfaction"
```

Rules for modeling means and intercepts in **Amos Basic**, in addition to those already stated in Example 13, are:

- If an *endogenous variable* is listed with a Sem.Intercept command, then an intercept will automatically be added to the regression equation for that variable. This function facilitates mean-level model specifications in **Amos Basic** *path* format.

- However, when regression *equations* appear in Sem.Structure statements, it is advisable to state the intercept term there, and use the Sem.Mean statements only for the *exogenous* variables. This way, it will be easier to keep track of which statement produced the intercept terms.

Results of the regression analysis

Text output

The present analysis is the same as the analysis of Example 4, but with the explicit estimation of three means and an intercept. The number of degrees of freedom is again zero, but the calculation goes a little differently. Sample means are required for this analysis, and so the *number of distinct sample moments* includes the sample means as well as the sample variances and covariances. There are four sample means, four sample variances and six sample covariances, for a total of 14 sample moments. As for the parameters to be estimated, there are three regression weights and an intercept. Also, the three predictors have among them three means, three variances and three covariances.

Finally, there is one error variance, for a total of 14 parameters to be estimated.

```
Computation of Degrees of Freedom

                   Number of distinct sample moments:    14
        Number of distinct parameters to be estimated:   14
                                          ------------------------
                                          Degrees of freedom:    0
```

With zero degrees of freedom, there is no hypothesis to be tested:

```
Chi-square =       0.000
Degrees of freedom =     0
Probability level cannot be computed
```

The estimates for regression weights, variances and covariances are the same as in Example 4, and so are the associated estimates for standard errors and the critical ratios.

```
Regression Weights:                  Estimate    S.E.     C.R.
-------------------                  --------   -------  -------

performance <-------- knowledge        0.258     0.054    4.822
performance <------------ value        0.145     0.035    4.136
performance <----- satisfaction        0.049     0.038    1.274


Standardized Regression Weights:     Estimate
--------------------------------     --------

performance <-------- knowledge        0.407
performance <------------ value        0.349
performance <----- satisfaction        0.101


Means:                               Estimate    S.E.     C.R.
------                               --------   -------  -------

                      knowledge        1.380     0.023   59.891
                          value        2.877     0.035   81.818
                   satisfaction        2.461     0.030   81.174


Intercepts:                          Estimate    S.E.     C.R.
-----------                          --------   -------  -------

                    performance       -0.834     0.140   -5.951


Covariances:                         Estimate    S.E.     C.R.
------------                         --------   -------  -------

knowledge <------------> value         0.028     0.008    3.276
knowledge <------> satisfaction        0.004     0.007    0.632
value <----------> satisfaction       -0.006     0.011   -0.593


Correlations:                        Estimate
-------------                        --------

knowledge <------------> value         0.353
knowledge <------> satisfaction        0.064
value <----------> satisfaction       -0.060

Variances:                           Estimate    S.E.     C.R.
----------                           --------   -------  -------

                      knowledge        0.051     0.007    6.964
                          value        0.120     0.017    6.964
                   satisfaction        0.089     0.013    6.964
                          error        0.012     0.002    6.964
```

In this case, the estimated means and intercepts do not appear to be especially interesting from a theoretical point of view. However, they would be needed in a prediction equation for the performance scores. This exercise shows how to obtain estimates of all parameters in the equation when needed.

Amos Graphics output

Below is the path diagram that contains the unstandardized estimates for this example. The intercept of −.83 is shown above the endogenous variable **performance**:

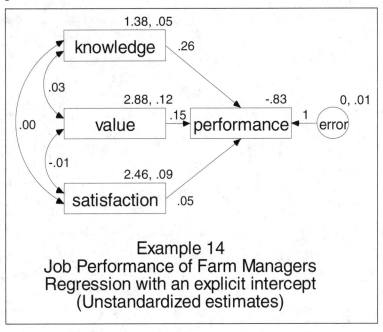

Example 14
Job Performance of Farm Managers
Regression with an explicit intercept
(Unstandardized estimates)

Example 15: Factor Analysis with Structured Means

Purpose

- Demonstrate how to estimate factor means in a common factor analysis of data from several populations.

Introduction

Conventionally, the common factor analysis model does not make any assumptions about the means of any variables. In particular, the model makes no assumptions about the means of the common factors. In fact, it is not even possible to estimate factor means or to test hypotheses in a conventional, single-sample factor analysis — unless you make some rather unrealistic assumptions.

However, Sörbom (1974) showed that it *is* possible to make inferences about factor means, as long as you are analyzing data simultaneously from several samples. Using Sörbom's approach, you cannot estimate the mean of every factor for every population, but it is still possible to assess any *differences* in factor means among two or more populations. For instance, our Example 12 analysis highlighted a common factor analysis model that fit simultaneously to a sample of girls and a sample of boys. For each group, there were two common factors, interpreted as *verbal ability* and *spatial ability*. The method used in Example 12 did not permit an examination of mean verbal ability or mean spatial ability. Sörbom's method (though not providing separate mean estimates for both girls and boys) gives us a way to estimate the *mean differences* due to the respondents' sex. In this example, we will fix the boys' mean verbal and spatial abilities, and then estimate the amount that the girls' mean abilities *differ* from the boys'. This method also provides a test of significance for differences of factor means.

Keep in mind that the identification status of the factor analysis model can be a difficult subject when estimating factor means. We feature Sörbom's original guidelines for achieving model identification in the present example.

The data

We will use the Holzinger and Swineford (1939) data introduced in Examples 8 and 12. We will then analyze data from the 73 girls in the Grant-White sample (Example 8), along with data from the 72 boys (Example 12). The files for these two groups are in **Grnt_fem.sav** and **Grnt_mal.sav**.

Model A for boys and girls

Modeling in Amos Graphics

Consider testing this hypothesis: "On average, the boys and girls from which these samples are drawn are equal in their spatial and verbal abilities (defined by three tests for each ability)." For starters, we must define the **spatial** and **verbal** factors in the same way for both groups, in order for the hypothesis to have any real meaning. Consequently, all regression *parameters* and *intercepts* must be *equal* in the two groups.

 Setting up this example is a lot like Example 12, Model B. In addition, however, you will need to click on the **Analysis properties** icon or menu and check the **Estimate means and intercepts** box (**Estimation** tab) before running the analysis. The **Amos Graphics** input file for Model A is **Ex15-a.amw**.

Model A imposes group-invariant factor loading and intercept patterns for the observed variables. Additionally, the *means* of the boys' **spatial** and **verbal** factor are fixed at zero (0).

The **Amos Graphics** input path diagram for the 73 girls is:

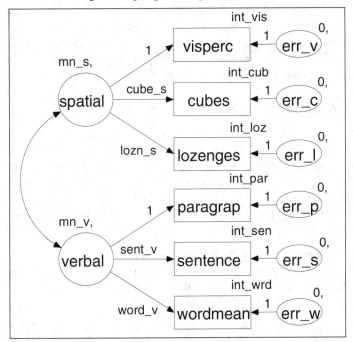

Next is the input path diagram for the 72 boys:

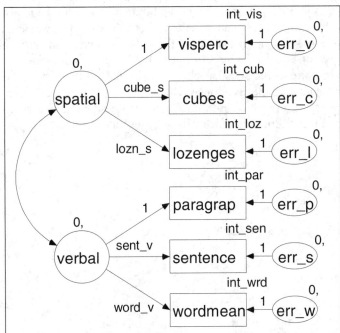

The two path diagrams show explicit intercepts for all observed variables, required to be the same for boys and girls. For example, the label `int_vis` is used to estimate the same intercept for the indicator variable **visperc** in the two groups. The path coefficients are also constrained to be the same for boys as for girls. For instance, the label `cube_s` is used in both groups to force the factor loading of the observed variable **cubes** to be group-invariant.

Understanding joint constraints

Are the joint constraints on intercepts and regression weights appropriate? One result of fitting this model will be a test of whether these constraints hold in the populations of girls and boys. The reason for starting out with these constraints is that (as Sörbom points out) it is necessary to impose *some* constraints on the intercepts and regression weights in order to make the model identified when estimating factor means. These are not the only constraints we could have used to make the model identified, but they are plausible ones.

The only difference in the setup for boys and girls is in the two common factor *means*, which are set to zero for the boys' group. In the girls' part of the model, both factor means are estimated, and the unique label `mn_s` and `mn_v` are used to identify these parameters in the input path diagram.

By specifying zero means for verbal ability and spatial ability among boys, we were able to make the model identified. Sörbom showed that, even with the constraints already imposed here on the intercepts and regression weights, it is still not possible to estimate factor means for both boys and girls simultaneously. Take verbal ability, for example. If you fix the boys' mean verbal ability at some constant (like zero), you can then estimate the girls' *relative* mean verbal ability. Alternatively, you could fix the girls' mean verbal ability at some constant, allowing you to estimate the boys' *relative* mean verbal ability. The bad news is that cannot estimate both means at once. The good news is that the difference between the boys' mean and the girls' mean will be the same no matter which mean is fixed. Further, the difference will stay constant no matter what value you fix the means at.

Modeling in Amos Basic

Defining the group-invariant factor analysis model for boys and girls (Model A) in **Amos Basic** is straightforward. The **Amos Basic** statements in file `Ex15-a.AmosBasic` correspond closely to the preceding path diagrams:

```
Sub Main()
   Dim Sem As New AmosEngine

   Sem.TextOutput
   Sem.Standardized
   Sem.Smc
   Sem.ModelMeansAndIntercepts

   Sem.BeginGroup "Grnt_fem.sav"
      Sem.GroupName "Girls"
      Sem.Structure "visperc  = (int_vis) +     (1) spatial + (1) err_v"
      Sem.Structure "cubes    = (int_cub) + (cube_s) spatial + (1) err_c"
      Sem.Structure "lozenges = (int_loz) + (lozn_s) spatial + (1) err_l"

      Sem.Structure "paragrap = (int_par) +     (1) verbal  + (1) err_p"
      Sem.Structure "sentence = (int_sen) + (sent_v) verbal  + (1) err_s"
      Sem.Structure "wordmean = (int_wrd) + (word_v) verbal  + (1) err_w"

      Sem.Mean "spatial", "mn_s"
      Sem.Mean "verbal", "mn_v"

   Sem.BeginGroup "Grnt_mal.sav"
      Sem.GroupName "Boys"
      Sem.Structure "visperc  = (int_vis) +     (1) spatial + (1) err_v"
      Sem.Structure "cubes    = (int_cub) + (cube_s) spatial + (1) err_c"
      Sem.Structure "lozenges = (int_loz) + (lozn_s) spatial + (1) err_l"

      Sem.Structure "paragrap = (int_par) +     (1) verbal  + (1) err_p"
      Sem.Structure "sentence = (int_sen) + (sent_v) verbal  + (1) err_s"
      Sem.Structure "wordmean = (int_wrd) + (word_v) verbal  + (1) err_w"

      Sem.Mean "spatial", "0"
      Sem.Mean "verbal", "0"

End Sub
```

The Sem.Structure sections show the measurement model for each observed variable, including intercept term, in equation format. The Sem.Mean statements in the girls' group specify that the means of the verbal ability and spatial ability factors are freely estimated, relative to the boys' factor means. The **Amos Basic** file uses the Sem.Mean statements once more to specify that verbal ability and spatial ability have zero means in the boys' group. However, **Amos Basic** would have automatically assumed zero means anyway, so this second set of Sem.Mean statements is actually redundant.

Results for Model A

Amos Basic output

There is no reason to reject Model A at any conventional significance level:

```
Chi-square =     22.593
Degrees of freedom =   24
Probability level =     0.544
```

Amos Graphics output

We are primarily interested in estimates of mean verbal ability and mean spatial ability, and not so much in estimates of the other parameters. However, as always, all the estimates should be inspected to make sure that they are reasonable. Here are the (unstandardized) parameter estimates for the 73 girls:

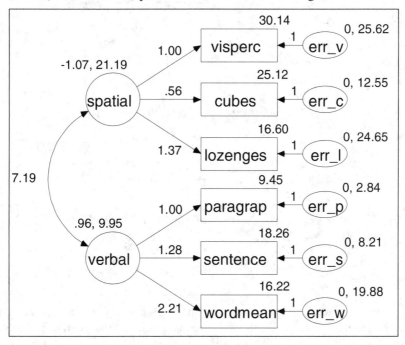

Many of the unstandardized parameter estimates for the boys' data are the same, except for the fixed means of the spatial and verbal factors, and the variances and covariances (which were not constrained):

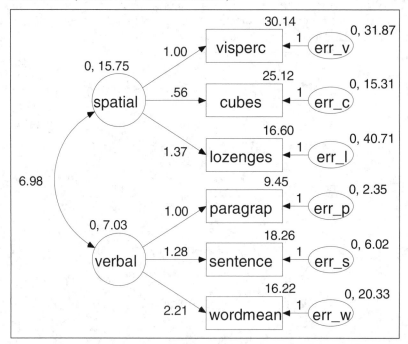

Girls have an estimated mean spatial ability of –1.066. We fixed the mean of boys' spatial ability at zero. Thus, the girls' spatial ability is estimated to be 1.066 units *below* the boys' spatial ability. This difference is not affected by the initial decision to fix the boys' mean at zero. If we had fixed the boys' mean at 10.000, the girls' mean would have been estimated to be 8.934. If we had fixed the girls' mean at zero, the boys' mean would have been estimated to be 1.066.

What unit should spatial ability be expressed in? A difference of 1.066 verbal ability units may be important or not, depending on the size of the unit. Since the regression weight for regressing **visperc** on spatial ability is equal to one, we can say that spatial ability is expressed in the same units as scores on the **visperc** test. Of course, this is useful information only if you happen to be familiar with the **visperc** test. There is another approach to evaluating the mean difference of 1.066, which does not involve **visperc**. Spatial ability has a standard deviation of about 4.0 among boys, and about 4.6 among girls. With standard deviations this large, a difference of 1.066 would not be considered very large for most purposes — certainly not when considering the moderate sample sizes of the Holzinger and Swineford study.

The statistical significance of the 1.066 unit difference between girls and boys is easy to evaluate. Since the boys' mean was fixed at zero, we only need to ask whether the girls' mean differs significantly from zero. Here are the girls' factor mean estimates given by **Amos Basic** together with standard error and critical ratio statistics:

```
Means:                 Estimate     S.E.      C.R.      Label
------                 --------    -------   -------   -------
          spatial      -1.066       0.881    -1.209     mn_s
          verbal        0.956       0.521     1.836     mn_v
```

The girls' mean spatial ability has a critical ratio of −1.209, so it is not significantly different from zero. In other words, it is not significantly different from the boys' mean.

Turning to verbal ability, the girls' mean is estimated 0.956 units *above* the boys' mean. For comparative purposes, verbal ability has a standard deviation of about 2.7 among boys, and about 3.15 among girls. Thus 0.956 verbal ability units is about one third of a standard deviation in either group. The difference between boys and girls approaches significance at the .05 level. The critical ratio for the girls' mean verbal ability is 1.836, close to the critical value for a standard normally distributed random variable.

Model B for boys and girls

In the discussion of Model A, we used critical ratios to carry out two tests of significance: a test for sex differences in spatial ability and a test for sex differences in verbal ability. We will now carry out a single test of the null hypothesis that all factor means are the same in both sexes. To do this, we will repeat the previous analysis, but add the constraint that boys and girls have the same average spatial and verbal abilities. Since the boys' means were fixed at zero in the previous analysis, requiring the girls' means to be the same as the boys' means amounts to setting the girls' means be equal to zero also.

Here is the listing of an **Amos Basic** input file, `Ex15-all.AmosBasic,` implementing the new Model B as a two-model comparison:

```
Sub Main()
  Dim Sem As New AmosEngine

  Sem.TextOutput
  Sem.Standardized
  Sem.Smc
  Sem.ModelMeansAndIntercepts

  Sem.BeginGroup "Grnt_fem.sav"
    Sem.GroupName "Girls"

    Sem.Structure "visperc  = (int_vis) +     (1) spatial + (1) err_v"
    Sem.Structure "cubes    = (int_cub) + (cube_s) spatial + (1) err_c"
    Sem.Structure "lozenges = (int_loz) + (lozn_s) spatial + (1) err_l"

    Sem.Structure "paragrap = (int_par) +     (1) verbal  + (1) err_p"
    Sem.Structure "sentence = (int_sen) + (sent_v) verbal  + (1) err_s"
    Sem.Structure "wordmean = (int_wrd) + (word_v) verbal  + (1) err_w"

    Sem.Mean "spatial", "mn_s"
    Sem.Mean "verbal", "mn_v"

  Sem.BeginGroup "Grnt_mal.sav"
    Sem.GroupName "Boys"

    Sem.Structure "visperc  = (int_vis) +     (1) spatial + (1) err_v"
    Sem.Structure "cubes    = (int_cub) + (cube_s) spatial + (1) err_c"
    Sem.Structure "lozenges = (int_loz) + (lozn_s) spatial + (1) err_l"

    Sem.Structure "paragrap = (int_par) +     (1) verbal  + (1) err_p"
    Sem.Structure "sentence = (int_sen) + (sent_v) verbal  + (1) err_s"
    Sem.Structure "wordmean = (int_wrd) + (word_v) verbal  + (1) err_w"

    Sem.Mstructure "spatial", "0"
    Sem.Mstructure "verbal", "0"

  Sem.Model "Model A"
  Sem.Model "Model B", "mn_s=0", "mn_v=0"

End Sub
```

With **Amos Graphics** input, the two models are defined in the model manager. Starting from the file **Ex15-a.amw** double click on Your model in the **Models** panel and define Models A as having no constraints and Model B with having these two parameter constraints:

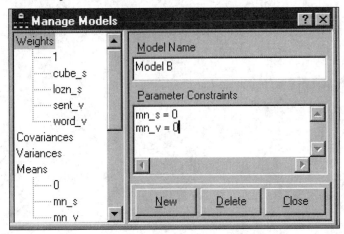

The file **Ex15-all.amw** contains this two-model setup.

Results for Model B

Had we not previously considered Model A, then we would now probably accept Model B at some conventional significance level:

```
Chi-square =      30.624
Degrees of freedom =    26
Probability level =      0.243
```

However, a stronger test of Model B is the comparison against Model A. The chi-square difference and its associated *p*-value is shown near the end of the list output in the two-model setup:

```
Model Comparisons
-----------------

Assuming Model_A to be correct:

                       df    chi-2      p
                       --    -----    -----
            Model_B     2    8.030    0.018
```

The test statistic for Model B, given Model A, is 8.030 with two degrees of freedom. The associated tail probability is only 0.018, indicating some evidence against Model B.

Example 16: Sörbom's Alternative to Analysis of Covariance

Purpose

- Demonstrate latent structural equation modeling with longitudinal observations in two or more groups.

- Provide examples of models that generalize traditional analysis of covariance techniques by incorporating latent variable terms and autocorrelated residuals (*cf.*, Sörbom, 1978).

- Show how specific assumptions employed by traditional analysis of covariance can be tested with this more general approach.

Introduction

Example 9 demonstrated an alternative to conventional analysis of covariance that works even with unreliable covariates. Unfortunately, analysis of covariance also depends on other assumptions besides the assumption of perfectly reliable covariates, and the method of Example 9 depends on those too. Sörbom (1978) developed a more general approach that allows us to test and relax many of those assumptions.

The present example uses the same data that Sörbom used to introduce his method. The modeling strategy in this example follows his exposition.

The data

We will again use the Olsson (1973) study introduced in Example 9. You will find the sample means, variances and covariances from the 108 experimental subjects in the Microsoft Excel worksheet **Olss_exp** in the workbook **UserGuide.xls**:

rowtype_	varname_	pre_syn	pre_opp	post_syn	post_opp
n		108	108	108	108
cov	pre_syn	50.084			
cov	pre_opp	42.373	49.872		
cov	post_syn	40.76	36.094	51.237	
cov	post_opp	37.343	40.396	39.89	53.641
mean		20.556	21.241	25.667	25.87

The sample means, variances and covariances from the 105 control subjects are in the worksheet **Olss_cnt**:

rowtype_	varname_	pre_syn	pre_opp	post_syn	post_opp
n		105	105	105	105
cov	pre_syn	37.626			
cov	pre_opp	24.933	34.68		
cov	post_syn	26.639	24.236	32.013	
cov	post_opp	23.649	27.76	23.565	33.443
mean		18.381	20.229	20.4	21.343

Note that both data sets contain the customary unbiased version of the variance and covariance estimates. That is, the elements in the covariance matrix were divided by $(N-1)$. This also happens to be Amos's default setting for *reading* covariance matrices. However, for the subsequent model fitting, Amos's default is the maximum likelihood version of the covariance matrix estimate (*i.e.*, divided by N). Amos performs the conversion automatically. You can change these settings if you want. We discuss the tradeoffs between analyzing ML vs. unbiased moment estimates in Appendix B of this User's Guide.

In **Amos Graphics**, you can click on the **Analysis properties** icon and the **Bias** tab to review these settings:

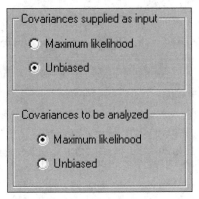

Amos's default setting yield results consistent with missing data modeling (discussed in Examples 17 and 18). Other SEM programs like LISREL (Jöreskog and Sörbom, 1989) and EQS (1985) analyze unbiased moments instead, resulting in slightly different solutions when sample sizes are small. In other words, checking both **Unbiased** options will cause Amos to produce the same estimates as LISREL or EQS.

Model A

Modeling in Amos Graphics

Consider Sörbom's initial model (Model A) for the Olsson data. The control group specification is:

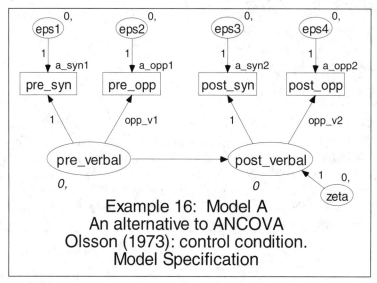

Example 16: Model A
An alternative to ANCOVA
Olsson (1973): control condition.
Model Specification

And for the experimental group, Model A looks like this:

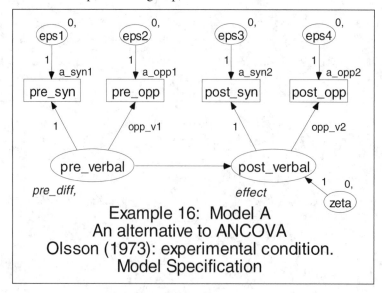

Example 16: Model A
An alternative to ANCOVA
Olsson (1973): experimental condition.
Model Specification

In each group, Model A specifies that **pre_syn** and **pre_opp** are indicators of a single latent variable called **pre_verbal**, and that **post_syn** and **post_opp** are indicators of another latent variable called **post_verbal**. The latent variable **pre_verbal** is interpreted as verbal ability at the beginning of the study, and **post_verbal** is interpreted as verbal ability at the conclusion of the study. This is Sörbom's *measurement* model.

The *structural* model specifies that **post_verbal** depends linearly on **pre_verbal**, although the slope and intercept of this regression is allowed to be different in the two groups.

The labels **opp_v1** and **opp_v2** for the regression weights and **a_syn1**, **a_opp1**, **a_syn2** and **a_opp2** for the intercepts of the measurement model set these parameters to the same values in the two groups. This assumption could turn out to be wrong. In fact, one result of the upcoming analyses will be a test of this assumption. As Sörbom points out, some assumptions have to be made about the parameters of the measurement model. This is so we can compare those parameters with the groups' parameters in the structural model. The assumption that the measurement model has the same regression weights in both groups is plausible, and Sörbom showed that it is sufficient.

For the *control* subjects, the mean of **pre_verbal** and the intercept of **post_verbal** are fixed at zero (0). This establishes the control group as a reference condition for the group comparison. You need to pick such a reference to make the factor mean structure(s) identifiable. For the *experimental* subjects, the mean and intercept parameters of the latent factors are allowed to be nonzero. The term *pre_diff* represents the difference in verbal ability prior to treatment (coaching), and the term *effect* represents the improvement of the experimental group relative to the control group. The **Amos Graphics** file for this example is **Ex16-a.amw**.

Also note that Sörbom's model imposes no between-group constraints on the variance terms of the six latent exogenous variables. Thus, the four observed variables may show different unique variance components in the control and experimental conditions. The common variance components, given by the variance estimates of **pre_verbal** and **zeta**, may also be different. We will investigate these assumptions more closely when we review Models X, Y and Z.

Modeling in Amos Basic

The **Amos Basic** file for Model A is `Ex16-a.AmosBasic`:

```
Sub Main()
  Dim Sem As New AmosEngine

  Sem.TextOutput
  Sem.Mods 4
  Sem.Standardized
  Sem.Smc
  Sem.ModelMeansAndIntercepts

  Sem.BeginGroup "UserGuide.xls", "Olss_cnt"
    Sem.GroupName "control"
    Sem.Structure "pre_syn  = (a_syn1) + (1)    pre_verbal  + (1) eps1"
    Sem.Structure "pre_opp  = (a_opp1) + (opp_v1) pre_verbal  + (1) eps2"
    Sem.Structure "post_syn = (a_syn2) + (1)     post_verbal + (1) eps3"
    Sem.Structure "post_opp = (a_opp2) + (opp_v2) post_verbal + (1) eps4"

    Sem.Structure "post_verbal = (0) + () pre_verbal + (1) zeta"

  Sem.BeginGroup "UserGuide.xls", "Olss_exp"
    Sem.GroupName "experimental"
    Sem.Structure "pre_syn  = (a_syn1) + (1)    pre_verbal  + (1) eps1"
    Sem.Structure "pre_opp  = (a_opp1) + (opp_v1) pre_verbal  + (1) eps2"
    Sem.Structure "post_syn = (a_syn2) + (1)     post_verbal + (1) eps3"
    Sem.Structure "post_opp = (a_opp2) + (opp_v2) post_verbal + (1) eps4"

    Sem.Structure "post_verbal = (effect) + () pre_verbal + (1) zeta"

    Sem.Mean "pre_verbal", "pre_diff"

End Sub
```

Results for Model A

Unfortunately, we cannot accept Model A at any conventional significance level:

```
Chi-square =      34.775
Degrees of freedom =     6
Probability level =     0.000
```

We also get the following message that helps confirm that Model A is wrong:

```
The following variances are negative

        zeta
        --------
         -2.868
This solution is not admissible.
```

The evidence against Model A is convincing because of both the chi-square statistic and because the solution is inadmissible. Can we modify Model A, so that it will fit the data while still permitting a meaningful comparison of the experimental and control groups? The statement Sem.Mods=4 in the previous input file produces a listing of modification indices that exceed 4. There will be a separate listing for the control group and for the experimental group. In the control group, no modification index exceeds 4, so the display for that group will be empty.

Here is the modification index output from the experimental group:

```
Modification Indices
--------------------


Covariances:                                 M.I.      Par Change
                                          ---------   ----------
        eps2 <----------------> eps4       10.508        4.700
        eps2 <----------------> eps3        8.980       -4.021
        eps1 <----------------> eps4        8.339       -3.908
        eps1 <----------------> eps3        7.058        3.310


Variances:                                   M.I.      Par Change
                                          ---------   ----------


Regression Weights:                          M.I.      Par Change
                                          ---------   ----------


Means:                                       M.I.      Par Change
                                          ---------   ----------


Intercepts:                                  M.I.      Par Change
                                          ---------   ----------
```

Model B

The largest modification index obtained with Model A is for the covariance between **eps2** and **eps4** in the experimental group. This indicates that the chi-square statistic will drop by at least 10.508 if **eps2** and **eps4** are allowed to have a nonzero covariance. The parameter change statistic of 4.700 indicates that the covariance estimate will be positive if set free. The term **eps2** represents unique variation of **pre_opp**, and **eps4** represents unique variation of **post_opp**, where the observed variables **pre_opp** and **post_opp** are obtained by administering the same test, *opposites*, on two different occasions. It is therefore reasonable to assume some positive correlation between **eps2** and **eps4**, on statistical as well as applied grounds.

Modeling in Amos Graphics

The next step is to consider the revised Model B, with unique terms **eps2** and **eps4** correlated in the experimental group. Do this in **Amos Graphics** by adding a two-headed arrow between **eps2** and **eps4**. Estimate the covariance of these two terms in the experimental group, but constrain it to zero in the control group. Follow the path **View/Set** → **Object Properties** → **Parameters** tab to be sure the **All groups** check box is empty. By leaving it unchecked, the constraint applies only to the control group:

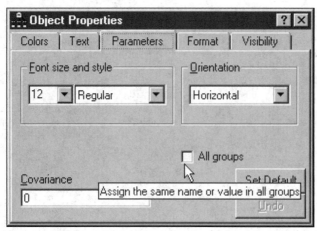

Model B for the *control* subjects is:

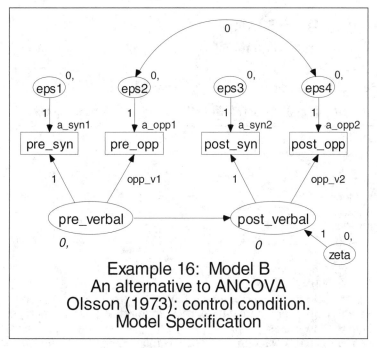

Example 16: Model B
An alternative to ANCOVA
Olsson (1973): control condition.
Model Specification

Model B for the *experimental* subjects is:

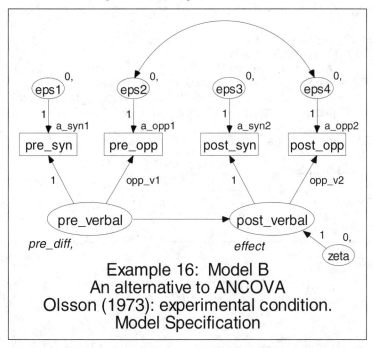

Example 16: Model B
An alternative to ANCOVA
Olsson (1973): experimental condition.
Model Specification

The **Amos Graphics** input file for this example is `Ex16-b.amw`.

Modeling in Amos Basic

To specify Model B in **Amos Basic**, just add the line:

```
eps2 <---> eps4
```

to the Sem.Structure statement for the experimental group.

The full specification of Model B, from file `Ex16-b.AmosBasic`, is:

```
Sub Main()
    Dim Sem As New AmosEngine

    Sem.TextOutput
    Sem.Mods 4
    Sem.Standardized
    Sem.Smc
    Sem.ModelMeansAndIntercepts

    Sem.BeginGroup "UserGuide.xls", "Olss_cnt"
        Sem.GroupName "control"
        Sem.Structure "pre_syn  = (a_syn1) + (1)     pre_verbal  + (1) eps1"
        Sem.Structure "pre_opp  = (a_opp1) + (opp_v1) pre_verbal  + (1) eps2"
        Sem.Structure "post_syn = (a_syn2) + (1)     post_verbal + (1) eps3"
        Sem.Structure "post_opp = (a_opp2) + (opp_v2) post_verbal + (1) eps4"

        Sem.Structure "post_verbal = (0) + () pre_verbal + (1) zeta"

    Sem.BeginGroup "UserGuide.xls", "Olss_exp"
        Sem.GroupName "experimental"
        Sem.Structure "pre_syn  = (a_syn1) + (1)     pre_verbal  + (1) eps1"
        Sem.Structure "pre_opp  = (a_opp1) + (opp_v1) pre_verbal  + (1) eps2"
        Sem.Structure "post_syn = (a_syn2) + (1)     post_verbal + (1) eps3"
        Sem.Structure "post_opp = (a_opp2) + (opp_v2) post_verbal + (1) eps4"

        Sem.Structure "post_verbal = (effect) + () pre_verbal + (1) zeta"

        Sem.Structure "eps2 <---> eps4"

        Sem.Mean "pre_verbal", "pre_diff"

End Sub
```

Results for Model B

In moving from Model A to Model B, the chi-square statistic dropped by 17.712 (more than the promised 10.508) while the number of degrees of freedom dropped by just one:

```
Chi-square =      17.063
Degrees of freedom =    5
Probability level =     0.004
```

Model B is certainly an improvement over Model A, but still does not fit the data well. Furthermore, the variance of **zeta** in the *control* group has a negative estimate (not shown here), just as it had for Model A. These two facts argue strongly against Model B. There is room for improvement, however, because the modification indices (produced by Sem.Mods 4) suggest further modifications of Model B. The listed modification indices for the control group are:

```
Modification Indices
--------------------


Covariances:                                      M.I.      Par Change
                                                --------    ----------
              eps2 <-----------------> eps4      4.727        2.141
              eps1 <-----------------> eps4      4.086       -2.384
```

The remaining modification indices, including those for the experimental group, are all less than four. The largest modification index (of 4.727) is for the covariance term between **eps2** and **eps4** in the control group, suggesting that the unique terms for the *opposites* test should be correlated not only in the experimental group, but in the control group as well.

Model C

Model C is just like Model B, except that the terms **eps2** and **eps4** are correlated in both control and experimental groups.

Modeling in Amos Graphics

To specify Model C, simply relax the covariance parameter between **eps2** and **eps4** in the control group of Model B. Here is the view of the new control group structure, as found in file **Ex16-c.amw**:

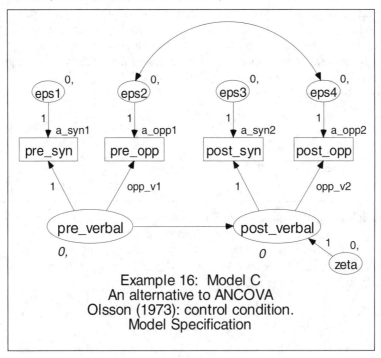

Example 16: Model C
An alternative to ANCOVA
Olsson (1973): control condition.
Model Specification

Modeling in Amos Basic

The **Amos Basic** input, from file **Ex16-c.AmosBasic**, for Model C is:

```
Sub Main()
    Dim Sem As New AmosEngine

    Sem.TextOutput
    Sem.Mods 4
    Sem.Standardized
    Sem.Smc
    Sem.ModelMeansAndIntercepts

    Sem.BeginGroup "UserGuide.xls", "Olss_cnt"
        Sem.GroupName "control"
        Sem.Structure "pre_syn  = (a_syn1) + (1)     pre_verbal  + (1) eps1"
        Sem.Structure "pre_opp  = (a_opp1) + (opp_v1) pre_verbal  + (1) eps2"
        Sem.Structure "post_syn = (a_syn2) + (1)     post_verbal + (1) eps3"
        Sem.Structure "post_opp = (a_opp2) + (opp_v2) post_verbal + (1) eps4"

        Sem.Structure "post_verbal = (0) + () pre_verbal + (1) zeta"

        Sem.Structure "eps2 <---> eps4"

    Sem.BeginGroup "UserGuide.xls", "Olss_exp"
        Sem.GroupName "experimental"
        Sem.Structure "pre_syn  = (a_syn1) + (1)     pre_verbal  + (1) eps1"
        Sem.Structure "pre_opp  = (a_opp1) + (opp_v1) pre_verbal  + (1) eps2"
        Sem.Structure "post_syn = (a_syn2) + (1)     post_verbal + (1) eps3"
        Sem.Structure "post_opp = (a_opp2) + (opp_v2) post_verbal + (1) eps4"

        Sem.Structure "post_verbal = (effect) + () pre_verbal + (1) zeta"

        Sem.Structure "eps2 <---> eps4"

        Sem.Mean "pre_verbal", "pre_diff"

End Sub
```

Results for Model C

When running the model in **Amos Graphics**, be sure you have checked the **Estimate means and intercepts** box found by following the path: <u>V</u>iew/Set → <u>A</u>nalysis Properties → **Estimation** tab.

Finally, we have a model that fits:

```
Chi-square =        2.797
Degrees of freedom =     4
Probability level =      0.592
```

From the point of view of statistical goodness of fit, there is no reason to reject Model C. Perhaps even more importantly, all the variance estimates are positive. Here are the parameter estimates for the 105 control subjects:

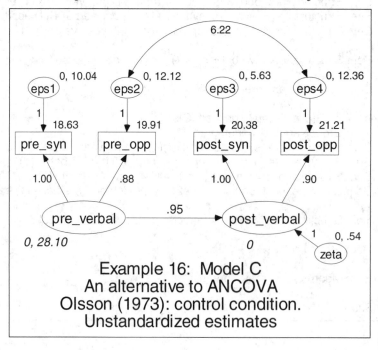

Example 16: Model C
An alternative to ANCOVA
Olsson (1973): control condition.
Unstandardized estimates

And here is a path diagram displaying the parameter estimates for the 108 experimental subjects:

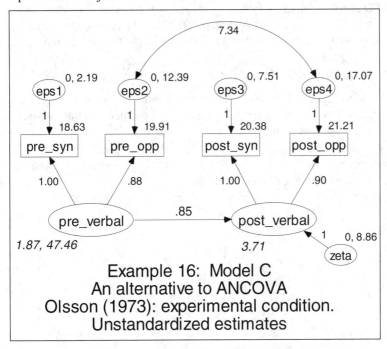

Example 16: Model C
An alternative to ANCOVA
Olsson (1973): experimental condition.
Unstandardized estimates

Most of these parameter estimates are not very interesting, though you may want to inspect whether they have *reasonable* values. We have already noted that the variance estimates are all positive. The path coefficients in the measurement model are likewise positive, which is reassuring. Mixed positive and negative regression weights in the measurement model would have been difficult to interpret and would cast doubt on the model. The covariance between **eps2** and **eps4** is positive in both groups, as expected.

Our primary concern is with the regression of **post_verbal** on **pre_verbal**. The intercept, fixed at zero in the control group, is estimated to be 3.71 in the experimental group. The regression weight is estimated at 0.95 in the control group and 0.85 in the experimental group. The regression weights for the two groups are close and might even be identical in the two populations. Identical regression weights would allow a greatly simplified evaluation of the treatment, limiting the comparison of the two groups to a comparison of their intercepts. It is therefore worthwhile to try such a model.

Model D

Model D specifies equal regression weights in the structural model. That is, Model D is just like Model C except that it specifies that the regression weight for predicting **post_verbal** from **pre_verbal** is the same for both groups.

Modeling in Amos Graphics

For the path diagram, we introduce one more parameter constrained to be equal in both groups: a common parameter for the path from **pre_verbal** to **post_verbal**, which will be named pre2post. The path diagram for the experimental subjects follows below. The diagram for the control subjects differs only in that the mean for **pre_verbal** and the intercept for **post_verbal** are both fixed at zero. The **Amos Graphics** input file is **Ex16-d.amw**.

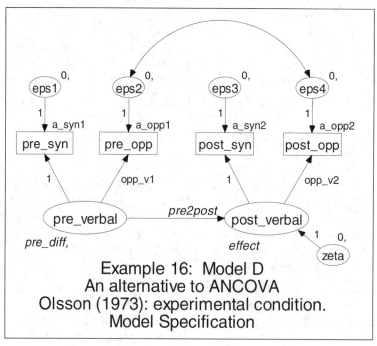

Example 16: Model D
An alternative to ANCOVA
Olsson (1973): experimental condition.
Model Specification

Modeling in Amos Basic

The **Amos Basic** input file `Ex16-d.AmosBasic` implements Model B:

```
Sub Main()
    Dim Sem As New AmosEngine

    Sem.TextOutput
    Sem.Mods 4
    Sem.Standardized
    Sem.Smc
    Sem.ModelMeansAndIntercepts

    Sem.BeginGroup "UserGuide.xls", "Olss_cnt"
        Sem.GroupName "control"
        Sem.Structure "pre_syn  = (a_syn1) + (1)     pre_verbal  + (1) eps1"
        Sem.Structure "pre_opp  = (a_opp1) + (opp_v1) pre_verbal  + (1) eps2"
        Sem.Structure "post_syn = (a_syn2) + (1)      post_verbal + (1) eps3"
        Sem.Structure "post_opp = (a_opp2) + (opp_v2) post_verbal + (1) eps4"

        Sem.Structure "post_verbal = (0) + (pre2post) pre_verbal + (1) zeta"

        Sem.Structure "eps2 <---> eps4"

    Sem.BeginGroup "UserGuide.xls", "Olss_exp"
        Sem.GroupName "experimental"
        Sem.Structure "pre_syn  = (a_syn1) + (1)     pre_verbal  + (1) eps1"
        Sem.Structure "pre_opp  = (a_opp1) + (opp_v1) pre_verbal  + (1) eps2"
        Sem.Structure "post_syn = (a_syn2) + (1)      post_verbal + (1) eps3"
        Sem.Structure "post_opp = (a_opp2) + (opp_v2) post_verbal + (1) eps4"

        Sem.Structure "post_verbal = (effect) + (pre2post) pre_verbal + (1) zeta"

        Sem.Structure "eps2 <---> eps4"

        Sem.Mean "pre_verbal", "pre_diff"

End Sub
```

Results for Model D

Model D would be accepted at conventional significance levels:

```
Chi-square =        3.976
Degrees of freedom =    5
Probability level =     0.553
```

Testing Model D against Model C gives a chi-square value of 1.179 (= 3.976 – 2.797) with 1 (= 5 – 4) degree of freedom. Again, you would accept the hypothesis of equal regression weights.

With equal regression weights, the comparison of treated and untreated subjects can now focus on the difference between their intercepts. Here are the parameter estimates for the 105 control subjects:

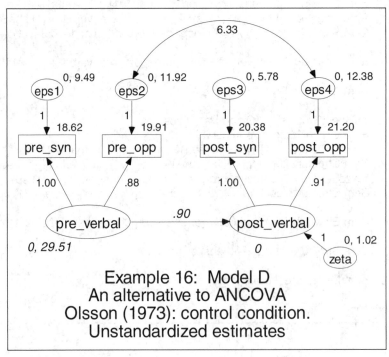

Example 16: Model D
An alternative to ANCOVA
Olsson (1973): control condition.
Unstandardized estimates

The estimates for the 108 experimental subjects are:

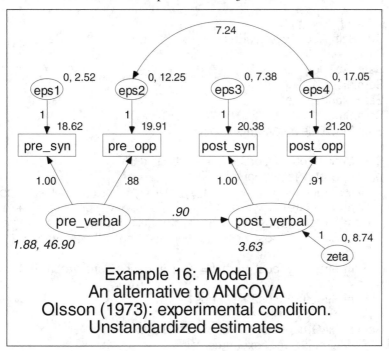

Example 16: Model D
An alternative to ANCOVA
Olsson (1973): experimental condition.
Unstandardized estimates

The parameter estimates look reasonable, so we will proceed to a discussion of the intercepts. The intercept (additive constant) for the experimental group is estimated as 3.627, with an associated critical ratio of 7.591. Thus, the intercept for the experimental group is significantly different from the intercept for the control group, which happens to be fixed at zero.

Model E

Another way of testing the difference in **post_verbal** intercepts is to repeat the Model D analysis with equality constraints added. Since the intercept for the control group is already fixed at zero, we need to add the requirement that the intercept be equal to zero in the experimental group as well. This restriction is used in Model E.

The **Amos Basic** input file, named `Ex16-e.AmosBasic`, is:

```
Sub Main()
  Dim Sem As New AmosEngine

  Sem.TextOutput
  Sem.Mods 4
  Sem.Standardized
  Sem.Smc
  Sem.ModelMeansAndIntercepts

  Sem.BeginGroup "UserGuide.xls", "Olss_cnt"
    Sem.GroupName "control"
    Sem.Structure "pre_syn  = (a_syn1) + (1)     pre_verbal  + (1) eps1"
    Sem.Structure "pre_opp  = (a_opp1) + (opp_v1) pre_verbal  + (1) eps2"
    Sem.Structure "post_syn = (a_syn2) + (1)     post_verbal + (1) eps3"
    Sem.Structure "post_opp = (a_opp2) + (opp_v2) post_verbal + (1) eps4"

    Sem.Structure "post_verbal = (0) + (pre2post) pre_verbal + (1) zeta"

    Sem.Structure "eps2 <---> eps4"

  Sem.BeginGroup "UserGuide.xls", "Olss_exp"
    Sem.GroupName "experimental"
    Sem.Structure "pre_syn  = (a_syn1) + (1)     pre_verbal  + (1) eps1"
    Sem.Structure "pre_opp  = (a_opp1) + (opp_v1) pre_verbal  + (1) eps2"
    Sem.Structure "post_syn = (a_syn2) + (1)     post_verbal + (1) eps3"
    Sem.Structure "post_opp = (a_opp2) + (opp_v2) post_verbal + (1) eps4"

    Sem.Structure "post_verbal = (0) + (pre2post) pre_verbal + (1) zeta"

    Sem.Structure "eps2 <---> eps4"

    Sem.Mean "pre_verbal", "pre_diff"

End Sub
```

The **Amos Graphics** specification of Model E is just like that of Model D, except that the intercept in the regression of **post_verbal** on **pre_verbal** is fixed at 0 in *both* groups. The **Amos Graphics** input file is `Ex16-e.amw` (not reproduced here).

Results for Model E

Model E has to be rejected:

```
Chi-square =      55.094
Degrees of freedom =    6
Probability level =     0.000
```

Comparing Model E against Model D yields a chi-square value of 51.018 (= 55.094 – 3.976) with 1 (= 6 – 5) degree of freedom. Model E has to be rejected in favor of Model D. Because the fit of Model E is significantly worse than that of Model D, the hypothesis of equal intercepts again has to be rejected.

In other words, the control and experimental groups differ at the time of the posttest in a way that cannot be accounted for by differences that existed at the time of the pretest. The experimenter thus attributes the difference at the time of the posttest to the intervening test coaching treatment.

Multiple model input

The previous five examples can be entered into a single file, using suitably modified parameter labels. The **Amos Basic** multiple-model specification, from the file **Ex16_a2e.AmosBasic**, is:

```
Sub Main()
   Dim Sem As New AmosEngine

   Sem.TextOutput
   Sem.Mods 4
   Sem.Standardized
   Sem.Smc
   Sem.ModelMeansAndIntercepts

   Sem.BeginGroup "UserGuide.xls", "Olss_cnt"
      Sem.GroupName "control"
      Sem.Structure "pre_syn  = (a_syn1) + (1)     pre_verbal  + (1) eps1"
      Sem.Structure "pre_opp  = (a_opp1) + (opp_v1) pre_verbal  + (1) eps2"
      Sem.Structure "post_syn = (a_syn2) + (1)      post_verbal + (1) eps3"
      Sem.Structure "post_opp = (a_opp2) + (opp_v2) post_verbal + (1) eps4"

      Sem.Structure "post_verbal = (0) + (c_beta) pre_verbal + (1) zeta"

      Sem.Structure "eps2 <---> eps4  (c_e2e4)"

   Sem.BeginGroup "UserGuide.xls", "Olss_exp"
      Sem.GroupName "experimental"
      Sem.Structure "pre_syn  = (a_syn1) + (1)     pre_verbal  + (1) eps1"
      Sem.Structure "pre_opp  = (a_opp1) + (opp_v1) pre_verbal  + (1) eps2"
      Sem.Structure "post_syn = (a_syn2) + (1)      post_verbal + (1) eps3"
      Sem.Structure "post_opp = (a_opp2) + (opp_v2) post_verbal + (1) eps4"

      Sem.Structure "post_verbal = (effect) + (e_beta) pre_verbal + (1) zeta"

      Sem.Structure "eps2 <---> eps4  (e_e2e4)"

      Sem.Mean "pre_verbal", "pre_diff"

   Sem.Model "Model A", "c_e2e4 = 0", "e_e2e4 = 0"
   Sem.Model "Model B", "c_e2e4 = 0"
   Sem.Model "Model C"
   Sem.Model "Model D", "c_beta = e_beta"
   Sem.Model "Model E", "c_beta = e_beta", "effect = 0"
End Sub
```

The corresponding multiple-model specification for **Amos Graphics** is given in the file **Ex16-a2e.amw** (not shown here).

This completes Sörbom's (1978) analysis of the Olsson data.

Comparison of Sörbom's method with the method of Example 9

Sörbom's alternative to analysis of covariance is more difficult to apply than the method of Example 9. If you are trying to choose between the two methods, realize that Sörbom's method is not just different from the method of Example 9, but superior in the sense of being more general. That is, you can duplicate the method of Example 9 by using Sörbom's method with suitable parameter constraints.

We end this example with three additional models called X, Y and Z. Comparisons among these new models will allow us to duplicate the results of Example 9. However, we will also find evidence that the method used in Example 9 was inappropriate. The purpose of this fairly complicated exercise is to call attention to the limitations of Example 9's alternative to an analysis of covariance, and to show that some of the assumptions of that method can be tested and relaxed in Sörbom's approach.

Model X

First, consider a new Model X, say, which requires that the variances and covariances of the observed variables are the same for the control and experimental conditions. The means of the observed variables may differ between the two populations. Model X does not specify any linear dependencies among the variables. The assumptions of Model X are rather basic, and the model may not appear interesting at all. However, the subsequent Models Y and Z *are* interesting, and we will want to know how well they fit the data, compared to Model X.

Modeling in Amos Basic

The **Amos Basic** specification of Model X, from file **Ex16-x.AmosBasic**, is:

```
Sub Main()
  Dim Sem As New AmosEngine

  Sem.TextOutput
  Sem.Mods 4
  Sem.Standardized
  Sem.Smc

  Sem.BeginGroup "UserGuide.xls", "Olss_cnt"
    Sem.GroupName "control"
    Sem.Structure "pre_syn (v_s1)"
    Sem.Structure "pre_opp (v_o1)"
    Sem.Structure "post_syn (v_s2)"
    Sem.Structure "post_opp (v_o2)"
    Sem.Structure "pre_opp <--> pre_syn (c_s1o1)"
    Sem.Structure "post_opp <--> pre_opp (c_o1o2)"
    Sem.Structure "post_syn <--> post_opp (c_s2o2)"
    Sem.Structure "pre_syn <--> post_syn (c_s1s2)"
    Sem.Structure "post_opp <--> pre_syn (c_s1o2)"
    Sem.Structure "post_syn <--> pre_opp (c_s2o1)"

  Sem.BeginGroup "UserGuide.xls", "Olss_exp"
    Sem.GroupName "experimental"
    Sem.Structure "pre_syn (v_s1)"
    Sem.Structure "pre_opp (v_o1)"
    Sem.Structure "post_syn (v_s2)"
    Sem.Structure "post_opp (v_o2)"
    Sem.Structure "pre_opp <--> pre_syn (c_s1o1)"
    Sem.Structure "post_opp <--> pre_opp (c_o1o2)"
    Sem.Structure "post_syn <--> post_opp (c_s2o2)"
    Sem.Structure "pre_syn <--> post_syn (c_s1s2)"
    Sem.Structure "post_opp <--> pre_syn (c_s1o2)"
    Sem.Structure "post_syn <--> pre_opp (c_s2o1)"

End Sub
```

The Sem.Mstructure statement is not used in this file, because Model X does not impose any assumptions on the population means. No intercepts are used either, since the model contains no regression equations. Model X simply requires estimating the population variances and covariances under the assumption that they are group-invariant, and Amos will compute fit statistics for this hypothesis. Thus, Amos does not need to estimate the means of the four observed variables.

Modeling in Amos Graphics

Because there are no intercepts or means to estimate, deselect the **Estimate Means and Intercepts** box (**Estimation** tab) in the **Analysis Properties** menu. The **Amos Graphics** file for Model X is **Ex16-x.amw**, with the group-invariant path diagram:

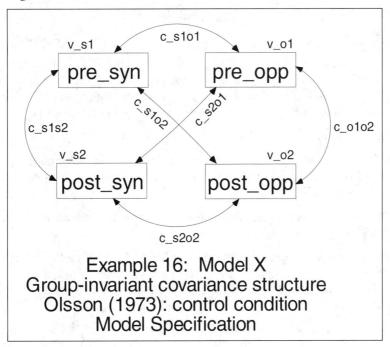

Example 16: Model X
Group-invariant covariance structure
Olsson (1973): control condition
Model Specification

Results for Model X

Model X has to be rejected at nearly any level of significance.

```
Chi-square =     29.145
Degrees of freedom =   10
Probability level =      0.001
```

The analyses that follow (Models Y and Z) are actually inappropriate now that we are satisfied that Model X is inappropriate. We will carry out the analyses as an exercise in order to demonstrate that they yield the same results as obtained in Example 9.

Model Y

Consider a model that is just like Model D, but with these additional constraints:

- Verbal ability at the pretest (**pre_verbal**) has the same variance in the control and experimental groups.

- The variances of **eps1**, **eps2**, **eps3**, **eps4** and **zeta** are the same for both groups.

- The covariance between **eps2** and **eps4** is the same for both groups.

Apart from the correlation between **eps2** and **eps4**, Model D required that **eps1**, **eps2**, **eps3**, **eps4** and **zeta** be uncorrelated among themselves and with every other exogenous variable. These new constraints amount to requiring that the variances and covariances of *all exogenous* variables be the same for both groups.

Altogether, the new model imposes two kinds of constraints:

- All regression weights and intercepts are the same for both groups, except possibly for the intercept used in predicting **post_verbal** from **pre_verbal** (Model D requirements).

- The variances and covariances of the exogenous variables are the same for both groups (additional Model Y requirements).

These are the same assumptions we made in Model B of Example 9. The difference this time is that the assumptions are made explicit and can be tested. We will skip the **Amos Graphics** input for Model Y, which can be found in the file `Ex16-y.amw`.

The **Amos Basic** input file (`Ex16-y.AmosBasic`) for Model Y follows:

```
Sub Main()
   Dim Sem As New AmosEngine

   Sem.TextOutput
   Sem.Mods 4
   Sem.Standardized
   Sem.Smc
   Sem.ModelMeansAndIntercepts

   Sem.BeginGroup "UserGuide.xls", "Olss_cnt"
      Sem.GroupName "control"
      Sem.Structure "pre_syn  = (a_syn1) + (1)     pre_verbal  + (1) eps1"
      Sem.Structure "pre_opp  = (a_opp1) + (opp_v1) pre_verbal  + (1) eps2"
      Sem.Structure "post_syn = (a_syn2) + (1)     post_verbal + (1) eps3"
      Sem.Structure "post_opp = (a_opp2) + (opp_v2) post_verbal + (1) eps4"

      Sem.Structure "post_verbal = (0) + (pre2post) pre_verbal + (1) zeta"

      Sem.Structure "eps2 <---> eps4 (c_e2e4)"
      Sem.Structure "pre_verbal (v_v1)"
      Sem.Structure "zeta      (v_z)"
      Sem.Structure "eps1      (v_e1)"
      Sem.Structure "eps2      (v_e2)"
      Sem.Structure "eps3      (v_e3)"
      Sem.Structure "eps4      (v_e4)"

   Sem.BeginGroup "UserGuide.xls", "Olss_exp"
      Sem.GroupName "experimental"
      Sem.Structure "pre_syn  = (a_syn1) + (1)     pre_verbal  + (1) eps1"
      Sem.Structure "pre_opp  = (a_opp1) + (opp_v1) pre_verbal  + (1) eps2"
      Sem.Structure "post_syn = (a_syn2) + (1)     post_verbal + (1) eps3"
      Sem.Structure "post_opp = (a_opp2) + (opp_v2) post_verbal + (1) eps4"

      Sem.Structure "post_verbal = (effect) + (pre2post) pre_verbal + (1) zeta"

      Sem.Structure "eps2 <---> eps4 (c_e2e4)"
      Sem.Structure "pre_verbal (v_v1)"
      Sem.Structure "zeta      (v_z)"
      Sem.Structure "eps1      (v_e1)"
      Sem.Structure "eps2      (v_e2)"
      Sem.Structure "eps3      (v_e3)"
      Sem.Structure "eps4      (v_e4)"

      Sem.Mean "pre_verbal", "pre_diff"

End Sub
```

Results for Model Y

We must reject Model Y:

```
Chi-square =      31.816
Degrees of freedom =   12
Probability level =    0.001
```

This is a good reason for being dissatisfied with the analysis of Example 9, since it depended upon Model Y (which, in Example 9, was called Model B) being correct. If you look back at Example 9, you will see that we accepted Model B there (χ^2 = 2.684, df = 2, p = .261). So how can we say that the same model has to be rejected here (χ^2 = 31.816, df = 1, p = .001)? The answer is that, while the null hypothesis is the same in both cases (Model B in Example 9 and Model Y in the present example), the alternative hypotheses are different. In Example 9, the alternative against which Model B is tested includes the assumption that the variances and covariances of the observed variables are the same for both values of the **treatment** variable (also stated in the *Technical Note* near the end of Example 1). In other words, the test of Model B carried out in Example 9 implicitly assumed homogeneity of variances and covariances for the control and experimental populations. This is the very assumption that is made explicit in Model X of the present example.

Model Y is a restricted version of Model X. It can be shown that the assumptions of Model Y (equal regression weights for the two populations, and equal variances and covariances of the exogenous variables) imply the assumptions of Model X (equal covariances for the observed variables). Models X and Y are therefore *nested* models, and it is possible to carry out a *conditional* test of Model Y given that Model X is true. Of course, it will only make sense to do that test if Model X really were true, and we have already concluded it is not. Nevertheless, we will continue by testing Model Y against Model X. The difference in chi-square values is 2.671 (*i.e.*, 31.816 – 29.145) with 2 (= 12 – 10) degrees of freedom. These figures are identical (within rounding error) to those of Example 9, Model B. The difference is that, in Example 9 we assumed that the test was appropriate. Now we are quite sure (because we rejected Model X) that it is not.

If you have any doubts that the current Model Y is the same as Model B of Example 9, you should compare the parameter estimates from the two analyses. Here are the Model Y parameter estimates for the 108 experimental subjects. Note that we followed the path: **View/Set → <u>A</u>nalysis Properties** and reselected the **Estimate Means and Intercepts** box to get these results. See if you can match up these estimates displayed here with the unstandardized (or *raw*) parameter estimates obtained by Model B of Example 9.

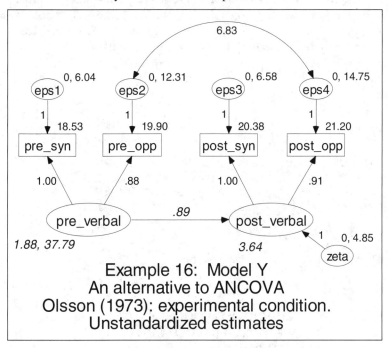

Example 16: Model Y
An alternative to ANCOVA
Olsson (1973): experimental condition.
Unstandardized estimates

Model Z

Finally, construct a new model (Model Z) by adding to Model Y the requirement that the intercept in the equation for predicting **post_verbal** from **pre_verbal** be the same in both populations. This model is equivalent to Model C of Example 9. The **Amos Graphics** model specification for the experimental condition, from file **Ex16-z.amw**, follows (the **Amos Basic** input file, **Ex16-z.AmosBasic**, is not shown). Once again, note that we checked the **Estimate Means and Intercepts** box in the **Analysis Properties** menu to get these results.

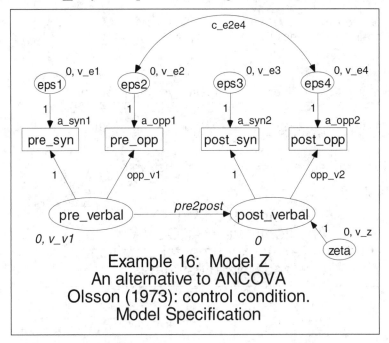

Example 16: Model Z
An alternative to ANCOVA
Olsson (1973): control condition.
Model Specification

Results for Model Z

We must also reject this model.

```
Chi-square =     84.280
Degrees of freedom =   13
Probability level =     0.000
```

Model Z also has to be rejected when compared to Model Y (χ^2-*difference* = $84.280 - 31.816 = 52.464$, *df* = 13 -12 = 1). Within rounding error, this is the same difference in chi-square values and degrees of freedom as in Example 9, when Model C was compared to Model B.

Example 17: Missing Data

Purpose

- Demonstrate the use of full information factor analysis when there are missing data.

Introduction

What happens when anticipated data values fail to materialize? Perhaps a subject fails to participate in part of a study. Or maybe a person filling out a questionnaire skips a couple of questions. Some people avoid giving their age and others refuse to report their income. Then there are the no-shows the day you measure reaction times. For one reason or another, your data set has gaps. What do you do?

One standard method for dealing with incomplete data is to just eliminate any observations where some data value is missing. This is often called *listwise* deletion (LD). For example, if respondents fail to report their income, you would simply eliminate them from your study. You would then proceed with a conventional analysis based on complete data — but with the reduced sample size. This method is unsatisfactory because you have to discard all the valuable information the person *did* give. And if you have lots of missing values (as commonly occurs), you may end up tossing out the bulk of your sample by using this method.

Then there is another standard approach, called *pairwise* deletion (PD). Pairwise deletion calculates each sample moment separately. This method excludes an observation from the calculation only when it is missing a value that is needed for the computation of that particular moment. For example, if you were calculating the sample mean income, you would exclude all people whose incomes you do not know. Similarly, in computing the sample covariance between age and income you

---

would exclude all observations where income is missing, plus all records without age information.

A third approach is data *imputation*. The concept here is to replace the missing values with some kind of guess, and then proceed with a conventional analysis appropriate for complete data. For example, you might compute the mean income of the persons who reported their income, and then attribute that income to all persons who did not report their income (means imputation, or MI for short). Beale and Little (1975) discuss methods for data imputation, which are implemented in many statistical packages.

Amos does not use any of these methods. Even in the presence of missing data, it computes full information maximum likelihood (FIML) estimates (Anderson, 1957) — a far more satisfying approach.

> *Because Amos computes full maximum likelihood estimates in the presence of missing data, you may prefer to use Amos to do a conventional analysis, such as a simple regression analysis (as in Example 4) or to estimate means only (as in Example 13).*

In order to discuss the advantages of FIML over MI, PD, and LD, it is useful to consider the mechanisms by which missing data can arise. Rubin (1976) and Little and Rubin (1987) distinguish the processes that generate the missing data with respect to the information they provide about the unobserved data. Missing values of a random variable Y can be *missing completely at random* (MCAR), *missing at random* (MAR), or *nonignorable*.

- MCAR means that whether the data are missing is entirely unrelated statistically to the values that would have been observed. MCAR is the most restrictive assumption. MCAR can sometimes be established in behavioral and social surveys by randomly assigning test booklets or blocks of survey questions to different respondents.

- MAR is a somewhat more relaxed condition. It means that missingness and data values are statistically unrelated, *conditional* on a set of predictor or stratifying variables X. One way to establish MAR processes is to include completely observed variables X that are highly predictive of incomplete data Y. For instance, initial (complete) measurement(s) in longitudinal designs can sometimes serve as a good choice of X.

- Under the third case, nonignorable missing data, missingness conveys probabilistic information about the values that would have been observed, beyond all the information already given in the observed data.

The performance of several or all of the four methods under the three types of missingness has been studied, among others, by Arbuckle (1996), Brown (1983), Brown (1994), Graham *et al.* (1997), Little and Rubin (1987), Little and Schenker (1995), Verleye (1996), and Wothke (1999).

For MCAR data, FIML, PD and LD all yield consistent solutions, but PD and LD are generally not as efficient as FIML. MI is consistent in the first moments but yields biased variance and covariance estimates. For structural equation model analyses, which happen to be based on variance and covariance information, means imputation is not a recommended approach.

When the data are only MAR, but not MCAR, Amos's FIML approach yields parameter estimates that are both consistent and efficient. In contrast, the MI, LD and PD methods can all produce severely biased results independent of the sample size, however large.

Finally, when the missing data process is nonignorable, all standard multivariate approaches can yield biased results. However, several authors suggest that FIML estimates will tend to be less biased than the other methods (Little and Rubin, 1989; Schafer, 1997; Muthén, Kaplan and Hollis, 1987).

In other words, Amos's missing data handling by FIML is the recommended estimation method of choice when the data are at least MAR, and may not be such a bad choice overall when the missingness is somewhat nonignorable. LD and PD, on the other hand, require that the missingness is MCAR, which is a much more difficult to establish than MAR.

The data

For this example we have modified the Holzinger and Swineford (1939) data used in Example 8. The original data set (in the SPSS file **Grnt_fem.sav**) contains the scores of 73 girls on six tests, for a total of 438 data values. Each one of the 438 data values was marked as missing with probability 0.30.

The result is contained in the SPSS file **Grant_x.sav**, where a data value of a period [.] indicates missing data. Here are the first few records of that data set:

	visperc	cubes	lozenges	paragrap	sentence	wordmean
1	33.00	.	17.00	8.00	17.00	10.00
2	30.00	.	20.00	.	.	18.00
3	.	33.00	36.00	.	25.00	41.00
4	28.00	.	.	10.00	18.00	11.00
5	.	25.00	.	11.00	.	8.00
6	20.00	25.00	6.00	9.00	.	.
7	17.00	21.00	6.00	5.00	10.00	10.00

Amos recognizes the periods in SPSS data sets and treats them as missing data. Technically speaking, Amos detects SPSS's missing data when they are coded as *system missing* (or **SYSMIS**).

Amos automatically recognizes missing data designations from many other data formats as well. For instance, an ASCII data set uses consecutive commas [, ,] to indicate missing data. The same data set sample as before would look like this in ASCII format (shown in the file **Grant_x.txt**):

```
visperc,cubes,lozenges,paragraph,sentence,wordmean
33,,17,8,17,10
30,,20,,,18
,33,36,,25,41
28,,,10,18,11
,,25,,11,,8
20,25,6,9,,,,
17,21,6,5,10,10
```

Approximately 27% of the data in **Grant_x.sav** are missing. Complete data are available for only seven cases. This is an example of how, under listwise deletion of missing values, the remaining sample size can become too small to estimate even simple multivariate models. With the full information approach, however, Amos can use all observed data values to estimate models with many parameters, including saturated models.

Modeling in Amos Graphics

We will now try to fit the common factor analysis model of Example 8 (shown below) to the Holzinger and Swineford data in file **Grant_x.sav**. The difference from the analysis in Example 8 is that this time 27% of the data are missing.

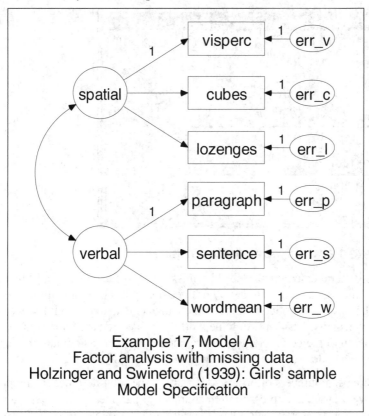

Example 17, Model A
Factor analysis with missing data
Holzinger and Swineford (1939): Girls' sample
Model Specification

Since the path diagram is identical to the one used in Example 8, you can copy the file **Ex08.amw**, and use it with three minor adjustments. First, follow the path: **View/Set → Analysis Properties → Estimation** and make sure that **Estimate Means and Intercepts** is checked. Second, specify the appropriate data set: **File → Data Files... → File Name → Grant_x.sav**.

Finally, because SPSS limits variable names to eight characters, the variable name paragraph needs to become paragrap. Make this change by double clicking on the variable and changing the **Variable <u>n</u>ame** to paragrap and the **Variable <u>l</u>abel** to paragraph, as shown below. By doing this, Amos will display the full name (paragraph) in any graphic model.

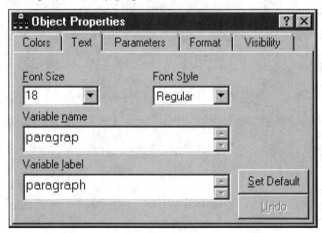

Saturated and independence models

Fitting structural equation models with missing data is technically a little different from the analysis of complete data. For once, many more computations are required, so you will notice that incomplete data can take quite a bit longer to analyze. Secondly, besides fitting the working model you are interested in, Amos also needs to fit the completely *saturated* model in order to compute the fit chi-square and derived statistics such as the AIC or RMSEA.

With increasing numbers of observed variables, the saturated model can quickly become very large, as expressed in the number of parameters to be estimated. This is because, for p observed variables, the saturated model has $p*(p+3)/2$ free parameters. For example, with 10 observed variables there are 65 parameters, with 20 variables there are 230 parameters, with 40 variables there are 860 parameters, and so on. If the sample size is small, there may not be enough information to estimate the saturated model for a large number of variables. As a general rule, the sample size should be greater than the number of free parameters.

In addition to the working and saturated models, the fit of the independence model is required for calculating the several fit indices such as CFI or NFI.

Amos Graphics output

When incomplete data are modeled with **Amos Graphics**, the program will automatically try to fit the working, independence and saturated models all at once. Afterwards all appropriate fit statistics are computed, based on which models were

---

successfully fitted. Here is the path diagram displaying the standardized estimates and the squared multiple correlations of the observed variables:

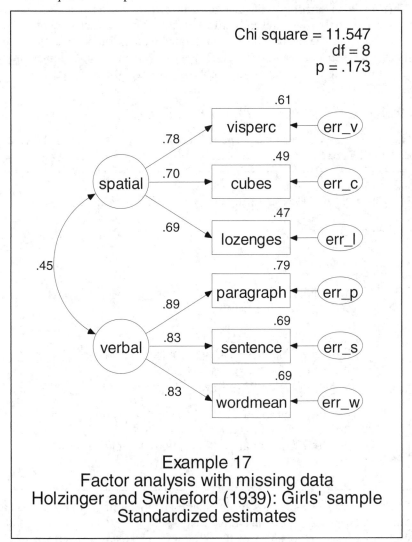

Chi square = 11.547
df = 8
p = .173

Example 17
Factor analysis with missing data
Holzinger and Swineford (1939): Girls' sample
Standardized estimates

The chi-square value of 11.547 is not very different from the value of 7.853 obtained in Example 8 with the complete data set. In both analyses, the *p*-values are above 0.05, and we would conclude that the model fits with the incomplete sample as well. The (standardized) parameter values can be compared to those obtained from the complete data in Example 8. Both sets of estimates are identical at the first decimal place. Considering the sizable percentage of missing data in **Grant_x.sav**, and the small size (N = 73) this sample had to begin with, the match is about as close as can possibly be expected.

Modeling in Amos Basic

When analyzing incomplete data with **Amos Basic**, the independence and saturated models have to be specified and estimated explicitly. This section presents in three steps setting up the factor model, the saturated model, and computing the fit chi square and its *p* value. After that, it is shown how the three modeling components can be integrated into a single, comprehensive **Amos Basic** program.

Model A: Confirmatory factor analysis

The confirmatory factor model can be specified in **Amos Basic** as shown in the file `Ex17-a.AmosBasic`:

```
Sub Main()
    Dim Sem As New AmosEngine

    With Sem
        .TextOutput
        .Standardized
        .Smc
        .AllImpliedMoments
        .ModelMeansAndIntercepts

        .BeginGroup "Grant_x.sav"
            .Structure "visperc  = ( ) + (1) spatial + (1) err_v"
            .Structure "cubes    = ( ) +     spatial + (1) err_c"
            .Structure "lozenges = ( ) +     spatial + (1) err_l"

            .Structure "paragrap = ( ) + (1) verbal  + (1) err_p"
            .Structure "sentence = ( ) +     verbal  + (1) err_s"
            .Structure "wordmean = ( ) +     verbal  + (1) err_w"
    End With
End Sub
```

This looks just like the **Amos Basic** input file from Example 8, except that all Amos statements appear in an **Amos Basic** "With" block. The main function of With blocks is to remove visual clutter and thus make the **Amos Basic** code more readable.

As a more important change from Example 8, each of the six regression equations following the .Structure statement contains a set of empty parentheses for the intercept term. When analyzing data with missing values you have to ask for an estimate of each additive constant except for those assumed to be zero. This is different from the analysis of complete data, where terms for the additive constants are not necessary unless the model specifies constraints among the intercepts.

Results for Model A

The parameter estimates, standard errors and critical ratios have the same interpretation as in an analysis of complete data:

```
Regression Weights:              Estimate    S.E.     C.R.
-------------------              --------   -------  -------

    visperc <-------- spatial     1.000
    cubes <---------- spatial     0.511     0.153    3.347
    lozenges <------- spatial     1.047     0.316    3.317
    paragraph <------ verbal      1.000
    sentence <------- verbal      1.259     0.194    6.505
    wordmean <------- verbal      2.140     0.326    6.572


Intercepts:                      Estimate    S.E.     C.R.
-----------                      --------   -------  -------

                     visperc     28.885     0.913   31.632
                       cubes     24.998     0.536   46.603
                    lozenges     15.153     1.133   13.372
                   paragraph     10.987     0.468   23.495
                    sentence     18.864     0.636   29.646
                    wordmean     18.097     1.055   17.146


Covariances:                     Estimate    S.E.     C.R.
------------                     --------   -------  -------

    verbal <--------> spatial     7.993     3.211    2.490


Variances:                       Estimate    S.E.     C.R.
----------                       --------   -------  -------

                     spatial     29.563    11.600    2.549
                      verbal     10.814     2.743    3.943
                       err_v     18.776     8.518    2.204
                       err_c      8.034     2.669    3.011
                       err_l     36.625    11.662    3.141
                       err_p      2.825     1.277    2.212
                       err_s      7.875     2.403    3.277
                       err_w     22.677     6.883    3.295
```

The fit of Model A to the data is summarized as follows:

```
Function of log likelihood =    1375.133
Number of parameters =   19
```

This Function of log likelihood value is displayed instead of the chi-square fit statistic usually obtained with complete data. In addition, at the beginning of the Summary of models section of the text output, Amos displays the warning:

```
The saturated model was not fitted to the data of at least one
group. For this reason, only the 'function of log likelihood', AIC
and BCC are reported. The likelihood ratio chi square statistic and
other fit measures are not reported.
```

Whenever Amos prints this note, the values in cmin column of the Summary of models section are no longer the familiar fit chi square statistics. To evaluate the fit of the factor model, its Function of log likelihood value has to be compared to that of some less constrained baseline model, such as the saturated model.

Model B: Saturated model

The saturated model has as many free parameters as there are first and second order moments. When complete data are analyzed, the saturated model always fits the sample data perfectly (with chi-square = 0.00 and df = 0). All structural equation models with the same six observed variables are either equivalent to the saturated model or are constrained versions of it. The saturated models will fit the sample data no worse than any constrained model, and so its Function of log likelihood value will be smaller. It will be interesting to see how much smaller.

Model B (from **Ex17-b.AmosBasic**) can be set up as follows:

```
Sub Main()
    Dim Saturated As New AmosEngine

    'Set up and estimate Saturated model:
    With Saturated
        .Title "Example 17 b: Saturated Model"
        .TextOutput
        .AllImpliedMoments
        .ModelMeansAndIntercepts

        .BeginGroup "Grant_x.sav"
            .Mean "visperc"
            .Mean "cubes"
            .Mean "lozenges"
            .Mean "paragrap"
            .Mean "sentence"
            .Mean "wordmean"
    End With
End Sub
```

Following the .BeginGroup statement, there are six .Mean commands requesting mean estimates of the exogenous variables. A useful property of the .Mean commands is that they automatically add variance and covariance terms of the referenced exogenous variables to the set of free model parameters. Thus, for p observed variables, the saturated model can be written with only p statements, instead of $p(p + 3)/2$. In the present Model B, the six .Mean commands specify 27 free parameters—six means, six variances and 15 covariances. This efficiency in model specification becomes even more pronounced as the number of observed variables increases.

Here are the unstandardized parameter estimates for Model B (*i.e.*, with no constraints on means, variances and covariances). Estimates, standard errors and critical ratios are interpreted in the same way as in an analysis of complete data.

```
Means:                          Estimate    S.E.      C.R.
------
                    visperc      28.883     0.910    31.756
                     cubes       25.154     0.540    46.592
                   lozenges      14.962     1.101    13.591
                   paragrap      10.976     0.466    23.572
                   sentence      18.802     0.632    29.730
                   wordmean      18.263     1.061    17.211

Covariances:                    Estimate    S.E.      C.R.
------------
        visperc <-------> cubes    17.484    4.614     3.789
        visperc <----> lozenges    31.173    9.232     3.377
        cubes <------> lozenges    17.036    5.459     3.121
        visperc <----> paragrap     8.453    3.705     2.281
        cubes <------> paragrap     2.739    2.179     1.257
        lozenges <---> paragrap     9.287    4.596     2.021
        visperc <----> sentence    14.382    5.114     2.813
        cubes <------> sentence     1.678    2.929     0.573
        lozenges <---> sentence    10.544    6.050     1.743
        paragrap <---> sentence    13.470    2.945     4.574
        visperc <----> wordmean    14.665    8.314     1.764
        cubes <------> wordmean     3.470    4.870     0.713
        lozenges <---> wordmean    29.655   10.574     2.804
        paragrap <---> wordmean    23.616    5.010     4.714
        sentence <---> wordmean    29.577    6.650     4.447

Variances:                      Estimate    S.E.      C.R.
----------
                    visperc      49.584     9.398     5.276
                     cubes       16.484     3.228     5.106
                   lozenges      67.901    13.404     5.066
                   paragrap      13.570     2.515     5.396
                   sentence      25.007     4.629     5.402
                   wordmean      73.974    13.221     5.595
```

And the .AllImpliedMoments command shown in the **Amos Basic** program displays these estimates (but not their standard errors) in tabular form:

```
Implied (for all variables) Covariances

          wordmean sentence paragrap lozenges cubes    visperc
          -------- -------- -------- -------- -------- --------
wordmean   73.974
sentence   29.577   25.007
paragrap   23.616   13.470   13.570
lozenges   29.655   10.544    9.287   67.901
cubes       3.470    1.678    2.739   17.036   16.484
visperc    14.665   14.382    8.453   31.173   17.484   49.584

Implied (for all variables) Means

          wordmean sentence paragrap lozenges cubes    visperc
          -------- -------- -------- -------- -------- --------
           18.263   18.802   10.976   14.962   25.154   28.883
```

These parameter estimates, even the estimated means, are different form those computed under either pairwise or listwise deletion methods. For example, in the case of the visual perception test, **visperc**, scores are available for 53 examinees. The sample mean of these 53 **visperc** scores is 28.245. One might reasonably expect the Amos estimate of the mean visual perception score to be 28.245 rather than 28.883. However, this is a case where intuition is incorrect.

Amos Basic presents this fit information for Model B:

```
Function of log likelihood =    1363.586
Number of parameters =   27
```

The `Function of log likelihood` values are used to compare the fit among two or more nested models. Model A (with a fit statistic of 1375.133 and 19 parameters) is structurally nested within Model B (with a fit statistic of 1363.586 and 27 parameters). In a case like this, where a stronger model is being compared to a weaker model, and where the stronger model is correct, you can say the following: The amount by which the `Function of log likelihood` increases when you switch from the weaker model to the stronger model is an observation on a *chi-square* random variable with degrees of freedom equal to the difference in the number of parameters of the two models. In the present example, Model A's Function of log likelihood exceeds that for Model B by 11.547 (= 1375.133 − 1363.586). At the same time, Model A requires estimating only 19 parameters while Model B requires estimating 27 parameters, for a difference of 8. In other words, if Model A is correct, 11.547 is an observation on a chi square variable with 8 degrees of freedom. We can check the statistical tables to see whether this chi-square is significant.

Model C: Rejection probability

Perhaps more convenient than looking up statistical tables, **Amos Basic**'s .ChiSquareProbability function can be used to determine the probability that a chi-square value of 11.547 or larger would have been observed by chance when the factor model fits exactly in the population.

Here is the **Amos Basic** code for calculating and displaying this *p*-value (from `Ex17-c.AmosBasic`):

```
Sub Main()
    Dim ChiSquare As Double, P As Double
    Dim Df As Integer

    ChiSquare = 1375.133 - 1363.586
    Df          =    27    -    19

    Dim FitTest As New AmosEngine
    P = FitTest.ChiSquareProbability (ChiSquare, CDbl(Df) )
    FitTest.Shutdown

    Debug.Print "Fit of factor model:"
    Debug.Print "Chi Square = "; Format$(ChiSquare,"#,##0.000")
    Debug.Print "DF = "; Df
    Debug.Print "P = "; Format$(P,"0.000")
End Sub
```

This **Amos Basic** program has three segments:

1. Compute the chi square value and its degrees of freedom.

2. Call the Amos Engine under the name FitTest and use the FitTest.ChiSquareProbability method to compute the upper tail probability of the chi square statistic. Use the FitTest.Shutdown method to suppress the Amos warning that actually "no model was specified."

3. Display the results in **Amos Basic**'s **Immediate** debug window, formatted at three-digit precision.

Note: In **Amos Basic**, **View** → **Always Split** has to be checked to view the results.

The **Amos Basic Immediate** window displays these results:

```
Fit of factor model:
Chi Square = 11.547
DF = 8
P = 0.173
```

The *p* value is 0.173, thus we accept (at the .05 level) the hypothesis that Model A is correct.

As the present example illustrates, in order to test a model with incomplete data, you have to compare its fit to that of another, alternative model. In this example, we wished to test Model A, and it was necessary also to fit Model B as a standard model of comparison. The alternative model has to meet two requirements. First, you have to be satisfied that it is correct. Model B certainly meets this criterion, since it places no constraints on the implied moments, and cannot be wrong. Second, it must be more general than the model you wish to test. Any model that can be obtained by removing some of the constraints on the parameters of the model under test will meet this second criterion. If you have trouble thinking up an alternative model, you can always use the saturated model that requires estimating all means, variances, and covariances without constraints.

Models A-C: One program for all tests

Amos Basic can, of course, compute all three submodels at once. The file **Ex17-all.AmosBasic** contains an **Amos Basic** program that first fits the confirmatory factor model, then the saturated model, and finally computes the fit statistic and *p* value. The first code section is the **Amos Basic** subroutine FitSaturated, which sets up and fits a saturated model of any desired size:

```
Sub FitSaturated(FileN, VarName, Converged, Admissible, Cmin, Nparms)

        Dim FirstVar As Integer, LastVar As Integer, ivar As Integer
        Dim Saturated As New AmosEngine

        FirstVar = LBound(VarName)
        LastVar = UBound(VarName)

        With Saturated
            .ModelMeansAndIntercepts

            .BeginGroup FileN

            For ivar = FirstVar To LastVar
                .Mean Trim(VarName(ivar))
            Next

            Converged = (.FitModel = 0)
            Admissible = .Admissible
            Cmin = .Cmin
            Nparms = .Npar
        End With
        Set Saturated = Nothing
        DoEvents
End Sub
```

The calling program calls FitSaturated with the name of the data file (in FileN) and an array of observed variable names (in VarName) as input arguments. FitSaturated calls the **Amos Engine** by the name Saturated, opens the data file with the .BeginGroup method, and executes the **Amos Engine**'s .Mean method for each observed variable listed in the VarName array. The .Fitmodel method fits the specified model, returning a value of zero (0) if the solution converged. FitSaturated stores the convergence and admissibility status, as well as the value of the fit function and the number of parameters. These values are returned to the calling routine via the last four subroutine arguments. Finally, the **Amos Basic** statement:

Set Saturated = Nothing

requests the **Amos Engine** to be unloaded from the operating system, and the **Amos Basic** command:

DoEvents

halts further program execution until the system has finished unloading the **Amos Engine**.

The somewhat shortened code of the calling (main) routine is:

```
Sub Main()
    Dim ObsVars As Variant, FileName As String, ChiSquare As Double
    Dim ModelAdmissible As Boolean, ModelConverged As Boolean
    Dim SaturatedAdmissible As Boolean, SaturatedConverged As Boolean
    Dim ModelCmin As Double, SaturatedCmin As Double, P As Double
    Dim ModelNparms As Integer, SaturatedNparms As Integer, Df As Integer

    FileName = "Grant_x.sav"
    ObsVars = Array("visperc", "cubes", "lozenges", _
            "paragrap", "sentence", "wordmean")
    Call FitSaturated(FileName,  ObsVars, SaturatedConverged, _
                SaturatedAdmissible, SaturatedCmin, SaturatedNparms)

    Dim Sem As New AmosEngine
    With Sem
        .Title "Example 17: Working Model"
        .TextOutput
        .ModelMeansAndIntercepts

        .BeginGroup FileName
        .Structure "visperc  = ( ) + (1) spatial + (1) err_v"
        .Structure "cubes    = ( ) +    spatial + (1) err_c"
        .Structure "lozenges = ( ) +    spatial + (1) err_l"
        .Structure "paragrap = ( ) + (1) verbal  + (1) err_p"
        .Structure "sentence = ( ) +    verbal  + (1) err_s"
        .Structure "wordmean = ( ) +    verbal  + (1) err_w"

        ModelConverged = (.FitModel = 0)
        ModelAdmissible = .Admissible
        ModelCmin = .Cmin
        ModelNparms = .Npar
    End With
    Set Sem = Nothing                          'Terminate AmosEngine objects
    DoEvents      'Let system unload AmosEngine objects before continuing

    If (ModelConverged And ModelAdmissible And _
        SaturatedConverged And SaturatedAdmissible) Then
        ChiSquare = ModelCmin - SaturatedCmin
        Df = SaturatedNparms - ModelNparms

        Dim FitTest As New AmosEngine
        P = FitTest.ChiSquareProbability (ChiSquare, CDbl(Df) )
        FitTest.Shutdown

        Debug.Print "Fit of factor model:"
        Debug.Print "Chi Square = "; Format$(ChiSquare,"#,##0.000")
        Debug.Print "DF = "; Df
        Debug.Print "P = "; Format$(P,"0.000")

        Set FitTest = Nothing
        DoEvents
    Else
        Debug.Print "Sorry, one or both models did not converge to an admissible solution."
    End If
End Sub
```

After a block of type definition (Dim) statements, the program initializes the FileName string and the ObsVars array of observed variable names and calls the FitSaturated routine. Then it initializes a new **Amos Engine** object by the name Sem, sets up the confirmatory factor model as the working model, and calculates its estimates. After checking that both working and saturated models converged to admissible solutions, the fit chi-square of the working model is computed and another **Amos Engine** object is initialized, this time by the name FitTest. FitTest computes the upper tail probability associated with the fit chi square statistic and displays its value in the **Immediate** window. Had one or both of the models not converged to an admissible solution, a warning message would have been displayed instead of the p value.

Note that after each use of the **Amos Engine**, the **Amos Engine** object is set to "Nothing" in order to unload it; a subsequent DoEvents statement causes the program to wait until the active object has in fact been removed from memory.

Example 18: More about Missing Data

Purpose

- Demonstrate the analysis of data in which some observations are missing *intentionally* by virtue of the measurement design.

- Highlight study situations where it may be advantageous to collect incomplete, instead of complete, data.

Introduction

Researchers do not ordinarily like missing data. They typically take great care to avoid these gaps whenever possible. But sometimes it is actually better *not* to observe every variable on every occasion. Matthai (1951) and Lord (1955) describe designs where certain data are intentionally missing.

> *The basic principle is that, when it is impossible or too costly to obtain sufficient observations on a variable, estimates with improved accuracy can be obtained by taking additional observations on other, correlated, variables.*

Such designs can be highly useful, but, because of computational difficulties, they have not previously been employed except in very simple situations. This example describes only one of many possible designs where some data are intentionally not collected. The method of analysis is the same as in Example 17.

The data

We have modified Attig's data (introduced in Example 1) by eliminating some of the data values and treating them as missing. The file **Atty_mis.sav**, listed below, contains scores of Attig's 40 young subjects on the two vocabulary tests **v_short** and **vocab**. As you can see from this excerpt, some observations for **vocab** are missing:

	v_short	vocab
7	6.00	51.00
8	9.00	52.00
9	8.00	60.00
10	5.00	48.00
11	13.00	.
12	12.00	.
13	14.00	.
14	4.00	.
15	5.00	.

The variable **vocab** is the raw score on the WAIS vocabulary test. **v_short** is the raw score on a small subset of the same test. In the file **Atty_mis.sav**, the **vocab** scores were deleted for 30 randomly picked subjects, and these missing values are displayed as periods in the SPSS Data Editor.

A second data file, **Atto_mis.sav**, contains vocabulary test scores for the 40 old subjects, again with 30 randomly picked **vocab** scores marked as missing:

	v_short	vocab
7	10.00	67.00
8	6.00	47.00
9	4.00	47.00
10	.00	40.00
11	12.00	.
12	14.00	.
13	13.00	.
14	6.00	.
15	7.00	.

Of course no sensible person deletes data that have already been collected. In order for this example to make sense, imagine the following scenario.

The variable **vocab** is one of the best tests of vocabulary knowledge. It is highly reliable and valid, and it is the customary instrument for important diagnoses. Unfortunately it is also an expensive test. Maybe it takes a long time to give the test, or maybe it has to be administered on an individual basis or it has to be scored by a highly trained person. A second vocabulary test, **v_short,** is available but is not as good. However, it is short, inexpensive and easy to administer to a large number of people at once. The cheap test, **v_short,** is given to 40 young and 40 old subjects. Then, 10 randomly picked subjects in each group are asked to take the expensive test (**vocab**). The purpose of the research is to:

- estimate the average **vocab** test score in the population of young subjects

- estimate the average **vocab** score in the population of old subjects

- test the hypothesis that the two populations have the same average **vocab** score.

There is no immediate research interest in similar statistics of the less reliable scores. However, as will be demonstrated below, the scores carry information that allows more efficient answers to the research questions about the **vocab** scores. This gain in efficiency can be surprisingly large.

Model A

The fact that the designer of the study, and not the test takers, randomly ignored 30 scores in each group does not affect the method of analysis. Model A estimates means, variances and covariances of the two vocabulary tests in both groups of subjects. The **Critical ratio for differences** option is used to obtain the critical ratio statistic for the difference of young and old subjects' **vocab** scores.

Modeling in Amos Graphics

Model A can be specified in **Amos Graphics** as a two-group model, similar to Model A of Example 10:

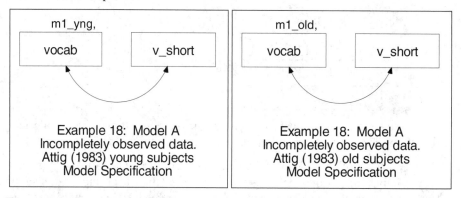

Two objects for the exogenous observed variables **vocab** and **v_short** appear in each group, connected by a two-headed (covariance) path. Model A places no restrictions on its ten parameters (two means, two variances and one covariance term in each of two groups). There is one free parameter for each of the first and second moments — the model is saturated.

The **Amos Graphics** input file for Model A is **Ex18-a.amw**. Follow the path: **File → Data Files...** and notice the **Data Files** dialog box references the data for the young and old subject groups as **Atty_mis.sav** and **Atto_mis.sav**, respectively. Because there are missing data, remember to keep the **Estimate means and intercepts** option checked. You will find this option in **View/Set → Analysis Properties** on the **Estimation** tab. The **Critical ratios for differences** on the **Output** tab apply to all model parameters in both groups. The output is a ten-by-ten lower-half matrix of 45 critical ratios for the differences between any two parameter estimates. Parameter labels, if supplied, are used as row and column headings of the output matrix. Because Model A focuses on the difference in group means of the **vocab** test, we are using the labels m1_yng and m1_old for the two parameters. These unique labels make it obvious where the critical value for the group difference appears in the matrix.

Modeling in Amos Basic

The **Amos Basic** input file **Ex18-a.AmosBasic** requests estimates of means, variances and covariances of both vocabulary tests in both groups of subjects:

```
Sub Main()
    Dim Sem As New AmosEngine

    Sem.TextOutput
    Sem.Crdiff
    Sem.ModelMeansAndIntercepts

    Sem.BeginGroup "Atty_mis.sav"
        Sem.GroupName "young_subjects"
        Sem.Mean "vocab", "m1_yng"
        Sem.Mean "v_short"

    Sem.BeginGroup "Atto_mis.sav"
        Sem.GroupName "old_subjects"
        Sem.Mean "vocab", "m1_old"
        Sem.Mean "v_short"

End Sub
```

The Sem.Crdiff command is included because we are interested in seeing the critical ratio for the difference between the mean **vocab** scores for young and old subjects. The parameter labels m1_yng and m1_old are supplied to identify this critical ratio in the matrix produced by the Sem.Crdiff command.

Output from Model A

Amos Graphics output

Here are the two path diagrams containing the means, variances, and covariances for the young and old subjects, respectively:

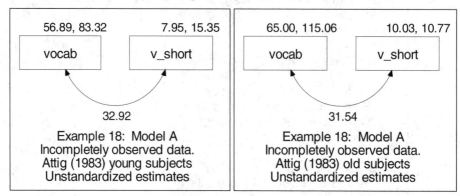

Amos Graphics computes the fit chi-square for this model as:

```
chi-square =              -.0.000
degrees of freedom =    0
```

Amos Basic output

The parameter estimates and standard errors for the young subjects are:

Means:		Estimate	S.E.	C.R.	Label
	vocab	56.891	1.765	32.232	m1_yng
	v_short	7.950	0.627	12.673	par-4
Covariances:		Estimate	S.E.	C.R.	Label
vocab <-----> v_short		32.916	8.694	3.786	par-3
Correlations:		Estimate			
vocab <-----> v_short		0.920			
Variances:		Estimate	S.E.	C.R.	Label
	vocab	83.320	25.639	3.250	par-7
	v_short	15.347	3.476	4.416	par-8

And for the old subjects:

```
Means:                      Estimate    S.E.     C.R.     Label
------                      --------    ----     ----     -----

                vocab        65.001    2.167    29.992    m1_old
              v_short        10.025    0.526    19.073    par-6


Covariances:                Estimate    S.E.     C.R.     Label
-----------                 --------    ----     ----     -----

 vocab <------> v_short       31.545    8.725     3.616    par-5


Correlations:               Estimate
-------------               --------

 vocab <------> v_short        0.896


Variances:                  Estimate    S.E.     C.R.     Label
----------                  --------    ----     ----     -----

                vocab       115.063    37.463    3.071    par-9
              v_short        10.774     2.440    4.416    par-10
```

The estimates for the mean of **vocab** are 56.891 in the young population and 65.001 in the old population. Notice that these are not the same as the sample means that would have been obtained from the 10 young and 10 old subjects who took the **vocab** test. The respective sample means of 58.5 and 62 are good estimates of the population means (the best that can be had from two samples of size 10), but the Amos estimates (56.891 and 65.001) use information contained in the **v_short** scores, and are more efficient.

How much more accurate are the mean estimates that include the information of the **v_short** scores? Some idea can be obtained by looking at estimated standard errors. For the young subjects the standard error for 56.891 shown above is about 1.765 whereas the standard error of the sample mean, 58.5, is about 2.21. For the old subjects the standard error for 65.001 is about 2.167 while the standard error of the sample mean, 62, is about 4.21. Although the standard errors just mentioned are only approximations, they still provide a reasonable basis for comparison. In the case of the young subjects, using the information contained in the **v_short** scores reduces the standard error of the estimated **vocab** mean by about 21%. In the case of the old subjects, the standard error was reduced by about 49%.

Another way to evaluate the additional information due to the **v_short** scores is by evaluating the sample size requirements. Suppose you did not use the information in the **v_short** scores, how many more young examinees would have to take the **vocab** test to reduce the standard error of its mean by 21%? Likewise, how many more old examinees would have to take the **vocab** test to reduce the standard error of its mean by 49%? The answer is that, because the standard error of the mean is inversely proportional to the square root of the sample size, it would require about 1.6 times as many young subjects and about 3.8 times as many old subjects. That is, it would require about 16 young subjects and 38 old subjects taking the **vocab** test, instead of 10 young and 10 old subjects taking both tests, and 30 young and 30 old subjects taking the short test alone. Of course this calculation treats the estimated standard errors as though they were exact standard errors, and so it gives only a rough idea of how much is gained by using scores on the **v_short** test.

We would now like to test how likely it is that the young and old populations have different mean **vocab** scores. The estimated mean difference is 8.11 (65.001 – 56.891). An approximate critical ratio statistic for this difference is produced by the Sem.Crdiff command:

```
Critical Ratios for Differences between Parameters

           m1_yng   m1_old   par-3    par-4    par-5    par-6    par-7
          --------  --------  --------  -------  -------  --------  ------
m1_yng      0.000
m1_old      2.901    0.000
par-3      -2.702   -3.581    0.000
par-4     -36.269  -25.286   -2.864    0.000
par-5      -2.847   -3.722   -0.111    2.697    0.000
par-6     -25.448  -30.012   -2.628    2.535   -2.462    0.000
par-7       1.028    0.712    2.806    2.939    1.912    2.858    0.000
par-8     -10.658  -12.123   -2.934    2.095   -1.725    1.514   -2.877
par-9       1.551    1.334    2.136    2.859    2.804    2.803    0.699
par-10    -15.314  -16.616   -2.452    1.121   -3.023    0.300   -2.817


            par-8    par-9    par-10
          -------  -------  -------
par-8       0.000
par-9       2.650    0.000
par-10     -1.077   -2.884    0.000
```

The first two rows and columns, labeled m1_yng and m1_old, refer to the group means of the **vocab** test. The critical ratio for the mean difference is 2.901, according to which the means differ significantly at the .05 level: the older population scores higher on the long test than the younger population.

Another test of equal **vocab** group means can be obtained by re-estimating the model with equality constraints imposed on these means. We will do that next. **Amos Graphics** will automatically compute the chi-square fit statistics for both models, so that no further computation is needed. With **Amos Basic**, however, we will have to explicitly compare the Function of log likelihood values of our models. Note the Function of log likelihood for Model A:

```
Function of log likelihood =     429.963
Number of parameters =    10
```

Model B

Model B adds the constraint that **vocab** has the same mean in the young and old populations.

Modeling in Amos Graphics

The group means of the **vocab** test can be constrained either by using the same parameter label in both groups or by equating the two parameter labels m1_yng and m1_old of Model A in Amos's **Model Manager**. The **Amos Graphics** input file **Ex18-b.amw** uses the latter approach, leaving Model A unconstrained and imposing one constraint in Model B: m1_yng = m1_old.

An advantage of using a multimodel format is that Amos will compute the χ^2 statistic and p value for the model comparison.

Modeling in Amos Basic

The **Amos Basic** input file of Model B, **Ex18-b.AmosBasic**, uses the *same* parameter label (mn_vocab) for the two group means of the **vocab** test:

```
Sub Main()
    Dim Sem As New AmosEngine

    Sem.TextOutput
    Sem.Crdiff
    Sem.ModelMeansAndIntercepts

    Sem.BeginGroup "Atty_mis.sav"
        Sem.GroupName "young_subjects"
        Sem.Mean "vocab", "mn_vocab"
        Sem.Mean "v_short"

    Sem.BeginGroup "Atto_mis.sav"
        Sem.GroupName "old_subjects"
        Sem.Mean "vocab", "mn_vocab"
        Sem.Mean "v_short"

End Sub
```

Output from Model B

Amos Graphics reports the fit of Model B as:

```
Chi-square =        7.849
Degrees of freedom =    1
Probability level =     0.005
```

If Model B is correct (*i.e.*, the young and old populations have the same mean **vocab** score), then 7.85 is an observation on a random variable that has a chi-square distribution with one degree of freedom. Since the probability level is vanishingly small (p = 0.005), Model B is rejected in favor of Model A — concluding that younger and older subjects differ in their mean **vocab** scores.

Amos Basic reports the fit of Model B as

```
Function of log likelihood =     437.813
Number of parameters =     9
```

The difference in fit measures between Models B and A is 7.85 (= 437.813 − 429.963), and the difference in the number of parameters is 1 (= 10 − 9). These are the same figures we obtained earlier with **Amos Graphics**.

Example 19: Bootstrapping

Purpose

- Demonstrate how to obtain robust standard error estimates by the bootstrap method.

Introduction

Bootstrapping (Efron, 1982) is a versatile method for evaluating the empirical sampling distribution of parameter estimates. In particular, bootstrapping can be used to obtain empirical standard error estimates of the model parameters, in addition to the regular standard error estimates that are part of the usual Amos output when maximum likelihood or generalized least squares estimation is employed. To calculate these latter standard errors, Amos uses formulas that depend on the normal-theory assumptions described in the Technical Note at the end of Example 1.

Bootstrapping is a completely different approach to the problem of estimating standard errors. Why do we need this alternate approach? To begin with, Amos does not have formulas for all the standard errors you might want, such as standard errors for squared multiple correlations. But with bootstrapping, lack of an explicit formula for standard errors is never a problem. Bootstrapping can be used to generate an approximate standard error for many statistics that Amos computes — regardless of whether a formula for the standard error is known. Even when Amos has formulas for standard errors, these formulas are only good under the assumptions of multivariate normality and when the correct model is employed. In contrast, approximate standard errors computed by bootstrapping do not suffer from these limitations.

Bootstrapping has its own shortcomings, however. For one thing, it requires fairly large samples. It is also computationally time-consuming. Fortunately, high-speed personal computers have made this almost a non-issue. For readers who are new to bootstrapping, we recommend the *Scientific American* article by Diaconis and Efron (1983).

The present example demonstrates bootstrapping with a factor analysis model but, of course, bootstrapping can be used with any model. Incidentally, Amos's bootstrapping capability can be beneficial not only with complex estimation problems but also with simple ones like that of Example 1.

The data

We will use the Holzinger and Swineford (1939) data, introduced and described in Example 8, for this example. The data are contained in the file **Grnt_fem.sav**.

A factor analysis model

Modeling in Amos Basic

The following input file is the same as the one in Example 8, except for the new Sem.Bootstrap command.

```
Sub Main()
    Dim Sem As New AmosEngine

    Sem.TextOutput

    Sem.Bootstrap 500
    Sem.Standardized
    Sem.Smc

    Sem.BeginGroup "Grnt_fem.sav"

        Sem.Structure "visperc  = (1) spatial + (1) err_v"
        Sem.Structure "cubes    =     spatial + (1) err_c"
        Sem.Structure "lozenges =     spatial + (1) err_l"

        Sem.Structure "paragrap = (1) verbal  + (1) err_p"
        Sem.Structure "sentence =     verbal  + (1) err_s"
        Sem.Structure "wordmean =     verbal  + (1) err_w"
        Sem.FitModel 1

End Sub
```

The command Sem.Bootstrap 500 requests 500 bootstrap replications for computing the bootstrapped standard errors.

You can also add another command, Sem.Seed <*number*>, to supply an initial seed value for the random number generator. Different seed values must be supplied with two or more Amos sessions, if these are supposed to generate independent sets of bootstrap samples. Conversely, in order to draw the exact same set of samples in each of several Amos sessions, the same seed number must be given each time. Currently, because the present example requires only one sample, the Sem.Seed command is left at its default value.

Modeling in Amos Graphics

The path diagram for this model is the same one used in Example 8:

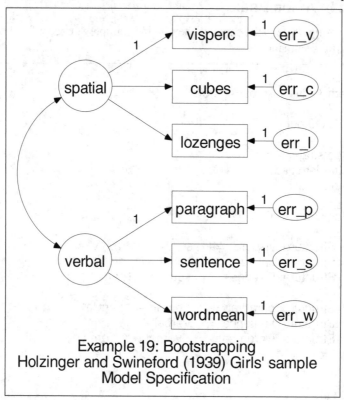

Example 19: Bootstrapping
Holzinger and Swineford (1939) Girls' sample
Model Specification

Remember that if you are working with an SPSS data set, you are limited to eight characters for variable names. In this example, we changed the variable name to paragrap and the variable label to paragraph, so the full word appears in the model specification:

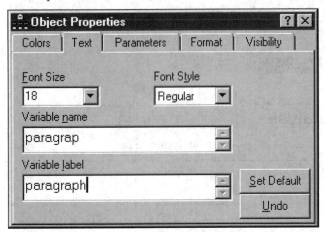

Then, to request 500 bootstrap replications, click on the **Analysis Properties** icon and go to the **Bootstrap** tab. Check the box for **Perform bootstrap** and enter "500" in the **Number of bootstrap samples** field:

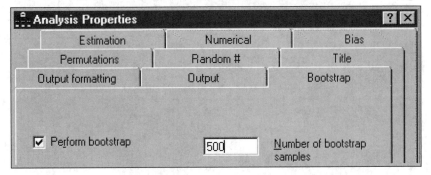

The input file for this example is **Ex19.amw**. None of the added features illustrated in this example are displayed in the path diagram — the bootstrap output is strictly text-based.

Speed of the analysis

Amos's speed at performing bootstrap simulations varies greatly, depending on how large a sample is used to begin with, and how quickly the model can be refitted to each bootstrap sample. Several components contribute to computing speed. The speed of floating point calculations supported by your computer hardware, how many parameters there are in the model, and how well these are

---

defined all affect computing speed. However, most Pentium systems will run this
500 bootstrap example in 15 seconds or less. While you are waiting, **Amos
Graphics** reports the bootstrapping progress in its **Computation summary** panel:

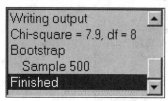

Results of the analysis

The model fit is, of course, the same as in Example 8:

```
Chi-square =        7.853
Degrees of freedom =     8
Probability level =      0.448
```

The unstandardized parameter estimates are also the same as in Example 8.
However, now the focus is on the standard error estimates computed by
normal-theory maximum likelihood, and on comparing them to standard errors
obtained by bootstrapping.

Here, again, are the maximum likelihood estimates of parameters and their standard errors:

```
Regression Weights:                  Estimate    S.E.     C.R.
-------------------                  --------  -------  -------

        visperc <------ spatial       1.000
        cubes <-------- spatial       0.610     0.143    4.250
        lozenges <----- spatial       1.198     0.272    4.405
        paragrap <------ verbal       1.000
        sentence <------ verbal       1.334     0.160    8.322
        wordmean <------ verbal       2.234     0.263    8.482


Standardized Regression Weights:     Estimate
--------------------------------     --------

        visperc <------ spatial       0.703
        cubes <-------- spatial       0.654
        lozenges <----- spatial       0.736
        paragrap <------ verbal       0.880
        sentence <------ verbal       0.827
        wordmean <------ verbal       0.841


Covariances:                         Estimate    S.E.     C.R.
------------                         --------  -------  -------

        spatial <------> verbal       7.315     2.571    2.846


Correlations:                        Estimate
-------------                        --------

        spatial <------> verbal       0.487


Variances:                           Estimate    S.E.     C.R.
----------                           --------  -------  -------

                        spatial      23.302    8.124    2.868
                         verbal       9.682    2.159    4.485
                          err_v      23.872    5.986    3.988
                          err_c      11.601    2.584    4.490
                          err_l      28.275    7.891    3.583
                          err_p       2.834    0.868    3.263
                          err_s       7.967    1.869    4.262
                          err_w      19.925    4.951    4.024

Squared Multiple Correlations:       Estimate
-----------------------------        --------
                        wordmean      0.708
                        sentence      0.684
                        paragrap      0.774
                        lozenges      0.542
                           cubes      0.428
                         visperc      0.494
```

The bootstrap output begins with summary diagnostics of the resampling process. For interpreting any bootstrap standard errors or confidence intervals, it is important to know whether there were bootstrap samples for which model estimates could not be computed and, if so, how many such aberrant cases were encountered. This information is reported concisely in the lines:

```
  0 bootstrap samples were unused because of a singular covariance matrix.
  0 bootstrap samples were unused because a solution was not found.
500 usable bootstrap samples were obtained.
```

If you are bootstrapping from a small or not continuously distributed sample, it is conceivable that one or more of your bootstrapped samples had singular covariance matrices. Similarly, Amos may not be able to find a solution for some of the bootstrap samples — at least not within the limits of the minimization algorithm (*cf.*, Sem.Iterations, Sem.Crit1, and Sem.Crit2 commands). Had such samples occurred, Amos would have reported them here, but would have left them out of any subsequent standard error calculations and bootstrap distribution graphs. If the message reports several problematic samples, then bootstrapping should perhaps not be performed for that particular problem.

The bootstrap estimates of the standard errors are:

```
Bootstrap Standard Errors
-------------------------
                                          S.E.                    S.E.
Regression Weights:           S.E.        S.E.    Mean    Bias    Bias
------------------           ------      -----   ------  ------  ------

visperc <------ spatial       0.000      0.000   1.000   0.000   0.000
cubes <-------- spatial       0.140      0.004   0.609  -0.001   0.006
lozenges <----- spatial       0.373      0.012   1.216   0.018   0.017
paragrap <------ verbal       0.000      0.000   1.000   0.000   0.000
sentence <------ verbal       0.176      0.006   1.345   0.011   0.008
wordmean <------ verbal       0.254      0.008   2.246   0.011   0.011

                                          S.E.                    S.E.
Standardized (Beta) Weights:  S.E.        S.E.    Mean    Bias    Bias
---------------------------   ------     ------   ------  ------  ------

visperc <------ spatial       0.123      0.004   0.709   0.006   0.005
cubes <-------- spatial       0.101      0.003   0.646  -0.008   0.005
lozenges <----- spatial       0.121      0.004   0.719  -0.017   0.005
paragrap <------ verbal       0.047      0.001   0.876  -0.004   0.002
sentence <------ verbal       0.042      0.001   0.826  -0.000   0.002
wordmean <------ verbal       0.050      0.002   0.841  -0.001   0.002

                                          S.E.                    S.E.
Covariances:                  S.E.        S.E.    Mean    Bias    Bias
------------                  ------     -------  -------  ------  ------

    spatial <------> verbal   2.393      0.076    7.241  -0.074   0.107

                                          S.E.                    S.E.
Correlations:                 S.E.        S.E.    Mean    Bias    Bias
-------------                 ------     --------  -------  ------  ------

    spatial <------> verbal   0.132      0.004    0.495   0.008   0.006

                                          S.E.                    S.E.
Variances:                    S.E.        S.E.    Mean    Bias    Bias
----------                    ------     --------  ------  ------  ------

               spatial        9.086      0.287   23.905   0.602   0.406
               verbal         2.077      0.066    9.518  -0.164   0.093
               err_v          9.166      0.290   22.393  -1.479   0.410
               err_c          3.195      0.101   11.190  -0.411   0.143
               err_l          9.940      0.314   27.797  -0.478   0.445
               err_p          0.878      0.028    2.772  -0.062   0.039
               err_s          1.446      0.046    7.597  -0.370   0.065
               err_w          5.488      0.174   19.123  -0.803   0.245

                                          S.E.                    S.E.
Squared Multiple Correlations: S.E.       S.E.    Mean    Bias    Bias
-----------------------------  -----     -------  ------  ------  ------

              wordmean        0.083      0.003   0.709   0.001   0.004
              sentence        0.069      0.002   0.685   0.001   0.003
              paragrap        0.081      0.003   0.770  -0.004   0.004
              lozenges        0.172      0.005   0.532  -0.010   0.008
              cubes           0.127      0.004   0.428   0.000   0.006
              visperc         0.182      0.006   0.517   0.023   0.008
```

The first column, labeled `S.E.`, gives the bootstrapped estimate of the standard error, which is simply the standard deviation of the parameter estimates computed across the 500 bootstrap samples. This figure should be compared to the approximate standard error estimates obtained by maximum likelihood. The second column, labeled `S.E.(S.E.)`, gives the approximate standard error of the bootstrap standard error estimate itself. As you can see, these entries are small throughout the second column, as they should be.

The column labeled `Mean` represents the average parameter estimate computed across bootstrap samples. This bootstrap mean is not necessarily identical to the original estimate. On the contrary, it can turn out being quite different. The fourth column, labeled `Bias`, gives the difference between the bootstrap mean and original estimate. If the average estimate of the bootstrapped samples is higher than the original estimate, then `Bias` will be positive. The last column, labeled `S.E.(Bias)`, gives the approximate standard error of the bias estimate.

Computational formulas for these statistics are documented under *Bootstrap standard errors* in the Amos 4.0 help file.

In the present example, many of the bootstrap standard errors are quite close to the approximate standard errors obtained originally by maximum likelihood. The three exceptions from this rule are associated with the two spatial tests, **lozenges** and **visperc**. The bootstrap standard error of the regression weight of **lozenges** on the **spatial** factor is 0.373, which is 37 percent larger than the maximum likelihood approximation. Similarly, the respective bootstrap standard errors for the residual variance terms for **visperc** and **lozenges** are 53 and 26 percent larger than the standard errors obtained by the maximum-likelihood method. The latter two parameter estimates are also significantly biased. In conclusion, the distribution of parameter estimates associated with the **spatial** common factor appears wider than expected under normal distribution assumptions.

We will not attempt to resolve why the bootstrap and normal-theory standard errors are different in this example. One promising next step would probably involve studying the joint and marginal distribution statistics of the three spatial tests. It could be that there are outliers in the data, or that there is a considerable amount of censoring in some of the tests, or that the distributions might simply be rather skewed. In any case, bootstrap simulations are a powerful tool to diagnose the presence of distribution problems in the data and to gauge their effects on the parameter estimates.

Note that because the Sem.Standardized and Sem.Smc commands were included in the input file, the bootstrap procedure produces standard errors and bias estimates for the standardized path coefficients, factor correlations, and squared multiple correlations. Amos does not provide normal-theory standard errors for these estimates. Yet, as the example demonstrates, it is easy to obtain empirical interval estimates for these parameters by bootstrapping.

Example 20: Bootstrapping for Model Comparison

Purpose

- Demonstrate the use of the bootstrap for model comparison.

Introduction

The problem addressed by this method is not that of evaluating an individual model in absolute terms, but of choosing among two or more competing models. Bollen and Stine (1992), Bollen (1982) and Stine (1989) suggested the possibility of using bootstrapping for model selection in analysis of moment structures. Linhart and Zucchini (1986) described a general schema for bootstrapping and model selection that is appropriate for a large class of models, including structural modeling. The Linhart and Zucchini approach is employed here.

The bootstrap approach to model comparison can be summarized as follows:

1. Generate several bootstrap samples by sampling with replacement from the original sample. In other words: the *original sample* serves as the *population* for purposes of bootstrap sampling.

2. Fit every competing model to every bootstrap sample. After each analysis, calculate the discrepancy between the implied moments obtained from the bootstrap sample and the moments of the bootstrap population.

---

3. For each model, calculate the average (across bootstrap samples) of the discrepancies from step 2.

4. Choose the model whose average discrepancy (from step 3) is smallest.

The data

The present example uses the combined male and female data from the Grant-White high school sample of the Holzinger and Swineford (1939) study, previously discussed in Examples 8, 12, 15, 17 and 19. We are using the same six psychological tests. The 145 combined observations are given in the file `Grant.sav`.

Five models

Five measurement models are applied to the six psychological tests. *Model 1* is an unrestricted factor analysis model with one factor:

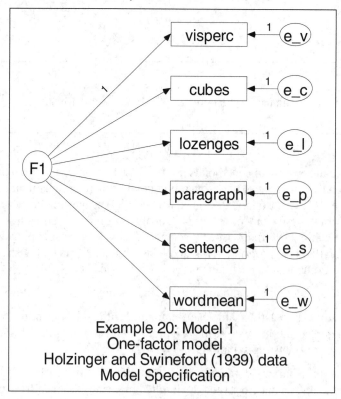

Example 20: Model 1
One-factor model
Holzinger and Swineford (1939) data
Model Specification

Model 2 is an unrestricted factor analysis with two factors. Note that the two zero constraints in the model are not restrictions, but fix the factors at some arbitrary orientation so that the model becomes identified (Anderson, 1984; Bollen and Jöreskog, 1985; Jöreskog, 1979):

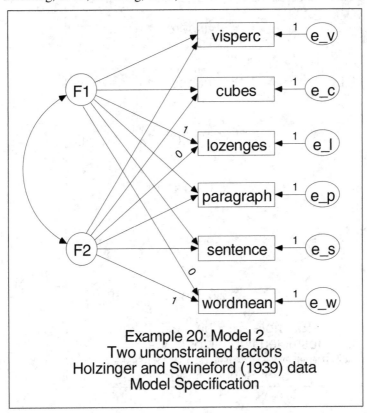

Example 20: Model 2
Two unconstrained factors
Holzinger and Swineford (1939) data
Model Specification

Model 2R is a restricted factor analysis model with two factors, in which the first three tests depend upon only one of the factors while the remaining three tests depend only upon the other factor:

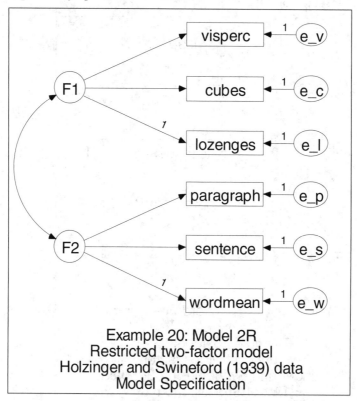

Example 20: Model 2R
Restricted two-factor model
Holzinger and Swineford (1939) data
Model Specification

The remaining two models provide the customary points of reference for comparing the fit of the previous models to the sample data. The *saturated model* simply restates the covariance structure:

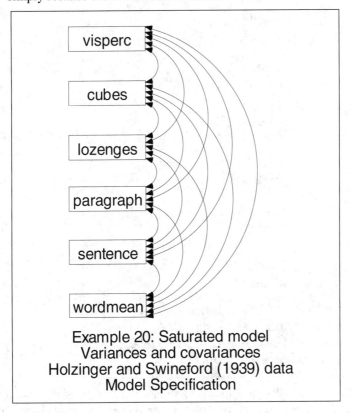

Example 20: Saturated model
Variances and covariances
Holzinger and Swineford (1939) data
Model Specification

And the *independence model* assumes that the six variables are uncorrelated:

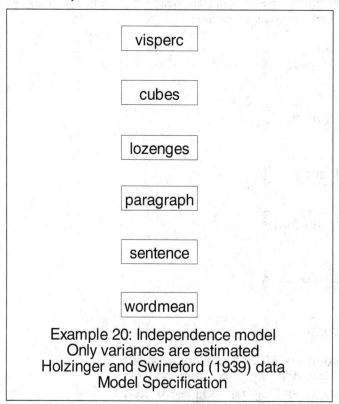

visperc

cubes

lozenges

paragraph

sentence

wordmean

Example 20: Independence model
Only variances are estimated
Holzinger and Swineford (1939) data
Model Specification

You would not ordinarily fit the saturated and independence models separately, since Amos automatically reports fit measures for those two models in the course of every analysis. However, it is necessary to specify explicitly the saturated and independence models in order to get bootstrap results for those models.

Five separate bootstrap analyses are performed, one for each model. For each of the five analyses, you will need to click on the **Analysis Properties** icon, go to the **Bootstrap** tab, check the **Perform bootstrap** box, and enter the **Number of bootstrap samples** at 1000:

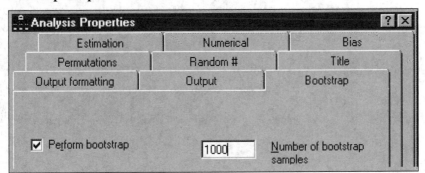

Then, click on the **Random #** tab and select a **Seed for random numbers**. It does not matter which seed number you choose, but in order to draw the exact same set of samples in each of several Amos sessions, the same seed number must be given each time. In this example, we have chosen 3:

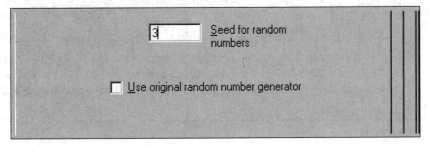

Occasionally during bootstrapping you may encounter samples where the computations will not converge. To keep overall computation times in check, click on the **Numerical** tab and limit the number of iterations to a realistic figure (say, 40) in the **Iteration limit** field:

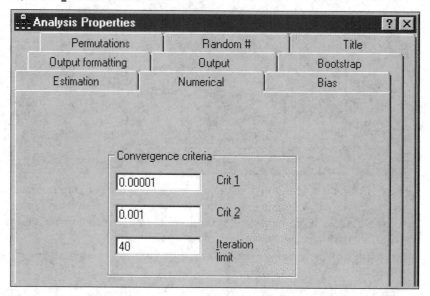

The **Amos Graphics** input files for the five models are called **Ex20-1.amw**, **Ex20-2.amw**, **Ex20-2r.amw**, **Ex20-sat.amw**, and **Ex20-ind.amw**. The **Amos Basic** input files use the same names but with the extension **.AmosBasic**.

Text output

From the analysis of Model 1, the following message indicates that it was not necessary to discard any bootstrap samples. All 1000 bootstrap samples were used:

```
   0 bootstrap samples were unused because of a singular covariance matrix.
   0 bootstrap samples were unused because a solution was not found.
1000 usable bootstrap samples were obtained.
```

For each of the five models and for each of the 1000 bootstrap samples, the bootstrap simulation shows by how much the implied sample moments differ from the population moments. The following output shows the distribution of

$$C_{ML}\left(\hat{\alpha}_b, \mathbf{a}\right) = C_{KL}\left(\hat{\alpha}_b, \mathbf{a}\right) - C_{KL}\left(\mathbf{a}, \mathbf{a}\right), \quad b = 1,\dots,1000,$$

where **a** contains the moments from the original sample of 145 Grant-White students (*i.e.*, the moment of the bootstrap population) and $\hat{\alpha}_b$ contains the implied moments obtained from fitting the model to the *b-th* bootstrap sample.

$C_{ML}(\hat{\alpha}_b, \mathbf{a})$ here is a measure of how much the population moments differ from the moments estimated from the *b-th* bootstrap sample using Model 1:

```
                        --------+--------------------
                         48.268|**
                         52.091|*********
                         55.913|*************
    ML discrepancy       59.735|*******************
    (implied vs pop)     63.558|*****************
                         67.380|************
                         71.202|********
        N = 1000         75.024|******
     Mean = 64.162       78.847|****
     S. e. = 0.292       82.669|*
                         86.491|**
                         90.313|**
                         94.136|*
                         97.958|*
                        101.780|*
                        --------+--------------------
```

The average of $C_{ML}(\hat{\alpha}_b, \mathbf{a})$ over the 1000 bootstrap samples is 64.162 with a standard error of .292. Similar histograms, along with means and standard errors, are displayed for the other four models, but are not reproduced here. The average discrepancies for the five competing models are shown in Table 20.1 along with values of the BCC, AIC, and CAIC criteria.

Model	Failures	Mean discrepancy	BCC	AIC	CAIC
1	0	64.16 (.29)	68.17	66.94	114.66
2	19	29.14 (.35)	36.81	35.07	102.68
2R	0	26.57 (.30)	30.97	29.64	81.34
Sat.	0	32.05 (.37)	44.15	42.00	125.51
Indep.	0	334.32 (.24)	333.93	333.32	357.18

Table 20.1: Fit Measures for Five Competing Models (Standard Errors in Parentheses)

The **Failures** column in Table 20.1 indicates that the likelihood function of Model 2 could not be maximized for 19 of the 1000 bootstrap samples, at least not with the iteration limit of 40. Nineteen additional bootstrap samples were generated for Model 2 in order to bring the total number of bootstrap samples to the target of 1000. The 19 samples where Model 2 could not be fitted successfully caused no problem with the other four models. Consequently, 981 bootstrap samples were common to all five models.

No attempt was made to find out why Model 2 estimates could not be computed for 19 bootstrap samples. As a rule, algorithms for analysis of moment structures tend to fail for models that fit the sample poorly. Conversely, if there were some other way to successfully estimate Model 2 from these 19 samples — say with hand-picked start values or a superior algorithm — it would likely have resulted in relatively large discrepancies. According to this line of reasoning, disregarding any bootstrap samples with estimation failure will likely lead to a downwards bias of the mean discrepancy for this model. Thus, you should be concerned by estimation failures during bootstrapping primarily when they occur for the model with the lowest mean discrepancy.

In this example, the lowest mean discrepancy (26.57) occurs for Model 2R, confirming the model choice based on the BCC, AIC, and CAIC criteria. The differences among the mean discrepancies are large compared to their standard errors. Since all models were fit to the same bootstrap samples (except for samples where Model 2 was not successfully fitted), you would expect to find positive correlations across bootstrap samples between discrepancies for similar models. Unfortunately, Amos does not report those correlations. Calculating the correlations by hand showed that they are quite close to one, so that standard errors for the differences between means in Table 20.1 are, on the whole, even smaller than the standard errors of the means.

Summary

Bootstrapping can be a practical aid in model selection for analysis of moment structures. The Linhart and Zucchini (1986) approach uses the expected discrepancy between implied and population moments as the basis for model comparisons. The method is conceptually simple and easy to apply. It does not employ any arbitrary "magic number" such as a significance level. Of course, the theoretical appropriateness of competing models and the reasonableness of their associated parameter estimates are not taken into account by the bootstrap procedure, and need to be given appropriate weight at some other stage in the model evaluation process.

Example 21: Bootstrapping to Compare Estimation Methods

Purpose

- Demonstrate how bootstrapping can be used to choose among competing estimation criteria.

Introduction

The discrepancy between the population moments and the moments implied by a model depends not only on the model, but also on the *estimation method*. We can adapt the technique used in Example 20 to compare models (with respect to their ability to recover population moments) to compare estimation methods. This capability is particularly needed when choosing among estimation methods that are known to be optimal only asymptotically, and whose relative merits in finite samples would be expected to depend on the model, the sample size and the population distribution. The principal obstacle to carrying out this program for comparing estimation methods is that it requires a prior decision about how to measure the discrepancy between the population moments and the moments implied by the model. There appears to be no way to make this decision without favoring some estimation criteria over others. Of course, if every choice of population discrepancy leads to the same conclusion, questions about which is the appropriate population discrepancy can be considered academic. The present example presents such a clear-cut case.

The data

The Holzinger-Swineford (1939) data from Example 20 (in file **Grant.sav**) are used in the present example.

The model

The present example estimates the parameters of Model 2R from Example 20 by four alternative methods: Asymptotically distribution-free (ADF), maximum likelihood (ML), generalized least squares (GLS), and unweighted least squares (ULS). To compare the four estimation methods, Amos needs to be run four times. In each of the four analyses, the factor specification for Model 2R is the same, and can be entered either in **Amos Graphics** or **Amos Basic**.

 To specify the estimation method and bootstrap parameters in **Amos Graphics**, begin by clicking on the **Analysis Properties** icon. Go to the **Random #** tab and select a **Seed for random numbers**. As we discussed in Example 20, it does not matter which seed number you choose, but in order to draw the exact same set of samples in each of several Amos sessions, the same seed number must be given each time. In this example, we have chosen 3:

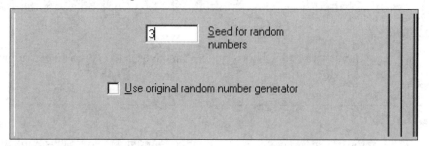

Next, select the **Estimation** tab and click on the <u>A</u>**symptotically distribution-free** discrepancy. This discrepancy specifies that ADF estimation should be used to fit the model to each bootstrap sample.

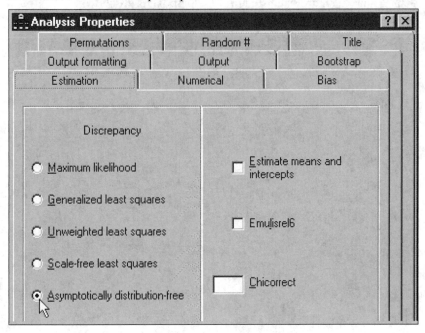

Finally, select the **Bootstrap** tab. Check the **Perform bootstrap** box, enter the **Number of bootstrap samples** at 1000, and select the desired output options. In our example, we are interested in **Bootstrap ADF**, **Bootstrap ML**, **Bootstrap GLS**, and **Bootstrap ULS**:

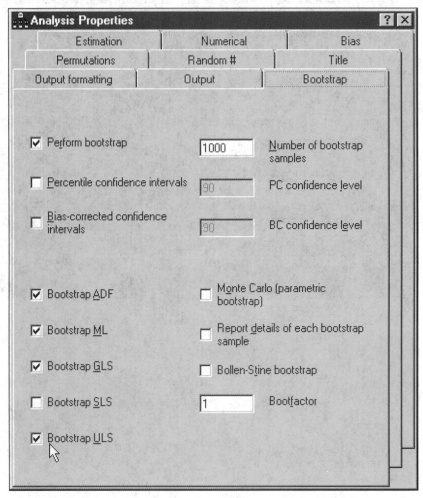

Amos will now evaluate the asymptotically distribution-free (ADF) estimation method using the same 1000 bootstrap samples that were used in Example 20.

The check boxes **Bootstrap ADF**, **Bootstrap ML**, **Bootstrap GLS**, **Bootstrap SLS**, and **Bootstrap ULS** specify that C_{ADF}, C_{ML}, C_{GLS}, and C_{ULS} should each be used to measure the discrepancy between the sample moments in the original sample and the implied moments from each bootstrap sample.

To evaluate the ML, GLS, and ULS estimation methods, repeat the analysis three more times, each time checking the appropriate discrepancy — **Maximum likelihood**, **Generalized least squares**, or **Unweighted least squares**:

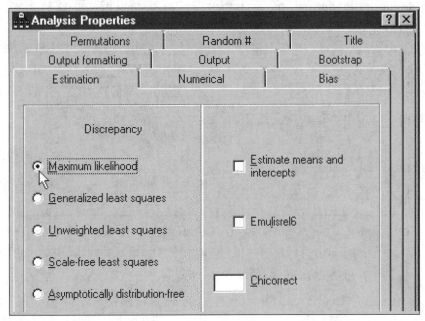

The **Amos Graphics** input files for this problem are **Ex21-adf.amw**, **Ex21-ml.amw**, **Ex21-gls.amw**, and **Ex21-uls.amw**, respectively. The **Amos Basic** files use the same naming convention, but with the extension **.AmosBasic**.

Text output

In the first of the four analyses (as found in **Ex21-adf.amw**), the ADF estimation discrepancy produces the following histogram output:

```
                          --------+-------------------
                   7.359 |*
                  10.817 |********
                  14.274 |****************
   ADF discrepancy  17.732 |********************
   (implied vs pop)  21.189 |*******************
                  24.647 |*************
                  28.104 |********
           N = 1000   31.562 |****
        Mean = 20.601  35.019 |**
        S. e. = 0.218  38.477 |**
                  41.934 |*
                  45.392 |*
                  48.850 |*
                  52.307 |*
                  55.765 |*
                          --------+-------------------
```

This portion of the output shows the distribution of the population discrepancy $C_{\text{ADF}}(\hat{\alpha}_b, \mathbf{a})$ across 1000 bootstrap samples, where $\hat{\alpha}_b$ contains the implied moments obtained by minimizing $C_{\text{ADF}}(\hat{\alpha}_b, \mathbf{a}_b)$, *i.e.*, the sample discrepancy. The average of $C_{\text{ADF}}(\hat{\alpha}_b, \mathbf{a})$ across 1000 bootstrap samples is 20.601, with a standard error of 0.218.

The output for this example (**Ex21-adf.amw**) also produces histograms for Bootstrap ML, Bootstrap GLS and Bootstrap ULS you get the following histograms:

```
                                --------+--------------------
                        11.272 |****
                        22.691 |********************
                        34.110 |********************
    ML discrepancy      45.530 |**********
    (implied vs pop)    56.949 |*****
                        68.368 |***
                        79.787 |**
        N = 1000        91.207 |*
     Mean = 36.860     102.626 |*
     S. e. = 0.571     114.045 |*
                       125.464 |
                       136.884 |
                       148.303 |
                       159.722 |
                       171.142 |*
                                --------+--------------------


                                --------+--------------------
                         7.248 |**
                        11.076 |*********
                        14.904 |**************
    GLS discrepancy     18.733 |********************
    (implied vs pop)    22.561 |**************
                        26.389 |**********
                        30.217 |*******
        N = 1000        34.046 |****
     Mean = 21.827      37.874 |**
     S. e. = 0.263      41.702 |***
                        45.530 |*
                        49.359 |*
                        53.187 |*
                        57.015 |*
                        60.844 |*
                                --------+--------------------


                                --------+--------------------
                      5079.897 |******
                     30811.807 |********************
                     56543.716 |********
    ULS discrepancy   82275.625 |****
    (implied vs pop) 108007.534 |**
                     133739.443 |*
                     159471.352 |*
        N = 1000     185203.261 |*
     Mean = 43686.444 210935.170 |
     S. e. = 1011.591 236667.079 |*
                     262398.988 |
                     288130.897 |
                     313862.806 |
                     339594.715 |
                     365326.624 |*
                                --------+--------------------
```

The four distributions just reported are summarized in the first row of Table 21.1. The remaining three rows show the results of estimation by minimizing C_{ML}, C_{GLS} and C_{ULS}, respectively.

		Population discrepancy for evaluation: $C(\hat{\alpha}_b, \mathbf{a})$			
		C_{ADF}	C_{ML}	C_{GLS}	C_{ULS}
Sample discrepancy for estimation $C(\hat{\alpha}_b, \mathbf{a}_b)$	C_{ADF}	20.60 (.22)	36.86 (.57)	21.83 (.26)	43686 (1012)
	C_{ML}	19.19 (.20)	26.57 (.30)	18.96 (.22)	34760 (758)
	C_{GLS}	19.45 (.20)	31.45 (.40)	19.03 (.21)	37021 (830)
	C_{ULS}	24.89 (.35)	31.78 (.43)	24.16 (.33)	35343 (793)

Table 21.1: Mean of $C(\hat{\alpha}_b, \mathbf{a})$ across 1000 Bootstrap Samples (Standard Errors in Parentheses)

The first column, labeled C_{ADF}, shows the relative performance of the four estimation methods according to the population discrepancy, C_{ADF}. Since 19.19 is the smallest mean discrepancy in the C_{ADF} column, C_{ML} is the best estimation method according to the C_{ADF} criterion. Similarly, examining the C_{ML} column of Table 21.1 shows that C_{ML} is the best estimation method according to the C_{ML} criterion.

Although the four columns of the table disagree on the exact ordering of the four estimation methods, ML is in all cases the method with the lowest mean discrepancy. The difference between ML estimation and GLS estimation is slight in some cases. Unsurprisingly, ULS estimation performed badly according to all of the population discrepancies employed. More interesting is the poor performance of ADF estimation, indicating that ADF estimation is unsuited to this combination of model, population and sample size.

Appendices

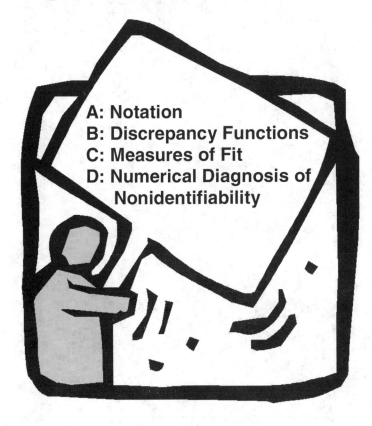

A: Notation
B: Discrepancy Functions
C: Measures of Fit
D: Numerical Diagnosis of
   Nonidentifiability

Appendix A: Notation

q = the number of parameters.

γ = the vector of parameters (of order q).

G = the number of groups.

$N^{(g)}$ = the number of observations in group g.

$N = \sum\limits_{g=1}^{G} N^{(g)}$, the total number of observations in all groups combined.

$p^{(g)}$ = the number of observed variables in group g.

$p*^{(g)}$ = the number of sample moments in group g. When means and intercepts are explicit model parameters, the relevant sample moments are means, variances and covariances, so that $p*^{(g)} = p^{(g)}\left(p^{(g)}+3\right)/2$. Otherwise, only sample variances and covariances are counted so that $p*^{(g)} = p^{(g)}\left(p^{(g)}+1\right)/2$.

$p = \sum\limits_{g=1}^{G} p*^{(g)}$, the number of sample moments in all groups combined.

$d = p-q$, the number of degrees of freedom for testing the model.

$x_{ir}^{(g)}$ = the r-th observation on the i-th variable in group g.

$\mathbf{x}_{r}^{(g)}$ = the r-th observation in group g.

$\mathbf{S}^{(g)}$ = the sample covariance matrix for group g.

$\Sigma^{(g)}(\gamma)$ = the covariance matrix for group g, according to the model.

$\mu^{(g)}(\gamma)$ = the mean vector for group g, according to the model.

$\Sigma_{0}^{(g)}$ = the population covariance matrix for group g.

$\mu_{0}^{(g)}$ = the population mean vector for group g.

$\mathbf{s}^{(g)} = \text{vec}\left(\mathbf{S}^{(g)}\right)$, the $p*^{(g)}$ distinct elements of $\mathbf{S}^{(g)}$ arranged in a single column vector.

$$\sigma^{(g)}(\gamma) = \text{vec}\left(\Sigma^{(g)}(\gamma)\right).$$

r = the nonnegative integer specified by the **Chicorrect** command. By default $r = G$. When the **Emulisrel6** command is used, $r = G$, and cannot be changed by using **Chicorrect**.

$n = N - r$.

a = the vector of order p containing the sample moments for all groups. That is, **a** contains the elements of $\mathbf{S}^{(1)}, \ldots, \mathbf{S}^{(G)}$, and also (if means and intercepts are explicit model parameters) $\overline{\mathbf{x}}^{(1)}, \ldots, \overline{\mathbf{x}}^{(G)}$.

$\boldsymbol{\alpha}_0$ = the vector of order p containing the population moments for all groups. That is, $\boldsymbol{\alpha}_0$ contains the elements of $\Sigma_0^{(1)}, \ldots, \Sigma_0^{(G)}$, and also (if means and intercepts are explicit model parameters) $\mu_0^{(1)}, \ldots, \mu_0^{(G)}$. The ordering of the elements of $\boldsymbol{\alpha}(\gamma)$ must match the ordering of the elements of **a**.

$\boldsymbol{\alpha}(\gamma)$ = the vector of order p containing the population moments for all groups according to the model. That is, $\boldsymbol{\alpha}(\gamma)$ contains the elements of $\Sigma^{(1)}(\gamma), \ldots, \Sigma^{(G)}(\gamma)$, and also (if means and intercepts are explicit model parameters) $\mu^{(1)}(\gamma), \ldots, \mu^{(G)}(\gamma)$. The ordering of the elements of $\boldsymbol{\alpha}(\gamma)$ must match the ordering of the elements of **a**.

$F(\boldsymbol{\alpha}(\gamma), \mathbf{a})$ = the function (of γ) that is minimized in fitting the model to the sample.

$\hat{\gamma}$ = the value of γ that minimizes $F(\boldsymbol{\alpha}(\gamma), \mathbf{a})$

$$\hat{\Sigma}^{(g)} = \Sigma^{(g)}(\hat{\gamma})$$

$$\hat{\mu}^{(g)} = \mu^{(g)}(\hat{\gamma})$$

$$\hat{\boldsymbol{\alpha}} = \boldsymbol{\alpha}(\hat{\gamma})$$

Appendix B: Discrepancy Functions

Amos minimizes discrepancy functions (Browne, 1982, 1984) of the form,

(D1)

$$C(\alpha,\, \mathbf{a}) = [N - r]\left(\frac{\sum_{g=1}^{G} N^{(g)} f\left(\mu^{(g)}, \Sigma^{(g)};\ \overline{\mathbf{x}}^{(g)}, \mathbf{S}^{(g)}\right)}{N}\right) = [N - r]F(\alpha,\, \mathbf{a}).$$

Different discrepancy functions are obtained by changing the way f is defined. If means and intercepts are unconstrained and do not appear as explicit model parameters, $\overline{\mathbf{x}}^{(g)}$ and $\mu^{(g)}$ will be omitted and f will be written $f\left(\Sigma^{(g)};\ \mathbf{S}^{(g)}\right)$.

The discrepancy functions C_{KL} and F_{KL} are obtained by taking f to be

$$f_{KL}\left(\mu^{(g)}, \Sigma^{(g)}; \overline{\mathbf{x}}^{(g)}, \mathbf{S}^{(g)}\right) = \log\left|\Sigma^{(g)}\right| + \mathrm{tr}\left(\mathbf{S}^{(g)}\Sigma^{(g)^{-1}}\right) + \left(\overline{\mathbf{x}}^{(g)} - \mu^{(g)}\right)' \Sigma^{(g)^{-1}}\left(\overline{\mathbf{x}}^{(g)} - \mu^{(g)}\right).$$

Except for an additive constant that depends only on the sample size, f_{KL} is -2 times the Kullback-Leibler information quantity (Kullback and Leibler, 1951). Strictly speaking, C_{KL} and F_{KL} do not qualify as discrepancy functions according to Browne's definition since $F_{KL}(\mathbf{a},\, \mathbf{a}) \neq 0$.

For *maximum likelihood* estimation (**ML**), C_{ML} and F_{ML} are obtained by taking f to be

(D2)

$$f_{ML}\left(\mu^{(g)}, \Sigma^{(g)}; \overline{\mathbf{x}}^{(g)}, \mathbf{S}^{(g)}\right) = f_{KL}\left(\mu^{(g)}, \Sigma^{(g)}; \overline{\mathbf{x}}^{(g)}, \mathbf{S}^{(g)}\right) - f_{KL}\left(\overline{\mathbf{x}}^{(g)}, \mathbf{S}^{(g)}; \overline{\mathbf{x}}^{(g)}, \mathbf{S}^{(g)}\right)$$

$$= \log\left|\Sigma^{(g)}\right| + \mathrm{tr}\left(\mathbf{S}^{(g)}\Sigma^{(g)^{-1}}\right) - \log\left|\mathbf{S}^{(g)}\right| - p^{(g)} + \left(\overline{\mathbf{x}}^{(g)} - \mu^{(g)}\right)' \Sigma^{(g)^{-1}}\left(\overline{\mathbf{x}}^{(g)} - \mu^{(g)}\right).$$

For *generalized least squares* estimation (**GLS**), C_{GLS} and F_{GLS} are obtained by taking f to be

(D3)
$$f_{GLS}\left(\Sigma^{(g)};\ \mathbf{S}^{(g)}\right) = \tfrac{1}{2}\,\mathrm{tr}\left[\mathbf{S}^{(g)^{-1}}\left(\mathbf{S}^{(g)} - \Sigma^{(g)}\right)\right]^{2}.$$

For *asymptotically distribution-free* estimation (**ADF**), C_{ADF} and F_{ADF} are obtained by taking f to be

(D4)
$$f_{ADF}\left(\Sigma^{(g)};\mathbf{S}^{(g)}\right) = \sum_{g=1}^{G}\left[\mathbf{s}^{(g)} - \mathbf{\sigma}^{(g)}(\gamma)\right]' \mathbf{U}^{(g)^{-1}}\left[\mathbf{s}^{(g)} - \mathbf{\sigma}^{(g)}(\gamma)\right],$$

where the elements of $\mathbf{U}^{(g)}$ are given by Browne (1984, Equations 3.1–3.4):

$$\bar{x}_i^{(g)} = \frac{1}{N_g}\sum_{r=1}^{N_g} x_{ir}^{(g)},$$

$$w_{ij}^{(g)} = \frac{1}{N_g}\sum_{r=1}^{N_g}\left(x_{ir}^{(g)} - \bar{x}_i^{(g)}\right)\left(x_{jr}^{(g)} - \bar{x}_j^{(g)}\right),$$

$$w_{ij,kl}^{(g)} = \frac{1}{N_g}\sum_{r=1}^{N_g}\left(x_{ir}^{(g)} - \bar{x}_i^{(g)}\right)\left(x_{jr}^{(g)} - \bar{x}_j^{(g)}\right)\left(x_{kr}^{(g)} - \bar{x}_k^{(g)}\right)\left(x_{lr}^{(g)} - \bar{x}_l^{(g)}\right),$$

$$\left[\mathbf{U}^{(g)}\right]_{ij,kl} = w_{ij,kl}^{(g)} - w_{ij}^{(g)}w_{kl}^{(g)}.$$

For *'scale free' least squares* estimation (**SLS**), C_{SLS} and F_{SLS} are obtained by taking f to be

(D5)
$$f_{SLS}\left(\Sigma^{(g)};\mathbf{S}^{(g)}\right) = \frac{1}{2}\text{tr}\left[\mathbf{D}^{(g)^{-1}}\left(\mathbf{S}^{(g)} - \Sigma^{(g)}\right)\right]^2,$$

where $\mathbf{D}^{(g)} = \text{diag}\left(\mathbf{S}^{(g)}\right)$.

For *unweighted least squares* estimation (**ULS**), C_{ULS} and F_{ULS} are obtained by taking f to be

(D6)
$$f_{ULS}\left(\Sigma^{(g)};\mathbf{S}^{(g)}\right) = \frac{1}{2}\text{tr}\left[\mathbf{S}^{(g)} - \Sigma^{(g)}\right]^2.$$

Amos's **Emulisrel6** command can be used to replace (D1) with

(D1a)
$$C = \sum_{g=1}^{G}\left(N^{(g)} - 1\right)F^{(g)}.$$

F is then calculated as $F = C/(N - G)$.

When $G = 1$ and $r = 1$, (D1) and (D1a) are equivalent, giving

$$C = \left(N^{(1)} - 1\right)F^{(1)} = (N - 1)F .$$

For maximum likelihood, asymptotically distribution-free, and generalized least squares estimation, both (D1) and (D1a) have a chi-square distribution for correctly specified models under appropriate distributional assumptions. Asymptotically, (D1) and (D1a) are equivalent. However, both formulas can exhibit some inconsistencies in finite samples.

Suppose you have two independent samples and a model for each. Furthermore, suppose that you analyze the two samples simultaneously, but that, in doing so, you impose no constraints requiring any parameter in one model to equal any parameter in the other model. Then if you minimize (D1a), the parameter estimates obtained from the simultaneous analysis of both groups will be the same as from separate analyses of each group alone.

Furthermore, the discrepancy function (D1a) obtained from the simultaneous analysis will be the sum of the discrepancy functions from the two separate analyses. Formula (D1) does not have this property when r is nonzero. Using formula (D1) to do a simultaneous analysis of the two groups will give the same parameter estimates as two separate analyses, but the discrepancy function from the simultaneous analysis will not be the sum of the individual discrepancy functions.

On the other hand, suppose you have a single sample to which you have fitted some model using Amos. Now suppose that you arbitrarily split the sample into two groups of unequal size and perform a simultaneous analysis of both groups, employing the original model for both groups, and constraining each parameter in the first group to be equal to the corresponding parameter in the second group. If you have minimized (D1) in both analyses, you will get the same results in both. However, if you use (D1a) in both analyses, the two analyses will produce different estimates and a different minimum value for F.

All of the inconsistencies just pointed out can be avoided by using (D1) with the choice $r = 0$, so that (D1) becomes

$$C = \sum_{g=1}^{G} N^{(g)} F^{(g)} = NF .$$

Appendix C: Measures of Fit

Model evaluation is one of the most unsettled and difficult issues connected with structural modeling. Bollen and Long (1993), MacCallum (1990), Mulaik, *et al.* (1989), and Steiger (1990) present a variety of viewpoints and recommendations on this topic. Dozens of statistics, besides the value of the discrepancy function at its minimum, have been proposed as measures of the merit of a model. Amos calculates most of them.

Fit measures are reported for each model specified by the user and for two additional models called the "saturated" model and the "independence" model. In the *saturated model*, no constraints are placed on the population moments. The saturated model is the most general model possible. It is a vacuous model in the sense that it is guaranteed to fit any set of data perfectly. Any Amos model is a constrained version of the saturated model. The *independence model* goes to the opposite extreme. In the independence model, the observed variables are assumed to be uncorrelated with each other. When means are being estimated or constrained, the means of all observed variables are fixed at zero. The independence model is so severely and implausibly constrained that you would expect it to provide a poor fit to any interesting set of data. It frequently happens that each one of the models that you have specified can be so constrained as to be equivalent to the independence model. If this is the case, the saturated model and the independence model can be viewed as two extremes between which your proposed models lie.

For every estimation method except maximum likelihood, Amos also reports fit measures for a *zero model*, in which every parameter is fixed at zero.

Measures of parsimony

Models with relatively few parameters (and relatively many degrees of freedom) are sometimes said to be high in parsimony, or simplicity. Models with many parameters (and few degrees of freedom) are said to be complex, or lacking in parsimony. This use of the terms, simplicity and complexity, does not always conform to everyday usage. For example, the saturated model would be called complex while a model with an elaborate pattern of linear dependencies but with highly constrained parameter values would be called simple.

While one can inquire into the grounds for preferring simple, parsimonious models (*e.g.*, Mulaik, *et al.*, 1989), there does not appear to be any disagreement that parsimonious models are preferable to complex ones. When it comes to parameters, all other things being equal, less is more. At the same time, well fitting models are preferable to poorly fitting ones. Many fit measures represent an attempt to balance these two conflicting objectives— simplicity and goodness of fit.

> "In the final analysis, it may be, in a sense, impossible to define one *best* way to combine measures of complexity and measures of badness-of-fit in a single numerical index, because the precise nature of the *best* numerical tradeoff between complexity and fit is, to some extent, a matter of personal taste. The choice of a model is a classic problem in the two-dimensional analysis of preference." (Steiger, 1990, p. 179)

NPAR

NPAR is the number of distinct parameters (q) being estimated. Two regression weights, say, that are required to be equal to each other count as one parameter, not two.

Note: Use the **\npar** text macro to display the number of parameters in the output path diagram.

DF

DF is the number of degrees of freedom for testing the model:

$$df = d = p - q.$$

where p is the number of sample moments and q is the number of distinct parameters. Rigdon (1994) gives a detailed explanation of the calculation and interpretation of degrees of freedom.

Note: Use the **\df** text macro to display the degrees of freedom in the output path diagram.

PRATIO

The parsimony ratio (James, Mulaik and Brett, 1982; Mulaik, *et al.*, 1989; Mulaik, *et al.*, 1989) expresses the number of constraints in the model being evaluated as a fraction of the number of constraints in the independence model:

$$\textbf{PRATIO} = \frac{d}{d_i},$$

where d is the degrees of freedom of the model being evaluated and d_i is the degrees of freedom of the independence model. The parsimony ratio is used in the calculation of **PNFI** and **PCFI** (see **Parsimony adjusted measures** on page 411).

Note: Use the **pratio** text macro to display the parsimony ratio in the output path diagram.

The minimum sample discrepancy function

The following fit measures are based on the minimum value of the discrepancy.

CMIN

CMIN is the minimum value, $\hat{C}$, of the discrepancy, C (see Appendix B).

Note: Use the **\cmin** text macro to display the minimum value $\hat{C}$ of the discrepancy function C in the output path diagram.

P

P is the probability of getting as large a discrepancy as occurred with the present sample (under appropriate distributional assumptions and assuming a correctly specified model). That is, **P** is a "*p* value" for testing the hypothesis that the model fits perfectly in the population.

One approach to model selection employs statistical hypothesis testing to eliminate from consideration those models that are inconsistent with the available data. Hypothesis testing is a widely accepted procedure and there is a lot of experience in its use. However, its unsuitability as a device for model selection was pointed out early in the development of analysis of moment structures (Jöreskog, 1969). It is generally acknowledged that most models are useful approximations that do not fit perfectly in the population. In other words, the null hypothesis of perfect fit is not credible to begin with and will in the end be accepted only if the sample is not allowed to get too big.

If you encounter resistance to the foregoing view of the role of hypothesis testing in model fitting, the following quotations may come in handy. The first two quotes predate the development of structural modeling, and refer to other model fitting problems.

> "The power of the test to detect an underlying disagreement between theory and data is controlled largely by the size of the sample. With a small sample an alternative hypothesis which departs violently from the null hypothesis may still have a small probability of yielding a significant value of χ^2. In a very large sample, small and unimportant departures from the null hypothesis are almost certain to be detected." (Cochran, 1952)

> "If the sample is *small* then the χ^2 test will show that the data are '*not* significantly different from' quite a wide range of very different theories, while if the sample is *large*, the χ^2 test will show that the data are *significantly* different from those expected on a given theory even though

the difference may be so very slight as to be negligible or unimportant on other criteria." (Gulliksen and Tukey, 1958, pp. 95–96)

"Such a hypothesis [of perfect fit] may be quite unrealistic in most empirical work with test data. If a sufficiently large sample were obtained this χ^2 statistic would, no doubt, indicate that any such non-trivial hypothesis is statistically untenable." (Jöreskog , 1969, p. 200)

"... in very large samples virtually all models that one might consider would have to be rejected as statistically untenable .... In effect, a nonsignificant chi-square value is desired, and one attempts to infer the validity of the hypothesis of no difference between model and data. Such logic is well-known in various statistical guises as attempting to prove the null hypothesis. This procedure cannot generally be justified, since the chi-square variate v can be made small by simply reducing sample size." (Bentler and Bonett, 1980, p. 591)

"Our opinion ... is that this null hypothesis [of perfect fit] is implausible and that it does not help much to know whether or not the statistical test has been able to detect that it is false." (Browne and Mels, 1992, p. 78).

See also **PCLOSE** on page 403.

Note: Use the **\p** text macro for displaying this *p* value in the output path diagram.

CMIN/DF

CMIN/DF is the minimum discrepancy, $\hat{C}$, (see Appendix B) divided by its degrees of freedom:

$$\frac{\hat{C}}{d} .$$

Several writers have suggested the use of this ratio as a measure of fit. For every estimation criterion except for **ULS** and **SLS**, the ratio should be close to one for correct models. The trouble is that it isn't clear how far from one you should let the ratio get before concluding that a model is unsatisfactory.

Rules of thumb:

"...Wheaton *et al.* (1977) suggest that the researcher also compute a *relative* chi-square (χ^2/df) .... They suggest a ratio of approximately five or less 'as beginning to be reasonable.' In our experience, however, χ^2 to degrees of freedom ratios in the range of 2 to 1 or 3 to 1 are indicative of an acceptable fit between the hypothetical model and the sample data." (Carmines and McIver, 1981, page 80)

"... different researchers have recommended using ratios as low as 2 or as high as 5 to indicate a reasonable fit." (Marsh and Hocevar, 1985).

"... it seems clear that a χ^2/df ratio > 2.00 represents an inadequate fit." (Byrne, 1989, p. 55).

Note: Use the **\cmindf** text macro to display the value of **CMIN/DF** in the output path diagram.

FMIN

FMIN is the minimum value, $\hat{F}$, of the discrepancy, F (see Appendix B).

Note: Use the **\fmin** text macro to display the minimum value $\hat{F}$ of the discrepancy function F in the output path diagram.

Measures based on the population discrepancy

Steiger and Lind (1980) introduced the use of the population discrepancy function as a measure of model adequacy. The population discrepancy function, F_0, is the value of the discrepancy function obtained by fitting a model to the population moments rather than to sample moments. That is,

$$F_0 = \min_{\gamma} \left[F(\alpha(\gamma), \alpha_0) \right]$$

in contrast to

$$\hat{F} = \min_{\gamma} \left[F(\alpha(\gamma), \mathbf{a}) \right].$$

Steiger, Shapiro and Browne (1985) showed that under certain conditions $\hat{C} = n\hat{F}$ has a noncentral chi-square distribution with d degrees of freedom and noncentrality parameter $\delta = C = nF$. The Steiger-Lind approach to model evaluation centers around the estimation of F_0 and related quantities.

This section of the User's Guide relies mainly on Steiger and Lind (1980) and Steiger, Shapiro and Browne (1985). The notation is primarily that of Browne and Mels (1992).

NCP

$NCP = \max(\hat{C} - d, 0)$ is an estimate of the noncentrality parameter, $\delta = C_0 = nF_0$.

The columns labeled **LO 90** and **HI 90** contain the lower limit (δ_L) and upper limit (δ_U) of a 90% confidence interval, on δ. δ_L is obtained by solving

$$\Phi\left(\hat{C} \mid \delta, d\right) = .95$$

for δ, and δ_U is obtained by solving

$$\Phi\left(\hat{C} \mid \delta, d\right) = .05$$

for δ, where $\Phi(x \mid \delta, d)$ is the distribution function of the noncentral chi-squared distribution with noncentrality parameter δ and d degrees of freedom.

Note: Use the **\ncp** text macro to display the value of the non-centrality parameter estimate in the path diagram, **\ncplo** to display the lower 90% confidence limit, and **\ncphi** for the upper 90% confidence limit.

F0

$$\text{F0} = \hat{F}_0 = \max\left(\frac{\hat{C} - d}{n}, 0\right) = \frac{\text{NCP}}{n} \text{ is an estimate of } \frac{\delta}{n} = F_0.$$

The columns labeled **LO 90** and **HI 90** contain the lower limit and upper limit of a 90% confidence interval on F_0:

$$\text{LO } 90 = \sqrt{\frac{\delta_L}{n}}$$

$$\text{HI } 90 = \sqrt{\frac{\delta_U}{n}} \; .$$

Note: Use the **\f0** text macro to display the value of $\hat{F}_0$ in the output path diagram, **\f0lo** to display its lower 90% confidence estimate, and **\f0hi** to display the upper 90% confidence estimate.

RMSEA

F_0 incorporates no penalty for model complexity and will tend to favor models with many parameters. In comparing two nested models, F_0 will never favor the simpler model. Steiger and Lind (1980) suggested compensating for the effect of model complexity by dividing F_0 by the number of degrees of freedom for testing the model. Taking the square root of the resulting ratio gives the population "root mean square error of approximation," called **RMS** by Steiger and Lind, and **RMSEA** by Browne and Cudeck (1993).

$$\text{population RMSEA} = \sqrt{\frac{F_0}{d}}$$

$$\text{estimated RMSEA} = \sqrt{\frac{\hat{F}_0}{d}}$$

The columns labeled **LO 90** and **HI 90** contain the lower limit and upper limit of a 90% confidence interval on the population value of **RMSEA**. The limits are given by

$$\text{LO } 90 = \sqrt{\frac{\delta_L/n}{d}}$$

$$\text{HI } 90 = \sqrt{\frac{\delta_U/n}{d}}$$

Rule of thumb:

"Practical experience has made us feel that a value of the RMSEA of about .05 or less would indicate a close fit of the model in relation to the degrees of freedom. This figure is based on subjective judgment. It cannot be regarded as infallible or correct, but it is more reasonable than the requirement of exact fit with the RMSEA = 0.0. We are also of the opinion that a value of about 0.08 or less for the RMSEA would indicate a reasonable error of approximation and would not want to employ a model with a RMSEA greater than 0.1." (Browne and Cudeck, 1993)

Note: Use the **\rmsea** text macro to display the estimated root mean square error of approximation in the output path diagram, **\rmsealo** for its lower 90% confidence estimate and **\rmseahi** for its upper 90% confidence estimate.

PCLOSE

$\text{PCLOSE} = 1 - \Phi\left(\hat{C} \mid .05^2 \, nd, d\right)$ is a "*p* value" for testing the null hypothesis that the population **RMSEA** is no greater than .05:

$$H_0 : \text{RMSEA} \leq .05 \ .$$

By contrast, the "*p* value" in the **P** column (see **P** on page 398) is for testing the hypothesis that the population **RMSEA** is zero:

$$H_0 : \text{RMSEA} = 0 \ .$$

Based on their experience with **RMSEA**, Browne and Cudeck (1993) suggest that a **RMSEA** of .05 or less indicates a "close fit." Employing this definition of "close fit," **PCLOSE** gives a test of close fit while **P** gives a test of exact fit.

Note: Use the **\pclose** text macro to display the "*p* value" for close fit of the population **RMSEA** in the output path diagram.

Information-theoretic measures

Amos reports several statistics of the form $\hat{C} + kq$ or $\hat{F} + kq$, where k is some positive constant. Each of these statistics creates a composite measure of badness of fit ($\hat{C}$ or $\hat{F}$) and complexity (q) by forming a weighted sum of the two. Simple models that fit well receive low scores according to such a criterion. Complicated, poorly fitting models get high scores. The constant k determines the relative penalties to be attached to badness of fit and to complexity.

The statistics described in this section are intended for model comparisons and not for the evaluation of an isolated model.

All of these statistics were developed for use with maximum likelihood estimation. Amos reports them for **GLS** and **ADF** estimation as well, although it is not clear that their use is appropriate there.

AIC

The Akaike information criterion (Akaike, 1973, 1987) is given by

$$\text{AIC} = \hat{C} + 2q \ .$$

See also **ECVI** on page 405.

Note: Use the **\aic** text macro to display the value of the Akaike information criterion in the output path diagram.

BCC

The Browne-Cudeck (1989) criterion is given by,

$$\text{BCC} = \hat{C} + 2q \frac{\displaystyle\sum_{g=1}^{G} b^{(g)} \frac{p^{(g)}\left(p^{(g)} + 3\right)}{N^{(g)} - p^{(g)} - 2}}{\displaystyle\sum_{g=1}^{G} p^{(g)}\left(p^{(g)} + 3\right)}$$

where $b^{(g)} = N^{(g)} - 1$ if the **Emulisrel6** command has been used, or $b^{(g)} = n\dfrac{N^{(g)}}{N}$ if it has not.

BCC imposes a slightly greater penalty for model complexity than does **AIC**.

BCC is the only measure in this section that was developed specifically for analysis of moment structures. Browne and Cudeck provided some empirical evidence suggesting that **BCC** may be superior to more generally applicable measures. Arbuckle (in preparation) gives an alternative justification for **BCC** and derives the above formula for multiple groups.

See also **MECVI** on page 406.

Note: Use the **\bcc** text macro to display the value of the Browne-Cudeck criterion in the output path diagram.

BIC

The Bayes information criterion (Schwarz, 1978; Raftery, 1993) is given by the formula,

$$\text{BIC} = \hat{C} + q \ln\left(N^{(1)} p^{(1)}\right).$$

In comparison to the **AIC**, **BCC** and **CAIC**, the **BIC** assigns a greater penalty to model complexity, and so has a greater tendency to pick parsimonious models. The **BIC** is reported only for the case of a single group where means and intercepts are not explicit model parameters.

Note: Use the **\bic** text macro to display the value of the Bayes information criterion in the output path diagram.

CAIC

Bozdogan's (1987) **CAIC** (consistent **AIC**) is given by the formula,

$$\text{CAIC} = \hat{C} + q\left(\ln N^{(1)} + 1\right).$$

CAIC assigns a greater penalty to model complexity than either **AIC** or **BCC**, but not as great a penalty as does **BIC**. **CAIC** is reported only for the case of a single group where means and intercepts are not explicit model parameters.

Note: Use the **\caic** text macro to display the value of the consistent **AIC** statistic in the output path diagram.

ECVI

Except for a constant scale factor, **ECVI** is the same as **AIC**:

$$\text{ECVI} = \frac{1}{n}(\text{AIC}) = \hat{F} + \frac{2q}{n}.$$

The columns labeled **LO 90** and **HI 90** give the lower limit and upper limit of a 90% confidence interval on the population **ECVI**:

$$LO\,90 = \frac{\delta_L + d + 2q}{n},$$

$$HI\,90 = \frac{\delta_U + d + 2q}{n}.$$

See also **AIC** on page 404.

Note: Use the **\ecvi** text macro to display the value of the expected cross-validation index in the output path diagram, **\ecvilo** to display its lower 90% confidence estimate, and **\ecvihi** for its upper 90% confidence estimate.

MECVI

Except for a scale factor, **MECVI** is identical to **BCC**:

$$\mathbf{MECVI} = \frac{1}{n}(\mathbf{BCC}) = \hat{F} + 2q\frac{\displaystyle\sum_{g=1}^{G} a^{(g)}\,\frac{p^{(g)}\left(p^{(g)}+3\right)}{N^{(g)}-p^{(g)}-2}}{\displaystyle\sum_{g=1}^{G} p^{(g)}\left(p^{(g)}+3\right)},$$

where $a^{(g)} = \dfrac{N^{(g)}-1}{N-G}$ if the **Emulisrel6** command has been used, or $a^{(g)} = \dfrac{N^{(g)}}{N}$ if it has not.

See also **BCC** on page 404

Note: Use the **\mecvi** text macro to display the modified **ECVI** statistic in the output path diagram.

Comparisons to a baseline model

Several fit measures encourage you to reflect on the fact that, no matter how badly your model fits, things could always be worse.

Bentler and Bonett (1980) and Tucker and Lewis (1973) suggested fitting the independence model or some other very badly fitting baseline model as an exercise to see how large the discrepancy function becomes. The object of the exercise is to put the fit of your own model(s) into some perspective. If none of your models fit very well, it may cheer you up to see a *really* bad model. For example, as the following output shows, Model A from Example 6 has a rather large discrepancy ($\hat{C} = 71.47$) in relation to its degrees of freedom. On the other hand, 71.544 does not look so bad compared to 2131.790 (the discrepancy for the independence model).

Model	NPAR	CMIN	DF	P	CMIN/DF
A	15	71.544	6	0.000	11.924
B	16	6.383	5	0.271	1.277
Saturated model	21	0.000	0		
Independence model	6	2131.790	15	0.000	142.119

This things-could-be-worse philosophy of model evaluation is incorporated into a number of fit measures. All of the measures tend to range between zero and one, with values close to one indicating a good fit. Only **NFI** (described below) is guaranteed to be between zero and one, with one indicating a perfect fit. (**CFI** is also guaranteed to be between zero and one, but this is because values bigger than one are reported as one, while values less than zero are reported as zero.)

The independence model is only one example of a model that can be chosen as the baseline model, although it is the one most often used, and the one that Amos uses. Sobel and Bohrnstedt (1985) contend that the choice of the independence model as a baseline model is often inappropriate. They suggest alternatives, as did Bentler and Bonett (1980), and give some examples to demonstrate the sensitivity of **NFI** to the choice of baseline model.

NFI

The Bentler-Bonett (1980) normed fit index (**NFI**), or Δ_1 in the notation of Bollen (1989) can be written

$$\text{NFI} = \Delta_1 = 1 - \frac{\hat{C}}{\hat{C}_b} = 1 - \frac{\hat{F}}{\hat{F}_b},$$

where $\hat{C} = n\hat{F}$ is the minimum discrepancy of the model being evaluated and $\hat{C}_b = n\hat{F}_b$ is the minimum discrepancy of the baseline model.

In Example 6 the independence model can be obtained by adding constraints to any of the other models. Any model can be obtained by constraining the saturated model. So Model A, for instance, with $\chi^2 = 71.544$, is unambiguously "in between" the perfectly fitting saturated model ($\chi^2 = 0$) and the independence model $\chi^2 = 2131.790$).

Model	NPAR	CMIN	DF	P	CMIN/DF
A	15	71.544	6	0.000	11.924
B	16	6.383	5	0.271	1.277
Saturated model	21	0.000	0		
Independence model	6	2131.790	15	0.000	142.119

Looked at in this way, the fit of Model A is a lot closer to the fit of the saturated model than it is to the fit of the independence model. In fact you might say that Model A has a discrepancy that is 96.6% of the way between the (terribly fitting) independence model and the (perfectly fitting) saturated model:

$$\text{NFI} = \frac{2131.790 - 71.54}{2131.790} = 1 - \frac{71.54}{2131.790} = .966 \ .$$

Rule of thumb:

> "Since the scale of the fit indices is not necessarily easy to interpret (*e.g.*, the indices are not squared multiple correlations), experience will be required to establish values of the indices that are associated with various degrees of meaningfulness of results. In our experience, models with overall fit indices of less than .9 can usually be improved substantially. These indices, and the general hierarchical comparisons described previously, are best understood by examples." (Bentler and Bonett, 1980, p. 600, referring to both the **NFI** and the **TLI**)

Note: Use the **\nfi** text macro to display the normed fit index value in the output path diagram.

RFI

Bollen's (1986) relative fit index (**RFI**) is given by

$$\text{RFI} = \rho_1 = 1 - \frac{\hat{C}/d}{\hat{C}_b/d_b} = 1 - \frac{\hat{F}/d}{\hat{F}_b/d_b} \ ,$$

where $\hat{C}$ and d are the discrepancy and the degrees of freedom for the model being evaluated, and $\hat{C}_b$ and d_b are the discrepancy and the degrees of freedom for the baseline model.

The **RFI** is obtained from the **NFI** by substituting F/d for F.

RFI values close to 1 indicate a very good fit.

Note: Use the **\rfi** text macro to display the relative fit index value in the output path diagram.

IFI

Bollen's (1989) incremental fit index (**IFI**) is given by

$$IFI = \Delta_2 = \frac{\hat{C}_b - \hat{C}}{\hat{C}_b - d},$$

where $\hat{C}$ and d are the discrepancy and the degrees of freedom for the model being evaluated, and $\hat{C}_b$ and d_b are the discrepancy and the degrees of freedom for the baseline model.

IFI values close to 1 indicate a very good fit.

Note: Use the **\ifi** text macro to display the incremental fit index value in the output path diagram.

TLI

The Tucker-Lewis coefficient (ρ_2 in the notation of Bollen, 1989) was discussed by Bentler and Bonett (1980) in the context of analysis of moment structures, and is also known as the Bentler-Bonett non-normed fit index (**NNFI**).

$$TLI = \rho_2 = \frac{\dfrac{\hat{C}_b}{d_b} - \dfrac{\hat{C}}{d}}{\dfrac{\hat{C}_b}{d_b} - 1},$$

The typical range for **TLI** lies between zero and one, but it is not limited to that range. **TLI** values close to 1 indicate a very good fit.

Note: Use the **\tli** text macro to display the value of the Tucker-Lewis index in the output path diagram.

CFI

The comparative fit index (**CFI**; Bentler, 1990) is given by.

$$CFI = 1 - \frac{\max\left(\hat{C} - d, 0\right)}{\max\left(\hat{C}_b - d_b, 0\right)} = 1 - \frac{NCP}{NCP_b},$$

where $\hat{C}, d$, and **NCP** are the discrepancy, the degrees of freedom and the noncentrality parameter estimate for the model being evaluated, and $\hat{C}_b, d_b$ and NCP_b are the discrepancy, the degrees of freedom and the noncentrality parameter estimate for the baseline model.

The **CFI** is identical to McDonald and Marsh's (1990) relative noncentrality index (**RNI**),

$$RNI = 1 - \frac{\hat{C} - d}{\hat{C}_b - d_b},$$

except that the **CFI** is truncated to fall in the range from 0 to 1. **CFI** values close to 1 indicate a very good fit.

Note: Use the **\cfi** text macro to display the value of the comparative fit index in the output path diagram.

Parsimony adjusted measures

James, *et al.* (1982) suggested multiplying the **NFI** by a "parsimony index" so as to take into account the number of degrees of freedom for testing both the model being evaluated and the baseline model. Mulaik (1989) suggested applying the same adjustment to the **GFI**. Amos also applies a parsimony adjustment to the **CFI**.

See also **PGFI** on page 413.

PNFI

The **PNFI** is the result of applying James, *et al.*'s (1982) parsimony adjustment to the **NFI**:

$$\text{PNFI} = (\text{NFI})(\text{PRATIO}) = \text{NFI}\frac{d}{d_b},$$

where d is the degrees of freedom for the model being evaluated, and d_b is the degrees of freedom for the baseline model.

Note: Use the **\pnfi** text macro to display the value of the parsimonious normed fit index in the output path diagram.

PCFI

The **PCFI** is the result of applying James, *et al.*'s (1982) parsimony adjustment to the **CFI**:

$$\text{PCFI} = (\text{CFI})(\text{PRATIO}) = \text{CFI}\frac{d}{d_b}$$

where d is the degrees of freedom for the model being evaluated, and d_b is the degrees of freedom for the baseline model.

Note: Use the **\pcfi** text macro to display the value of the parsimonious comparative fit index in the output path diagram.

GFI and related measures

The **GFI** and related fit measures are described here.

GFI

The **GFI** (goodness of fit index) was devised by Jöreskog and Sörbom (1984) for **ML**and **ULS** estimation, and generalized to other estimation criteria by Tanaka and Huba (1985). The **GFI** is given by

$$GFI = 1 - \frac{\hat{F}}{\hat{F}_b}$$

where $\hat{F}$ is the minimum value of the discrepancy function defined in Appendix B and $\hat{F}_b$ is obtained by evaluating F with $\Sigma^{(g)} = \mathbf{0}$, $g = 1, 2,..., G$. An exception has to be made for maximum likelihood estimation, since (D2) in Appendix B is not defined for $\Sigma^{(g)} = \mathbf{0}$. For the purpose of computing **GFI** in the case of maximum likelihood estimation, $f\left(\Sigma^{(g)}; \mathbf{S}^{(g)}\right)$ in Appendix B is calculated as

$$f\left(\Sigma^{(g)}; \mathbf{S}^{(g)}\right) = \frac{1}{2} \text{tr}\left[\mathbf{K}^{(g)^{-1}}\left(\mathbf{S}^{(g)} - \Sigma^{(g)}\right)\right]^2$$

with $\mathbf{K}^{(g)} = \Sigma^{(g)}(\hat{\gamma}_{ML})$, where $\hat{\gamma}_{ML}$ is the maximum likelihood estimate of γ.

GFI is always between zero (0) and unity (1), where unity indicates a perfect fit.

Note: Use the **\gfi** text macro to display the value of the goodness-of-fit index in the output path diagram.

AGFI

The **AGFI** (adjusted goodness of fit index) takes into account the degrees of freedom available for testing the model. It is given by

$$AGFI = 1 - (1 - GFI)\frac{d_b}{d},$$

where

$$d_b = \sum_{g=1}^{G} p^{*(g)}.$$

The **AGFI** is bounded above by one, which indicates a perfect fit. It is not, however, bounded below by zero, as the **GFI** is.

Note: Use the **\agfi** text macro to display the value of the adjusted GFI in the output path diagram.

PGFI

The **PGFI** (parsimony goodness of fit index), suggested by Mulaik, *et al.* (1989), is a modification of the **GFI** that takes into account the degrees of freedom available for testing the model:

$$\text{PGFI} = \text{GFI}\frac{d}{d_b},$$

where d is the degrees of freedom for the model being evaluated, and

$$d_b = \sum_{g=1}^{G} p^{*(g)}$$

is the degrees of freedom for the baseline zero model.

Note: Use the **\pgfi** text macro to display the value of the parsimonious GFI in the output path diagram.

Miscellaneous measures

Miscellaneous fit measures are described here.

HI 90

See **LO 90** on page 414.

HOELTER

Hoelter's (1983) "critical N" is the largest sample size for which one would accept the hypothesis that a model is correct. Hoelter does not specify a significance level to be used in determining the critical N, although he uses .05 in his examples. Amos reports a critical N for significance levels of .05 and .01. Here are the critical N's displayed by Amos for each of the models in Example 6.

```
                         HOELTER     HOELTER
             Model          .05         .01
----------------         ----------  ----------
                 A          164         219
                 B         1615        2201
Independence model          11          14
```

Model A, for instance, would have been accepted at the .05 level if the sample moments had been exactly as they were found to be in the Wheaton study, but with a sample size of 164. With a sample size of 165, Model A would have been rejected. Hoelter argues that a critical N of 200 or better indicates a satisfactory fit. In an analysis of multiple groups, he suggests a threshold of 200 times the number of groups. Presumably this threshold is to be used in conjunction with a significance level of .05. This standard eliminates Model A and the independence model in Example 6. Model B is satisfactory according to the Hoelter criterion. I am not myself convinced by Hoelter's arguments in favor of the 200 standard. Unfortunately, the use of critical N as a practical aid to model selection requires some such standard. Bollen and Liang (1988) report some studies of the critical N statistic.

Note: Use the **\hfive** text macro to display Hoelter's critical N in the output path diagram for $\alpha = 0.05$, or the **\hone** text macro for $\alpha = 0.01$.

LO 90

Amos reports a 90% confidence interval for the population value of several statistics. The upper and lower boundaries are given in columns labeled **HI 90** and **LO 90**.

RMR

The **RMR** (root mean square residual) is the square root of the average squared amount by which the sample variances and covariances differ from their estimates obtained under the assumption your model is correct:

$$\text{RMR} = \sqrt{\sum_{g=1}^{G} \left\{ \sum_{i=1}^{P_g} \sum_{j=1}^{j \le i} \left(\hat{s}_{ij}^{(g)} - \sigma_{ij}^{(g)} \right) \right\} \Bigg/ \sum_{g=1}^{G} p *^{(g)} } .$$

The smaller the **RMR** is, the better. An **RMR** of zero indicates a perfect fit.

The following output from Example 6 shows that, according to the **RMR**, Model A is the best among the models considered except for the saturated model:

```
            Model        RMR         GFI        AGFI        PGFI
-------------------   ----------  ----------  ----------  ----------
                A        0.284       0.975       0.913       0.279
                B        0.758       0.998       0.990       0.238
  Saturated model       0.000       1.000
Independence model     12.356       0.494       0.292       0.353
```

Note: Use the **\rmr** text macro to display the value of the root mean square residual in the output path diagram.

Selected list of fit measures

If you want to focus on a few fit measures, you might consider the implicit recommendation of Browne and Mels (1992), who elect to report only the following fit measures:

CMIN on page 398

P on page 398

FMIN on page 400

F0 on page 402, with 90% confidence interval

PCLOSE on page 403

RMSEA on page 402, with 90% confidence interval

ECVI on page 405, with 90% confidence interval (See also: AIC on page 404)

For the case of maximum likelihood estimation, Browne and Cudeck (1989, 1992) suggest substituting **MECVI** (page 406) for **ECVI**.

Appendix D: Numerical Diagnosis of Nonidentifiability

In order to decide whether a parameter is identified, or whether an entire model is identified, Amos examines the rank of the matrix of approximate second derivatives, and of some related matrices. The method used is similar to that of McDonald and Krane (1977). There are objections to this approach in principle (Bentler and Weeks, 1980; McDonald, 1982). There are also practical problems in determining the rank of a matrix in borderline cases. Because of these difficulties, you should judge the identifiability of a model on *a priori* grounds if you can. With complex models, this may be impossible, so that you will have to rely on Amos's numerical determination. Fortunately, Amos is pretty good at assessing identifiability in practice.

Bibliography

Akaike, H. (1973). Information theory and an extension of the maximum likelihood principle. In Petrov, B.N. and Csaki, F. [Eds.], *Proceedings of the 2nd International Symposium on Information Theory*. Budapest: Akademiai Kiado, 267–281.

Akaike, H. (1987). Factor analysis and AIC. *Psychometrika, 52*, 317–332.

Anderson, T.W. (1957). Maximum likelihood estimates for a multivariate normal distribution when some observations are missing. *Journal of the American Statistical Association, 52*, 200–203.

Anderson, T.W. (1984). *An introduction to multivariate statistical analysis*. New York: Wiley.

Arbuckle, J.L. (in preparation). Bootstrapping and model selection for analysis of moment structures.

Arbuckle, J.L. (1994a). Advantages of model-based analysis of missing data over pairwise deletion. Presented at the RMD Conference on Causal Modeling, West Lafayette, IN.

Arbuckle, J.L. (1994b). A permutation test for analysis of covariance structures. Presented at the annual meeting of the Psychometric Society, University of Illinois, Champaign, IL.

Arbuckle, J.L. (1996). Full information estimation in the presence of incomplete data. In G.A. Marcoulides and R.E. Schumacker [Eds.] *Advanced structural equation modeling.* Mahwah, New Jersey: Lawrence Erlbaum Associates.

Attig, M.S. (1983). The processing of spatial information by adults. Presented at the annual meeting of The Gerontological Society, San Francisco.

Beale, E.M.L. and Little, R.J.A. (1975). Missing values in multivariate analysis. *Journal of the Royal Statistical Society Series B, 37,* 129–145.

Bentler, P.M. (1980). Multivariate analysis with latent variables: Causal modeling. *Annual Review of Psychology, 31,* 419–456.

Bentler, P.M. (1985). *Theory and Implementation of EQS: A Structural Equations Program.* Los Angeles: BMDP Statistical Software.

Bentler, P.M. (1990). Comparative fit indexes in structural models. *Psychological Bulletin, 107,* 238–246.

Bentler, P.M. and Bonett, D.G. (1980). Significance tests and goodness of fit in the analysis of covariance structures. *Psychological Bulletin, 88,* 588–606.

Bentler, P.M. and Chou, C. (1987). Practical issues in structural modeling. *Sociological Methods and Research, 16,* 78–117.

Bentler, P.M. and Freeman, E.H. (1983). Tests for stability in linear structural equation systems. *Psychometrika, 48,* 143–145.

Bentler, P.M. and Weeks, D.G. (1980). Linear structural equations with latent variables. *Psychometrika, 45,* 289–308.

Bentler, P.M. and Woodward, J.A. (1979). Nonexperimental evaluation research: Contributions of causal modeling. In Datta, L. and Perloff, R. [Eds.], *Improving Evaluations.* Beverly Hills: Sage.

Bollen, K.A. (1986). Sample size and Bentler and Bonett's nonnormed fit index. *Psychometrika, 51,* 375–377.

Bollen, K.A. (1987). Outliers and improper solutions: A confirmatory factor analysis example. *Sociological Methods and Research, 15,* 375–384.

Bollen, K.A. (1989a). *Structural equations with latent variables.* New York: Wiley.

Bollen, K.A. (1989b). A new incremental fit index for general structural equation models. *Sociological Methods and Research, 17,* 303–316.

Bollen, K.A. and Jöreskog, K.G. (1985). Uniqueness does not imply identification: A note on confirmatory factor analysis. *Sociological Methods and Research,* 14, 155–163.

Bollen, K.A. and Liang, J. (1988). Some properties of Hoelter's CN. *Sociological Methods and Research, 16,* 492–503.

Bollen, K.A. and Long, J.S. [Eds.] (1993). *Testing structural equation models.* Newbury Park, California: Sage.

Bollen, K.A. and Stine, R.A. (1992). Bootstrapping goodness-of-fit measures in structural equation models. *Sociological Methods and Research*, *21*, 205–229.

Boomsma, A. (1987). The robustness of maximum likelihood estimation in structural equation models. In Cuttance, P. and Ecob, R. [Eds.] *Structural Modeling by Example: Applications in Educational, Sociological, and Behavioral Research*. Cambridge University Press, 160–188.

Botha, J.D., Shapiro, A. and Steiger, J.H. (1988). Uniform indices-of-fit for factor analysis models. *Multivariate Behavioral Research*, *23*, 443–450.

Bozdogan, H. (1987). Model selection and Akaike's information criterion (AIC): The general theory and its analytical extensions. *Psychometrika*, *52*, 345–370.

Brown, C.H. (1983). Asymptotic comparison of missing data procedures for estimating factor loadings. *Psychometrika*, *48(2)*, 269-291.

Brown, R.L. (1994). Efficacy of the indirect approach for estimating structural equation models with missing data: A comparison of five methods. *Structural Equation Modeling: A Multidisciplinary Journal*, *1*, 287-316.

Browne, M.W. (1982). Covariance structures. In Hawkins, D.M. [Ed.] *Topics in applied multivariate analysis*. Cambridge: Cambridge University Press, 72–141.

Browne, M.W. (1984). Asymptotically distribution-free methods for the analysis of covariance structures. *British Journal of Mathematical and Statistical Psychology*, *37*, 62–83.

Browne, M.W. and Cudeck, R. (1989). Single sample cross-validation indices for covariance structures. *Multivariate Behavioral Research*, *24*, 445–455.

Browne, M.W. and Cudeck, R. (1993). Alternative ways of assessing model fit. In Bollen, K.A. and Long, J.S. [Eds.] *Testing structural equation models*. Newbury Park, California: Sage, 136–162.

Browne, M.W. and Mels, G. (1992). RAMONA User's Guide. The Ohio State University, Columbus, OH.

Byrne, B.M. (1989). *A primer of LISREL: Basic applications and programming for confirmatory factor analytic models*. New York: Springer-Verlag.

Carmines, E.G. and McIver, J.P. (1981). Analyzing models with unobserved variables. In Bohrnstedt, G.W. and Borgatta, E.F. [Eds.] *Social measurement: Current issues*. Beverly Hills: Sage.

Cliff, N. (1973). Scaling. *Annual Review of Psychology*, *24*, 473–506.

Cliff, N. (1983). Some cautions concerning the application of causal modeling methods. *Multivariate Behavioral Research*, *18*, 115–126.

Cochran, W.G. (1952). The χ^2 test of goodness of fit. *Annals of Mathematical Statistics*, *23*, 315–345.

Cook, T.D. and Campbell, D.T. (1979). *Quasi-experimentation: Design and analysis issues for field settings*. Chicago: Rand McNally.

Cudeck, R. and Browne, M.W. (1983). Cross-validation of covariance structures. *Multivariate Behavioral Research, 18*, 147–167.

Davis, W.R. (1993). The FC1 rule of identification for confirmatory factor analysis: A general sufficient condition. *Sociological Methods and Research, 21*, 403–437.

Diaconis, P. and Efron, B. (1983). Computer-intensive methods in statistics. *Scientific American, 248(5)*, 116–130.

Dolker, M., Halperin, S. and Divgi, D.R. (1982). Problems with bootstrapping Pearson correlations in very small samples. *Psychometrika, 47*, 529–530.

Draper, N.R. and Smith, H. (1981). *Applied regression analysis. (2nd Ed.)* New York: Wiley.

Edgington, E.S. (1987). *Randomization Tests* (Second edition). New York: Marcel Dekker.

Efron, B. (1979). Bootstrap methods: Another look at the jackknife. *Annals of Statistics, 7*, 1–26.

Efron, B. (1982). *The jackknife, the bootstrap and other resampling plans.* (SIAM Monograph #38) Philadelphia: Society for Industrial and Applied Mathematics.

Efron, B. (1987). Better bootstrap confidence intervals. *Journal of the American Statistical Association, 82*, 171–185.

Efron, B. and Gong, G. (1983). A leisurely look at the bootstrap, the jackknife, and cross-validation. *American Statistician, 37*, 36–48.

Efron, B. and Hinkley, D.F. (1978). Assessing the accuracy of the maximum likelihood estimator: Observed versus expected Fisher information. *Biometrika, 65*, 457-87.

Efron, B. and Tibshirani, R.J. (1993). *An introduction to the bootstrap*. New York: Chapman and Hall.

Felson, R.B. and Bohrnstedt, G.W. (1979). "Are the good beautiful or the beautiful good?" The relationship between children's perceptions of ability and perceptions of physical attractiveness. *Social Psychology Quarterly, 42*, 386–392.

Fox, J. (1980). Effect analysis in structural equation models. *Sociological Methods and Research, 9*, 3–28.

Graham, J.W., Hofer, S.M., Donaldson, S.I. Mackinnon, D.P. and Schafer, J.L. (1997). Analysis with missing data in prevention research. In K. Bryant, M. Windle and S. West [Eds.] *The science of prevention: Methodological advances from alcohol and substance abuse research.* Washington, DC: American Psychological Association.

Graham, J.W., Hofer, S.M. and MacKinnon, D.P. (1996). Maximizing the usefulness of data obtained with planned missing value patterns: An application of maximum likelihood procedures. *Multivariate Behavorial Research, 31*, 197-218.

Gulliksen, H. and Tukey, J.W. (1958). Reliability for the law of comparative judgment. *Psychometrika, 23,* 95–110.

Hamilton, L.C. (1990). *Statistics with Stata.* Pacific Grove, California: Brooks/Cole.

Hayduk, L.A. *Structural equation modeling with LISREL.* (1987). Baltimore: Johns Hopkins University Press.

Hoelter, J.W. (1983). The analysis of covariance structures: Goodness-of-fit indices. *Sociological Methods and Research, 11,* 325–344.

Holzinger, K.J. and Swineford, F.A. (1939). A study in factor analysis: The stability of a bi-factor solution. *Supplementary Educational Monographs,* No. 48. Chicago: University of Chicago, Dept. of Education.

Hubert, L.J. and Golledge, R.G. (1981). A heuristic method for the comparison of related structures. *Journal of Mathematical Psychology, 23,* 214–226.

Huitema, B.E. (1980). *The analysis of covariance and alternatives.* New York: Wiley.

James, L.R., Mulaik, S.A. and Brett, J.M. (1982). *Causal analysis: Assumptions, models and data.* Beverly Hills: Sage.

Jöreskog, K.G. (1967). Some contributions to maximum likelihood factor analysis. *Psychometrika, 32,* 443–482.

Jöreskog, K.G. (1969). A general approach to confirmatory maximum likelihood factor analysis. *Psychometrika, 34,* 183–202.

Jöreskog, K.G (1971). Simultaneous factor analysis in several populations. *Psychometrika, 36,* 409–426.

Jöreskog, K.G. (1979). A general approach to confirmatory maximum likelihood factor analysis with addendum.. In Jöreskog, K.G. & Sörbom, D. [Eds.] *Advances in factor analysis and structural equation models.* Cambridge, MA: Abt Books, 21–43.

Jöreskog, K.G. and Sörbom, D. (1984). *LISREL-VI user's guide* (3rd ed.). Mooresville, IN: Scientific Software.

Jöreskog, K.G. and Sörbom, D. (1989). *LISREL-7 user's reference guide.* Mooresville, IN: Scientific Software.

Kaplan, D. (1989). Model modification in covariance structure analysis: Application of the expected parameter change statistic. *Multivariate Behavioral Research, 24,* 285–305.

Kendall, M.G. and Stuart, A. (1973). *The advanced theory of statistics* (vol. 2, 3rd edition). New York: Hafner.

Kullback, S. and Leibler, R.A. (1951). On information and sufficiency. *Annals of Mathematical Statistics, 22,* 79–86.

Lee, S. and Hershberger, S. (1990). A simple rule for generating equivalent models in covariance structure modeling. *Multivariate Behavioral Research, 25,* 313–334.

Linhart, H. and Zucchini, W. (1986). *Model selection*. New York: Wiley.

Little, R.J.A. and Rubin, D.B. (1987). *Statistical analysis with missing data*. New York: Wiley.

Little, R.J.A. and Rubin, D.B. (1989). The analysis of social science data with missing values. *Sociological Methods and Research, 18*, 292–326.

Little, R.J.A. and Schenker, N. (1995). Missing data. In G. Arminger, C.C. Clogg and M.E. Sobel [Eds.] *Handbook of statistical modeling for the social and behavioral sciences*. New York: Plenum.

Loehlin, J.C. (1992). *Latent variable models: An introduction to factor, path, and structural analysis* (2nd edition). Mahwah, New Jersey: Lawrence Erlbaum Associates.

Lord, F.M. (1955). Estimation of parameters from incomplete data. *Journal of the American Statistical Association, 50*, 870–876.

MacCallum, R.C. (1986). Specification searches in covariance structure modeling. *Psychological Bulletin, 100*, 107–120.

MacCallum, R.C. (1990). The need for alternative measures of fit in covariance structure modeling. *Multivariate Behavioral Research, 25*, 157–162.

MacCallum, R.C., Roznowski, M. and Necowitz, L.B. (1992). Model modifications in covariance structure analysis: The problem of capitalization on chance. *Psychological Bulletin, 111*, 490–504.

MacCallum, R.C., Wegener, D.T., Uchino, B.N. and Fabrigar, L.R. (1993). The problem of equivalent models in applications of covariance structure analysis. *Psychological Bulletin, 114*, 185–199.

Manly, B.F.J. (1991). *Randomization and Monte Carlo Methods in Biology*. London: Chapman and Hall.

Mantel, N. (1967). The detection of disease clustering and a generalized regression approach. *Cancer Research, 27*, 209–220.

Mantel, N. and Valand, R.S. (1970). A technique of nonparametric multivariate analysis. *Biometrics, 26*, 47–558.

Mardia, K.V. (1970). Measures of multivariate skewness and kurtosis with applications. *Biometrika, 57*, 519–530.

Mardia, K.V. (1974). Applications of some measures of multivariate skewness and kurtosis in testing normality and robustness studies. *Sankhya*, Series B, *36*, 115–128.

Marsh, H.W. and Hocevar, D. (1985). Application of confirmatory factor analysis to the study of self-concept: First- and higher-order factor models and their invariance across groups. *Psychological Bulletin, 97*, 562–582.

Matthai, A. (1951). Estimation of parameters from incomplete data with application to design of sample surveys. *Sankhya, 11*, 145–152.

McArdle, J.J. and Aber, M.S. (1990). Patterns of change within latent variable structural equation models. In A. von Eye [Ed.] *Statistical methods in longitudinal research, Volume I: Principles and structuring change.* New York: Academic Press, 151-224.

McDonald, R.P. (1978). A simple comprehensive model for the analysis of covariance structures. *British Journal of Mathematical and Statistical Psychology, 31,* 59–72.

McDonald, R.P. (1982). A note on the investigation of local and global identifiability. *Psychometrika, 47,* 101–103.

McDonald, R.P. (1989). An index of goodness-of-fit based on noncentrality. *Journal of Classification, 6,* 97–103.

McDonald, R.P. and Krane, W.R. (1977). A note on local identifiability and degrees of freedom in the asymptotic likelihood ratio test. *British Journal of Mathematical and Statistical Psychology, 30,* 198–203.

McDonald, R.P. and Marsh, H.W. (1990). Choosing a multivariate model: Noncentrality and goodness of fit. *Psychological Bulletin, 107,* 247-255.

McDonald, R.P. and Krane, W.R. (1979). A Monte-Carlo study of local identifiability and degrees of freedom in the asymptotic likelihood ratio test. *British Journal of Mathematical and Statistical Psychology, 32,* 121–132.

Mulaik, S.A. (1990). An analysis of the conditions under which the estimation of parameters inflates goodness of fit indices as measures of model validity. Paper presented at the Annual Meeting, Psychometric Society, Princeton, New Jersey, June 28–30, 1990.

Mulaik, S.A., James, L.R., Van Alstine, J., Bennett, N., Lind, S. and Stilwell, C.D. (1989). Evaluation of goodness-of-fit indices for structural equation models. *Psychological Bulletin, 105,* 430–445.

Muthén, B., Kaplan, D., and Hollis, M. (1987) On structural equation modeling with data that are not missing completely at random. *Psychometrika, 52,* 431–462

Olsson, S. (1973). *An experimental study of the effects of training on test scores and factor structure.* Uppsala, Sweden: University of Uppsala, Department of Education.

Raftery, A.E. (1993). Bayesian model selection in structural equation models. In Bollen, K.A. and Long, J.S. [Eds.] *Testing structural equation models.* Newbury Park, California: Sage, 163–180.

Rigdon, E.E. (1994a). Calculating degrees of freedom for a structural equation model. *Structural Equation Modeling, 1,* 274–278.

Rigdon, E.E. (1994b). Demonstrating the effects of unmodeled random measurement error. *Structural Equation Modeling, 1,* 375–380.

Rock, D.A., Werts, C.E., Linn, R.L. and Jöreskog, K.G. (1977). A maximum likelihood solution to the errors in variables and errors in equations model. *Journal of Multivariate Behavioral Research, 12,* 187–197.

Rubin, D.E. (1976). Inference and missing data. *Biometrika, 63,* 581–592.

Rubin, D.E. (1987). *Multiple imputation for nonresponse in surveys*. New York: Wiley

Runyon, R.P. and Haber, A. (1980). *Fundamentals of behavioral statistics*, 4th ed. Reading, Mass.: Addison-Wesley.

Saris, W.E, Satorra, A. and Sörbom, D (1987). The detection and correction of specification errors in structural equation models. In Clogg, C.C. [Ed.]. *Sociological methodology 1987*. San Francisco: Jossey-Bass.

Schafer, J.L. (1997). *Analysis of incomplete multivariate data*. London, UK: Chapman and Hall.

Schwarz, G. (1978). Estimating the dimension of a model. *The Annals of Statistics, 6*, 461–464.

Sobel, M.E. and Bohrnstedt, G.W. (1985). Use of null models in evaluating the fit of covariance structure models. In Tuma, N.B [Ed.] *Sociological methodology 1985*. San Francisco: Jossey-Bass, 152–178.

Sörbom, D. (1974). A general method for studying differences in factor means and factor structure between groups. *British Journal of Mathematical and Statistical Psychology, 27*, 229–239.

Sörbom, D. (1978). An alternative to the methodology for analysis of covariance. *Psychometrika, 43*, 381–396.

Steiger, J.H. (1989). *EzPATH: Causal modeling*. Evanston, IL: Systat.

Steiger, J.H. (1990). Structural model evaluation and modification: An interval estimation approach. *Multivariate Behavioral Research, 25*, 173–180.

Steiger, J.H., Shapiro, A. and Browne, M.W. (1985). On the multivariate asymptotic distribution of sequential chi-square statistics. *Psychometrika, 50*, 253–263.

Stelzl, I. (1986). Changing a causal hypothesis without changing the fit: Some rules for generating equivalent path models. *Multivariate Behavioral Research, 21*, 309–331.

Stine, R.A. (1989). An introduction to bootstrap methods: Examples and ideas. *Sociological Methods and Research, 18*, 243–291.

Swain, A.J. (1975). Analysis of parametric structures for variance matrices. Unpublished Ph.D. thesis, University of Adelaide.

Tanaka, J.S. and Huba, G.J. (1985). A fit index for covariance structure models under arbitrary GLS estimation. *British Journal of Mathematical and Statistical Psychology, 38*, 197–201.

Tanaka, J.S. and Huba, G.J. (1989). A general coefficient of determination for covariance structure models under arbitrary GLS estimation. *British Journal of Mathematical and Statistical Psychology, 42*, 233–239.

Tucker, L.R and Lewis, C. (1973). A reliability coefficient for maximum likelihood factor analysis. *Psychometrika, 38*, 1–10.

Verleye, G. (1996). *Missing at random data problems in attitude measurements using maximum likelihood structural equation modeling*. Unpublished dissertation. Frije Universiteit Brussels, Department of Psychology.

Warren, R.D., White, J.K. and Fuller, W.A. (1974). An errors-in-variables analysis of managerial role performance. *Journal of the American Statistical Association, 69*, 886–893.

Wheaton, B. (1987). Assessment of fit in overidentified models with latent variables. *Sociological Methods and Research, 16*, 118–154.

Wheaton, B., Muthén, B., Alwin, D.F. and Summers, G.F. (1977). Assessing reliability and stability in panel models. In Heise, D.R. [Ed.] *Sociological methodology 1977*. San Francisco: Jossey-Bass, 84–136.

Wichman, B.A. and Hill, I.D. (1982). An efficient and portable pseudo-random number generator. Algorithm AS 183. *Applied Statistics, 31*, 188–190.

Winer, B.J. (1971). *Statistical principles in experimental design*. New York: McGraw-Hill.

Wothke, W. (1993). Nonpositive definite matrices in structural modeling. In Bollen, K.A. and Long, J.S. [Eds.], *Testing structural equation models* (pp. 256–293). Newbury Park, California: Sage.

Wothke, W. (1999) Longitudinal and multi-group modeling with missing data. In T.D. Little, K.U. Schnabel and J. Baumert [Eds.] *Modeling longitudinal and multiple group data: Practical issues, applied approaches and specific examples*. Mahwah, New Jersey: Lawrence Erlbaum Associates.

Index

Fox, J., 171, 183, 422
FoxPro (.dbf) file, 4
Free parameter, 72, 102-104, 233-336, 340
Freeman, E.H., 183, 420
Fresco, D., 7
Friendly, M., 6
F-test, 276
Full information analysis of missing data, 2, 331-338, 343, 419-420, 424
Fuller, W.A., 107, 124, 280, 427
Function of log likelihood, 339-342, 356-358
Generalized least squares
  Amos Graphics, 383
German language option, 3, 7
GFI
  goodness of fit index, 411-415
  text macro, 412
GLS, Generalized least squares, 2, 78, 359, 380-383, 391-393
Golledge, R.G., 423
Gong, G., 422
Goodness of fit, 81, 215, 420-421, 425
Goodness of fit index (GFI), 411-415
Graham, J.W., 332, 422
Graphics Automation demo, 11
Group
  text macro, 227, 241
Group manager, 213, 222
Group name, 211-213, 217, 221, 227-229, 235, 239, 254, 258, 269, 274-275, 293, 298, 306, 310-313, 317-327, 353, 357
Group-invariance
  factor patterns, 234
  regression weights, 234
GroupName
  Amos Basic command, 211, 217, 221, 229, 235, 239, 254, 258, 269, 274-275, 293, 298, 306, 310-313, 317-327, 353, 357
Gulliksen, H., 399, 423
Haber, A., 74, 426
Halperin, S., 422

Hamilton, L.C., 14-19, 36, 39-40, 55-56, 423
Hancock, G., 7
Hawkins, D.M., 421
Hayduk, L.A., 423
Heise, D.R., 427
Help, 9-13, 17, 26, 35, 57-59, 66, 85, 90, 122, 368
Hershberger, S., 423
Heyder, A., 7
HFIVE
  text macro, 414
HI 90 (confidence limit), 401-405, 414
Hill, I.D., 427
Hinkley, D.F., 422
Hocevar, D., 400, 424
HOELTER (fit measure), 414, 420
Hoelter, J.W., 414, 420-423
Hofer, S.M., 422
Hollis, M., 333, 425
Holzinger, K.J., 185, 189-193, 251-252, 257, 261, 290, 296, 333-335, 360, 370, 380, 423
Homogeneity of within-group regressions, 233
HONE
  text macro, 414
Hox, J., 7
Huba, G.J., 412, 426
Hubert, L.J., 423
Huitema, B.E., 233, 423
Hypotheses about means, 265
Hypothesis testing, 2, 74, 78, 97-99, 106, 147, 398
Identifiability, 107, 112, 118, 187, 417, 425
Identification, 83, 112-119, 127-129, 133-139, 146, 151, 160, 176, 181, 187-188, 199, 202, 282, 290, 420, 422
Identified model, 148, 427
IFI
  incremental fit index, 168, 409
  text macro, 409

.wk1 file, 4, 124, 133, 137
.wk3 file, 4
.wk4 file, 4
Lower 90% bound of
ECVI (ECHILO), 406
MacCallum, R.C., 153, 395, 424
Mackinnon, D.P., 422
Macro
Amos Graphics, 11, 248, 378
Macros
automating Amos Graphics functions,
11, 248, 378
Macros (text macros), 96, 97, 227, 240-
241, 396-415
Main-effects model, 233
Manage groups
Amos Graphics, 213, 222
Manage models
Amos Graphics, 164-166, 206, 222
Manly, B.F.J., 424
MANOVA, 265, 276-277
Mantel, N., 424
Marcoulides, G.A., 419-420
Mardia, K.V., 424
Marsh, H.W., 400, 410, 424-425
Martinez, C., 7
Matrix representation
Amos Graphics, 217-219, 237
Matrix view, 4, 237
Matthai, A., 349, 424
Maximum likelihood
Amos Basic, 91
Amos Graphics, 78, 94-97, 302, 364,
368, 380-383
Maximum likelihood (ML), 412
McArdle, J.J., 425
McDonald, R.P., 188, 410, 417, 425
McIver, J.P., 399, 421
Mean
Amos Basic command, 269-270, 274-
275, 283-284, 293-294, 298, 306,
310-313, 317-322, 327, 340, 344,
353, 357

and intercept model, 2, 10, 265-270,
281-297, 305, 314, 325, 329-330,
335, 352, 389-391, 405, 426
expected change, 307
hypothesis tests, 265
imputation of missing data, 2, 332-333
model, 121, 265-270, 274-275, 279-
294, 298, 305-330, 338-340, 344-
346, 353, 357
modeling, 2, 10, 265-282, 286-297,
305, 314, 325, 329-330, 335, 352,
389-391, 405, 426
modification index, 307
of unobserved variables, 289-290, 294
parameter, 5, 121-123, 265-276, 281-
298, 306, 310-346, 352-357, 378,
389-391, 395, 405
population, 324, 355
sample, 2, 108, 124, 144, 174, 266-270,
280, 284, 302, 331, 342, 355
structure, 269-270, 274-275, 283, 293,
298, 306, 310-313, 317, 320-340,
344-346, 353, 357
Mean-level model, 2, 10, 265-270, 281-
297, 305, 314, 325, 329-330, 335-
352, 389-391, 405, 426
default for identification, 284
Measurement error, 109, 123-126, 145,
152, 192, 196, 425
Measurement model, 126-131, 169,
294, 305, 315, 370
Measures of fit, 395, 424
MECVI
fit measure, 405-406, 416
text macro, 406
Mels, G., 399-401, 416, 421
Methods for retrieving results, 90
Minimization history, 27, 93
Minimization parameter
crit1, 366
crit2, 366
number of iterations, 366
Minimum discrepancy function C
(CMIN), 168, 398, 407-408, 416

Normed fit index (NFI), 168, 336, 407-408, 411

NPAR

Amos Basic command, 344-346

number of parameters, 168, 344-346, 396, 407-408

text macro, 396

Null hypothesis, 74-76, 97-100, 105-106, 168, 297, 328, 398-399, 403

Number of

bootstrap samples, 363, 375-377, 382

Object

changing shape, 25, 110

dragging properties, 85, 176, 247

duplicating, 65, 131, 188

erasing, 25, 68

moving, 23, 25, 66, 85, 110, 150, 176, 247

selecting all, 131, 188, 247

Object properties

Amos Graphics, 22-25, 67-68, 82-84, 101, 113, 132, 164, 201, 222, 236, 272, 308

Parameters, 222, 273, 308, 390

Covariance, 76, 84, 91, 101, 110, 115, 132, 268

Mean, 267

Orientation, 128

Regression weight, 4, 15, 24, 55, 112-114, 118, 236-268, 305

Variance, 2, 4, 24, 72-73, 78, 82-84, 89-91, 100, 104, 112, 119-122, 149, 156, 164, 168, 234, 267-268, 305, 326, 354, 415, 422

Text, 68, 201

Variable label, 22, 336, 363

Variable name, 4, 19, 22, 39, 68, 132, 201, 273, 336, 363

Observed

variable, 2, 15, 20, 39, 65-68, 78, 89-100, 107, 113-121, 126, 132, 136, 144-147, 169-170, 181, 187, 212, 237, 244-246, 290-294, 305, 308, 323-324, 328, 332, 336-340, 344, 347, 352, 389, 395

ObsVars (Amos Basic command), 346, 347

Olinsky, A., 7

Olsson, S., 196-203, 302-304, 322, 425

Omitted variable, 124

Open

Amos Basic, 37, 40, 71

Orientation of parameters, 128

Outlier diagnostic, 2, 368, 420

Output, 61, 93, 147, 270

all implied moments, 167

Amos Basic, 44, 57, 90-91, 116-117, 150, 168, 222, 241, 270, 294

Amos Graphics, 4, 27-34, 59, 69-70, 76-77, 92-98, 103-105, 112, 119-121, 135, 148, 152-154, 166-168, 179-180, 192, 200, 215, 222-223, 233, 240-243, 257, 267-268, 272, 287, 295, 336, 352-354, 358, 363, 382-385, 396-412, 415

format

table view, 43, 72, 76

text output, 39-42, 55, 89, 137, 146, 161, 177, 199, 204-205, 217, 221, 229, 235, 239, 254, 258, 269, 274-275, 282-283, 293, 298, 306, 310-313, 317-327, 338-340, 346, 353, 357, 361

implied moments, 91,-94, 344, 369, 382-384

printing, 42

residual moments, 93-94

sample moments, 382

view

table, 11, 30-31, 43-44, 70-73, 77, 117, 167

text, 4, 11, 29, 34, 41-43, 77, 90-94, 103, 116, 121, 151, 180, 199, 207, 284, 339, 376, 384

P

Amos Basic command, 343, 346

probability level, 74, 160, 168, 275, 299, 337-338, 343-347, 357, 398-399, 403 text macro, 97, 280, 399, 403, 411

Page
layout (interface properties), 128
orientation, 128

Pairwise deletion of missing data, 2, 331, 332-333, 341, 419

Palascewski, B., 7

Parameter, 2, 4, 24, 38, 69-75, 82-84, 91-92, 97, 101-104, 113-118, 127, 134-140, 147-162, 188-190, 209-211, 215-222, 229-230, 236, 255, 260, 264-276, 284-286, 290-295, 305-308, 334-345, 352, 356-359, 363-368, 380, 389-391, 396, 402-405, 424-425
Amos Basic, 217
Amos Graphics dialog, 24, 72, 82-84, 101-104, 113, 147, 211, 222, 236, 267-268, 273, 292, 305-308, 352, 368, 380, 390, 391, 396, 405
constraint, 4, 91, 102, 138, 140, 166, 204-207, 264, 281, 299, 323
critical ratios for differences, 153-156, 233, 352, 356
estimate, 2-4, 31-33, 39, 69, 73-74, 78, 82, 91, 103, 112, 121, 127, 134-135, 139, 151-154, 160, 169, 181, 202-203, 209, 215-216, 223, 230-232, 242, 256, 261-264, 271, 295-296, 314-319, 329, 333, 339-341, 352-354, 359, 364, 368, 378, 393, 401, 410
expected change, 149, 150, 200, 307, 311
free, 72, 102-104, 233, 336, 340
label, 83, 89, 155, 163, 217-222, 235-239, 260, 268, 273, 322, 352-353, 357
name, 4, 83, 221-222, 259, 273
number of free parameters, 344-346
unnamed, 211
unstandardized/standardized, 32, 77, 95, 216
value, 35, 70, 83, 211, 251, 257, 337, 396

value returned, 55

Parameter estimation
direct, indirect and total effects, 157
fitting a single model, 39, 55, 344-346, 361
implied moments, 157, 338-341
all, 88, 122, 282-283
intercept, 284
iteration limit, 366
mean, 269-270, 274-275, 283-284, 293-294, 298, 306, 310-313, 317-322, 327, 340, 344, 353, 357
mean structure, 298, 324
mean-level model, 269-270, 274-275, 283, 293, 298, 306, 310-322, 327, 338-340, 344-346, 353, 357
modification indices, 146-149, 199-200, 204-205, 306-313, 317-327
nested models, 162, 205-207, 221, 239, 275, 283, 298, 306, 313, 317, 322, 357
p value of chi-square statistic, 343-346
residual moments, 88
sample moments reported, 88, 282-283
squared multiple correlations reported, 39, 42, 119, 133, 137, 157, 177, 181, 189, 191, 199, 204-205, 254, 258, 282-283, 293, 298, 306, 310-313, 317-327, 338, 361, 368
standardized parameter estimates, 39, 76, 88, 133-137, 157, 177, 181, 189, 199, 204-205, 217, 221, 254, 258, 282-283, 293, 298, 306, 310-313, 317--327, 338, 361, 368
structure specification, 39, 42, 55, 72, 89-90, 116, 133, 137, 146, 150, 157, 161, 177-178, 189, 199-207, 211, 217, 221, 229, 235, 239, 254, 258, 269, 274-275, 282-284, 293-294, 298, 306, 310-313, 317-327, 338, 346, 361

Parameter Value
Amos Basic command, 55

intercept, 270, 279, 282
model, 15, 24, 123, 127, 281, 284
parameter, 116, 236, 290
weight, 4, 15, 24, 29, 32, 39-42, 55,
112-127, 134-139, 146-156, 176,
181-183, 187, 191, 198-204, 229-
236, 242, 254-257, 265-268, 279-
286, 292, 296, 305, 315-318, 326-
328, 365, 368, 396
    modification index, 307
    parameter, 339, 365-367
Regression weights
in factor analysis, 187
Reinhard, M., 7
Rejected model, 148, 328
Relation
causal, 419-421, 426
Relative fit index (RFI), 168, 408-409
Relative noncentrality index (RNI),
410
Reliability, 123, 136, 143, 152, 192,
423-427
Residual
moments, 88, 93-94
ResidualMoments
Amos Basic command, 88
Results retrieved
admissible solution, 344-346
chi-square statistic, 55, 344-346
critical ratio
    differences among parameters, 353-
    357
number of free parameters, 344-346
parameter value, 55
RFI
relative fit index, 168, 408-409
text macro, 409
Rigdon, E.E., 5, 6, 7, 124, 396, 425
Rindskopf, D., 7
RMR
root mean square residual, 415
text macro, 415
RMSEA
root mean square of approximation,
336, 402-403, 416

text macro, 403
RMSEAHI
text macro, 403
RMSEALO
text macro, 403
RNI
relative noncentrality index, 410
Robust estimation (bootstrap), 363,
375, 382
**Robust standard error estimates
(bootstrap)**, 359
Rock, D.A., 124, 136, 425
Root mean square residual (RMR),
415
Rotate
Amos Graphics, 130
Roznowski, M., 153, 424
R-square, 27-32, 39-42, 119-124, 133,
137-140, 152, 157, 177, 181-182,
189-192, 199, 203-205, 254, 258,
282-283, 293, 298, 306, 310-313,
317-327, 337-338, 359-361, 365,
367-368, 408
Rubin, D.B., 332-333, 424-426
Runyon, R.P., 74, 426
Safren, S.A., 7
Sample
correlation, 100, 174
covariance, 75, 92-97, 108, 118, 147,
170, 215, 269-270, 284, 302, 331,
389
mean, 2, 108, 124, 144, 174, 266-270,
284, 302, 331, 342, 355
moment, 91-94, 103-104, 108, 118,
134, 138, 147-150, 159, 190, 215,
222, 230, 255, 260, 270, 276, 284-
285, 331, 376, 382, 389-390, 396,
401, 414
moments, 88, 282-283, 382
size, 389-390
variance, 75, 92-94, 108, 118, 124, 147,
170, 215, 270, 284, 302, 389, 415
SampleMoments
Amos Basic command, 88, 282-283
Saris, W.E., 426

Text macros, 96, 97, 227, 240-241, 396-415
\agfi, 413
\aic, 404
\bcc, 405
\bic, 405
\caic, 405
\cfi, 410
\cmin, 97, 398
\cmindf, 400
\df, 97, 396
\ecvi, 406
\ecvihi, 406
\ecvilo, 406
\f0, 402
\f0hi, 402
\f0lo, 402
\fmin, 400
\format, 96, 240
\gfi, 412
\group, 227, 241
\hfive, 414
\hone, 414
\ifi, 409
\mecvi, 406
\model, 241
\ncp, 401
\ncphi, 401
\ncplo, 401
\nfi, 408
\npar, 396
\p, 97, 280, 399, 403, 411
\pcfi, 411
\pclose, 403
\pgfi, 413
\pnfi, 411
\pratio, 397
\rfi, 409
\rmr, 415
\rmsea, 403
\rmseahi, 403
\rmsealo, 403
\tli, 409

Text output
Amos Basic, 41-44, 90-91, 116, 151, 339
Amos Graphics, 4, 11, 29, 34, 77, 94, 103, 121, 180, 199, 207, 284, 376, 384
minimization history
Amos Graphics, 27, 93
modification indices
Amos Basic, 307
Amos Graphics, 200, 311
Textbooks on SEM, 5, 192
TextOutput
Amos Basic command, 39, 42, 55, 89, 133, 137, 146, 157, 161, 177, 189, 199, 204-205, 211, 217, 221, 229, 235, 239, 254, 258, 269, 274-275, 282-283, 293, 298, 306, 310-313, 317-327, 338-340, 346, 353, 357, 361
Tibshirani, R.J., 422
Title
Amos Basic command, 340, 346
figure caption, 4, 96, 240
Title of analysis, 340, 346
TLI
text macro, 409
Tucker-Lewis index, 168, 408-409
Total effects, 5, 143, 167, 171
Totaleffects
Amos Basic command, 157
Tucker, L.R, 407-409, 426
Tucker-Lewis index (NNFI), 409
Tucker-Lewis index (TLI), 168, 408-409
Tukey, J.W., 399, 423
Tuma, N.B., 426
Uchino, B.N., 424
Undo the previous change
Amos Graphics, 25-26
Undo the previous undo
Amos Graphics, 26
Unique
factors, 187-189
variable, 113, 126, 132, 147, 187, 198

Univariate normality (estimation), 2
Unnamed parameters, 211
Unobserved
  variable, 21, 110, 118-132, 144-147,
    170, 176, 187, 199-202, 421
  mean, 289-290, 294
Unreliability (variables), 123
Unstable model, 182-183
Unstandardized estimates, 33, 95-96,
    105, 216, 231, 240, 287
Unweighted least squares, 2, 380, 383
  Amos Graphics, 383
Unweighted least squares (ULS), 392,
    399, 412
Upper 90% bound of
  ECVI (ECHIHI), 406
Valand, R.S., 424
Value constraint, 83, 146, 270
Van Alstine, J., 425
Variable
  dependent, 39, 42, 123, 132, 173, 282
  endogenous, 110-113, 119-121, 152,
    178, 182, 234-237, 267, 284-287
  error, 109-113, 118, 123-126, 145, 152,
    177, 192, 196, 201, 425
  exogenous, 2, 72, 78-79, 110-115, 121-
    124, 133, 174, 233-234, 250, 267-
    269, 270-272, 283-284, 305, 326-
    328, 340
  factor, 115, 126, 147, 187-189, 191-
    193, 234, 252-257, 261, 289-297,
    305, 331, 335-347, 360-361, 368-
    372, 380, 421
  in data set, 67, 132, 246
    Amos Graphics, 246
  indicator, 129
  label
    object properties, 22, 336, 363
  latent, 7, 15, 24, 115, 130, 143, 198,
    260, 301, 305, 420, 424-427
  name, 67, 72, 91, 99, 132
    object properties, 3, 4, 19, 22, 39, 68,
    132, 201, 273, 336, 363
  observed, 2, 15, 20, 39, 65-68, 78, 89-
    90, 100, 107, 113-121, 126, 132,

136, 144-147, 169-170, 181, 187,
    212, 237, 244-246, 290-294, 305-
    308, 323-324, 328, 332, 336-340,
    344-347, 352, 389, 395
  omitted, 124
  predictor, 39, 79, 109-110, 115, 124,
    282
  random, 78
  reflect indicators, 132
  unique, 113, 126, 132, 147, 187, 198
  unobserved, 21, 110, 118-132, 144-147,
    170, 176, 187, 199-202, 421
Variance
  common, 305
  constraint, 97
  expected change, 307
  implied, 94, 170
  implied by model, 94, 169
  modification index, 307
  negative, 203, 307
  parameter, 2, 4, 24, 29, 41, 61, 65-84,
    89-95, 100-104, 112-123, 134-137,
    144-157, 164, 168-170, 180-181,
    191-192, 201-202, 206, 210-211,
    215-219, 223, 230-234, 242, 249-
    250, 254-257, 265-276, 282-286,
    296, 302-305, 311-315, 323-328,
    333, 339-344, 352-355, 365-368,
    389, 415, 422
  sample, 75, 92-94, 104, 108, 118, 124,
    147, 170, 215, 270, 280, 284, 302,
    389, 415
  unique, 305
Verleye, G., 332, 427
View
  data, 3, 4, 11, 64, 86
  input path diagram, 215
  output path diagram, 32, 69, 77, 95,
    215
  path diagrams in directory, 3, 11, 15
  spreadsheet
    Amos Graphics, 4
  Table output
    Amos Graphics, 30, 77
  tables (estimation results), 3, 11